THE STRUGGLE FOR A FREE
STAGE IN LONDON

THE STRUGGLE
FOR A FREE STAGE IN
LONDON

BY

WATSON NICHOLSON
M.A. (HARVARD), PH.D. (YALE)
Instructor in English in Yale University

Benjamin Blom
New York

First Published Boston 1906
Reissued 1966, by
Benjamin Blom, Inc., New York 10452
Library of Congress Catalog Card No. 65-27915

Printed in U.S.A. by
NOBLE OFFSET PRINTERS, INC.
NEW YORK 3, N. Y.

PREFACE

ON the 22d of August, 1843, royal sanction was given to the Theatre Regulation Bill, depriving the two patent theatres — Drury Lane and Covent Garden — of the monopoly they had possessed, for nearly two centuries, of playing Shakespeare and the national drama, and extending the privilege to the minor, or independent, theatres which had sprung up and multiplied in London in spite of the "inviolable rights" of the patentees. The monopoly had been bolstered up by special legislation, revivals of vagrant acts, chicanery, and evasions of every sort, in the face of a growing public demand for an unrestricted stage for the regular drama. The subject of this volume is the story of the long struggle to free London of the theatrical monopoly, a struggle which began almost within the lifetime of the second Charles himself, and culminated in the parliamentary act of 1843.

From the necessities of the case, I have gone
to the sources for my materials. The most valuable of these have been the theatrical columns
of the London newspapers and magazines containing playbills, stage criticisms, police court
records, and correspondence; memoirs, diaries,
biographies, and letters; copies of documents in
the Lord Chamberlain's office, of theatrical patents and licenses, of proceedings in Parliament,
King's Bench, and Privy Council; pamphlets
relating to the stage, contracts between managers and actors, petitions to King and Parliament, minutes of meetings, reports of commit-
tees, etc., etc.

As a result of this research among the sources,
naturally, much new material has been un-
earthed, mistakes of former historians have been
corrected, and new relations of well-known facts
established. Even when treating of epochs of
theatrical history perfectly familiar to the student of the drama, it has been my aim to throw
more light on the field, and to bring into prominence the main significance of the events. For
example, in the first chapter, the Union of 1682,

Betterton's revolt, the rise of Vanbrugh's Opera House, the ejectment of Christopher Rich from Drury Lane Theatre, and Steele's contest with the Crown over his patent, have not only had additional materials gathered to them, but they have all been interpreted in relation to the meaning of monopolistic rights and crown prerogative over theatrical amusements.

Again, to single out a few prominent topics at random, the revolts of the actors from the patent theatres in 1733 and 1743 have been placed in the light of new evidence; the relation of Henry Fielding to the other causes which brought about the Licensing Act of 1737 has been given a coherent place in the political and theatrical events of the eighteenth century; the story of John Palmer's Royalty Theatre has been given a logical connection in the struggle for a free stage in London; the so-called " O. P." riots of 1809 have been examined with a view to their real meaning in the struggle; the development of that dramatic hybrid, known as "burletta," has been traced from its innocent beginning to its final importance as a monopoly breaker.

Among the more general topics of interest to the student of English dramatic history may be mentioned the account of the warfare of encroachments between the summer and winter theatres, and the importance of the English opera in this contest; the attempts to establish a third theatre in London under the protection of Government; the spirited struggle between the majors and minors (*i. e.* patent and independent theatres); the parts played by dramatic authors and actors against the monopoly; the various *rôles* taken by the different Lord Chamberlains; and the final downfall of the patent houses as the combined result of all the influences waged against them for nearly two centuries.

In every instance, I believe, where the source of my authority for statements of fact is not apparent from the context, a footnote reference will be found. For the convenience of scholars desiring further knowledge of the subject than would be possible to present in a volume of limited size, I have collected these references in an Appendix. I have in my possession copies of many of the original documents used in this investigation, and these may be published in a separate volume, should it appear advisable, at some future time. While I have included Wyndham's " Annals of Covent Garden Theatre " in my bibliography, I have not examined it, being unable to secure a copy before the present work was in press.

Relative to the Index, it has been my object to furnish as complete analysis as possible for the more important lines of investigation, and to give perspective, so to speak, to the various topics comprising the work. If I have succeeded in this, a mere glance at this part of the book should serve to reveal the comparative importance to the subject of the various titles therein contained. This method, it would seem, is better calculated to guide the reader to the real contents of the book than a senseless repetition of the pages which happen to contain proper names. It should not be surprising, therefore, if Charles II, though appearing scores of times in the pages of the book, should be mentioned in the Index only in relation to some act of importance connected with his name. On the other hand, the monopoly which he created, forming one of the main interests of the investigation, should be found exhaustively analyzed. For similar reasons, the titles of farces, operas, etc., which bear but slightly on the larger features of the subject have been omitted from the Index.

In the way of acknowledgments, my sincere thanks are due the entire staff of the Yale University Library; to Professor Henry A. Beers, who read and criticised the first draft of the manuscript; to Professors W. L. Cross and W. L. Phelps, both of whom read and criticised portions of the book in manuscript; to Mr. Andrew Keogh, whose expert knowledge of bibliographical materials saved me many hours of labor; to Professor George P. Baker, who read critically the entire manuscript; and to Professor Thomas R. Lounsbury, who first aroused my interest in the subject, and has been my constant adviser and sympathetic critic during the progress of the work.

WATSON NICHOLSON.

NEW HAVEN, CONN.,
September 7, 1906.

CONTENTS

THE STRUGGLE FOR A FREE
STAGE IN LONDON

THE STRUGGLE FOR A FREE
STAGE IN LONDON

CHAPTER I

INTRODUCTORY

THE THEORY AND PRACTICE OF THEATRICAL
MONOPOLY DURING THE FIRST HALF CEN-
TURY OF THE PATENT THEATRES

OF all the follies committed by Charles II,
after his restoration to the throne of his
father, " of glorious memory," none seemed
more innocent than the creation of the monopoly
over the acted, national drama in London and
Westminster. And none, probably, was of more
far-reaching consequences, either as to the difficulties involved, or the duration of the controversies arising out of the simple, irresponsible
act of the King, when, on August 21, 1660, he
granted his letters patent to Thomas Killigrew
and Sir William Davenant, making them the
sole guardians of theatrical amusements in the
metropolis. For the monopoly thus created lasted
until near the middle of the nineteenth century;
and the train of strifes which it entailed gathered
in size and momentum to the end of the long

struggle waged against it. The causes alleged
by King Charles for this particular act form
not only a humorous commentary in themselves,
— when we recall the character of the brilliant
dramas written for the delectation of the Merrie
Monarch and his Court, — but they also, inad-
vertently as it were, contain the fulcrum on
which, later, the opponents to the monopoly operated to oust all patent rights connected with
the London theatres. In the preamble to the
grant to Killigrew and Davenant appears the
ostensible *raison d'être* of the theatrical monopoly created by Charles. "Whereas wee are
given to understand," so runs the document,
"that certain persons in and about our City of
London, or the suburbs thereof, doe frequently
assemble for the performing and acting of Playes
and Enterludes for reevards, to which divers of
our subjects doe for their entertainment resort,
which said Playes, as wee are informed, doe con-
taine much matter of prophanation and scurrility, soe that such kinds of entertainment, which,
if well managed, might serve as morall instructions in humane life, as the same are now used
doe for the most part tende to the debauchinge
of the manners of such as are present at them,
and are very scandalous and offensive to all pious
and well-disposed persons."

It is of little import to the later history of the

London stage, that the real reason why Killigrew was given such great privileges was that he
was " our trusty and well-beloved, . . . one of
the Groomes of our Bed-chamber," or that Sir
William Davenant was included in the grant because he had been a stanch supporter of Charles
I; the essential facts are the monopoly itself,
and the purposes for which it was created, as
recorded in the preamble just quoted. For although the separate patents issued to Killigrew
and Davenant on the 15th of January and 25th
of April, 1662, respectively, did not contain the
references to " morall instructions in humane
life," nevertheless, the grant of 1660 has ever
been looked upon as the origin of the theatrical
monopoly, and its enemies constantly made use
of it in after days as a weapon against the thing
they would destroy.

But the story of the struggle against the theatrical monopoly in London, to be understood,
must be followed in the order of its progress.
And, although the opposition to the monopoly
began almost within the second Charles's own
lifetime, it should be pointed out at once that for
the first fifty years of the history of the Patent
Theatres (the two built by Killigrew and Davenant, and designated as Drury Lane and Covent
Garden), there was no concerted action against
the monopoly, as such ; for it is doubtful whether

many concerned themselves about theatrical
privileges at that time. So long as the theatre-
going public were supplied with sufficient entertainment in kind and quantity, they cared
little, and knew less, about the principle on which
that entertainment was founded. Furthermore,
private speculation (as understood to-day) in
theatricals was a thing unknown in the period of
the Restoration, and this was a strong negative
factor calculated to support the monopoly. However, the practical operation of the monopoly, as
created by Charles, had its obstacles to contend
with, and these are as truly episodes in the struggle for a free stage in London, as if they had
been consciously aimed at the monopoly itself.
It is my purpose in this chapter to pass over in
review those incidents in the first fifty years of
the Patent Theatres, which tended to weaken the
monopoly and laid the foundation for the later,
conscious attacks upon it.

Killigrew's company of actors at Drury Lane
were taken under the fostering care of Charles
himself, while the Duke of York acted as patron
to Davenant's theatre. Both the King and his
brother exercised an active interest in the welfare of their respective " servants," and, to avoid
friction between the two theatres, the patents
themselves provided that the manager of neither
company should be permitted to receive actors

from the other house. To insure further the
amicable relations between the two theatres,
Cibber tells us in his "Apology," that " no play
acted at one house, should ever be attempted at
the other ; " to accomplish which, the plays of
the old dramatists, Shakespeare, Jonson, etc.,
were divided between the two companies. Under
such favoring conditions, both theatres prospered
for some years on equal terms. But as soon as
the stock plays were exhausted, this parity was
broken, the public showing its preference for
the King's company, which included the veteran
actors Hart and Mohun, Lacy, Kynaston, and
many others. To counteract the disadvantage in
which he found himself, Davenant had recourse
to music and dancing, expensive scenes, ma-
chines, and spectacles ; but as soon as the novelty
of these attractions wore off, he was left in the
same situation as before.

Over at the King's theatre, too, a reaction
was going on : the two greatest actors there,
Hart and Mohun, were growing too old to remain longer on the stage, and their exits were
sure to leave the Drury Lane Theatre in a crip-
pled state. The success of both companies being
thus decidedly on the wane, to save them, the
King, by suggestion or command, caused them
to be merged into one in 1682. Every precaution taken in 1660 to avoid a destructive compe-

tition had proved of little avail in the face of
human nature and practical affairs. Relative to
the situation as thus brought about, Cibber,
with his usual critical acumen, makes the following summary conclusion. It is directly opposed to the argument used the next century for
a free stage, but it is none the less applicable to
the conditions in 1682. He says: " I know that
it is the common Opinion, That the more Playhouses, the more Emulation; I grant it; but
what has this Emulation ended in? Why, a
daily Contention which shall soonest surfeit you
with the best Plays; so that when what *ought*
to please, can no *longer* please, your Appetite,
is again to be raised by such monstrous Pre-
sentations, as dishonour the Taste of a civiliz'd
People. If, indeed, to our several Theatres we
could raise a proportionable Number of good
Authors, to give them all different Employment,
then, perhaps, the Publick might profit from
their Emulation: But while good Writers are so
scarce, and undaunted Criticks so plenty, I am
afraid a good Play and a blazing Star, will be
equal Rarities."

The union of 1682 is the real beginning of the
theatrical monopoly in practice; for although
it had existed in fact before, it was not until
the patents were in one hand that the evil effects of the monopoly could appear. Then, for

the first time, the patentees might impose their own terms on the actors. But the combined companies were scarcely more successful than before the union ; for the same causes which led to a falling-off in the audiences in the first instance were still operative after 1682. To correct the deficit in the treasury, the patentees adopted the foolish policy of reducing the salaries of their leading actors, the mainstays of the theatre, and of shelving them for the feeble reason of giving young aspirants a chance in the leading parts.[1]

In a wild endeavor to better the financial situation of the theatre, shares were sold to speculators, who, knowing nothing of the dramatic and histrionic arts, favored a still further reduction of salaries. This step was looked upon as tyrannous by the actors, and, led by Betterton, Mrs. Barry, and Mrs. Bracegirdle, they revolted and laid their grievances before the chief officer of the King's Household, the Lord Chamberlain, then the Earl of Dorset, who, in the words of the old prompter, John Downes, " Espousing the Cause of the Actors, with the assistance of *Sir Robert Howard*, finding their Complaints just," carried the petition of the seceders to King William.[2]

A series of accidents greatly aided the cause

[1] *Apology*, pp. 152 ff.

[2] John Downes, *Roscius Anglicanus*, 1st ed., 1708, p. 43.

of the revolters. Before the matter could be
fully investigated by the King, the death of
Queen Mary, on the 28th of December, 1694,
necessitated a postponement of action on the
memorial. Meantime, public opinion gathered
on the side of the actors, so that, early in 1695,
when Betterton and his colleagues secured an
audience of his Majesty, it was not difficult to
convince him of the justice of their complaint.
The legal questions involved were submitted to
the King's lawyers, who gave it as their opinion,
"that no patent for acting plays given by one
Prince could prevent a succeeding one from
granting a similar privilege to those with whom
he could trust it." [1] Thereupon, King William
authorized a license to be issued to Betterton
and a select number of actors to erect a theatre
and establish a company independent of the patentees. A subscription was immediately filled,
a theatre was constructed out of Gibbon's Tennis
Court, and, from its location, named the "New
Theatre in Lincoln's - Inn - Fields." [2] Another
circumstance favorable to the revolters was the
enlistment of Congreve to the venture, who
brought with him his new play, *Love for Love*,
with which the new house was opened on the last

[1] Cibber, *Apology*, p. 157.

[2] Thus Downes; but *The Daily Courant* (e. g. December 28,
1702) invariably speaks of this theatre as the " New Theatre in
Little-Lincoln's-Inn-Fields."

day of April, 1695, and which proved so successful that " it took 13 Days successively." Downes
forgets to state, however, that *Love for Love*
had been written for the patent house, and that
on the secession of the leading actors, for whom
the chief characters had been written, Congreve
had no choice, thus causing a double blow to the
patentees.

The revolt of 1694–95 forms the first land-
mark in the history of resistance to the theatrical monopoly created by Charles II. What the
ultimate effect of this revolt might have been
on the monopoly, had the success of Betterton's
company, which started out so auspiciously, continued indefinitely, is a question which belongs
to the domain of unprofitable conjecture. The
facts are that Betterton was too old to manage
a theatre with vigor ; democracy was rampant
among his performers ; and to hasten the dis-
integrating influences already at work, Betterton
fell a victim to the public demand for novelty,
and imported, at enormous expense, dancers and
singers decked out in French furbelows. It is
no surprise, therefore, to read that the patent
house soon led in the estimation of the public,
and that within five or six years after the revolt,

> " . . . the peaceful tattle of the town
> Is how to join both houses into one." [1]

[1] Prologue to *The Unhappy Penitent.*

At this juncture in the declining state of the new company, Sir John Vanbrugh came forward and offered to relieve Betterton from his difficulties. Vanbrugh had but recently completed his fine, new Opera House in the Haymarket, and had opened it with an Italian troupe on the 9th of April, 1705. But the foreigners proved a failure, and so for both Vanbrugh and Betterton it was an opportune time to transfer the Lincoln's-Inn-Fields actors and license to the Opera House in the Haymarket. The building, however, was too large for the regular drama, and within a year from the opening, Vanbrugh abdicated, leaving his actors to manage for themselves. During the following summer (1706), Vanbrugh succeeded in unloading his theatrical burdens on the shoulders of one Owen Swiney, who, in all probability, was acting merely as the agent of Christopher Rich. Rich had purchased the theatrical patents from the Davenant heirs in 1690, and this clandestine move, as proved by events, was for the purpose of once more securing single control of the two companies. Wilks, Johnson, Mills, and Mrs Oldfield were permitted to join the company at the Opera House, though to outward appearances their abandonment of Drury Lane looked like a revolt. Foreseeing the trend of circumstances, Rich availed himself of the situation, and, to all in-

tents and purposes, the dramatic companies were
. again united at this time (October, 1706), though
the fact was not generally known until 1708,
when the actors, in despair, left the big house
in the Haymarket and returned to Drury Lane.
It was at this time that the arrangement was
made between the managers, whereby the Opera
House was to be appropriated exclusively to
Italian opera, the patent house to waive all
claims to that species of entertainment.

By the union of 1708 theatrical management
in London was brought back to the situation of
1682, and, as then, the monopoly was once more
complete. Betterton's revolt was a failure, due
to the inherent weaknesses of the management,
on the one hand, and to the tact and pertinacity
of Rich, on the other. One victory, however, of
inestimable value had been won against the principle of exclusive privilege in theatrical management, namely, that a tyrannical exercise of that
privilege might be successfully resisted. And
this position was supported by the legal sanction
of the King's counselors, a precedent better understood and used in later conflicts than could
have been foreseen in 1694.

It was an overweening confidence in the efficacy of his monopoly that had led Rich to oppress his actors in 1694; and now, with supreme
power once more in his hands (for the original

patents were presumably still in his possession),
he began to assume his old-time arrogance.
Once more he arbitrarily reduced the salaries of
his players, and once more they appealed to the
Lord Chamberlain for redress, with the result
that Rich was commanded to pay his actors in
full. This he stubbornly refused to do. Queen
Anne at once issued a silencing mandate (June
6, 1709), and ordered the Drury Lane Theatre
closed until further instructions. The unpaid
actors again resorted to the Opera House and
reëngaged with Swiney, who, it seems, after all,
had not played into Rich's hands. Just what
factors were at work in the present case different
from those which elicited King William's interference in 1694–95, it is not my purpose to inquire into here. There can be little doubt that
the declining state of theatrical representations
was sufficient cause for the crown to bring public amusements once more within the jurisdiction
of the Lord Chamberlain. And it is quite as certain that political influences coöperated to work
Rich's downfall. A short time before the troubles
of 1709, Captain Brett had been a shareholder in
the patent; but Rich's penchant for sole power
soon forced him out of the management. Brett's
political influence may have had something to
do with closing the patent house. But the essential thing is that Queen Anne did not hesitate

to silence the patents issued by Charles II, and that the restriction was not removed during her lifetime. The patents were null and void from June 6, 1709, until after the accession of George I in 1714, when John Rich, son of Christopher, was permitted to open his new Lincoln's-Inn-Fields Theatre under one of them.

Closely associated with the affair which led to the closing of the patent theatre there is an episode of peculiar interest. It is to be found in a report made to Queen Anne by her attorney and solicitor-general, in pursuance to an Order in Council of February 18, 1709, to inquire into the difficulties at the patent theatre. The report itself bears date of November 8, 1711. It contains Rich's excuse for not obeying the Chamberlain's order to pay the actors, viz., "because that officer's name was not mentioned in the patent; but that he readily assented to her Majesty's pleasure in shutting up the house, and had not since acted." The report further informs us that Rich continued in the capacity of tenant at Drury Lane until November 22, 1709, when William Collier (who was a lawyer, member of Parliament, and an intriguing politician) came to the door of the theatre with an armed band, " and in a riotous and violent manner " broke into the theatre, turned out Rich, and took possession. So much for Rich's testimony. Collier, on his side, produced a letter, dated November 19, 1709, containing her Majesty's permission for the said Collier to perform at the theatre on the 23d of November, and also stating that a license for him was in preparation. The letter further instructed Collier "not to permit Rich, or any other person claiming under him, to interfere with him [Collier] or his company." Collier was advised that a patent was of no effect unless supported by the crown; and that if any one claiming rights under the patent of Charles II should submit to her Majesty's pleasure, and waive all claims to the patent, the Queen would permit such an one to open the theatre. Now, it appears that this Collier was a shareholder in the patent, and, having made the required submission, had received the royal sanction to act on the date mentioned.[1]

The foregoing incident marks the second stage in the history of the theatrical monopoly, and forms the second precedent of the superiority of crown prerogative over patent rights. It would be rash, however, to conclude that the patents issued by Charles II, and still in Rich's possession, had been made nugatory by the silencing act of Queen Anne, or by the superseding license issued to Collier. But, certainly, the peremptory

[1] An abstract of this curious incident may be found in the *Dramatic Censor* for 1811, cols. 101–126.

conduct of the Queen had an unsettling effect on theatrical affairs for the time being.

Wilks, Colley Cibber, and Doggett, the three leading actors at the patent house at this time (1709), now entered into an arrangement with Swiney at the Opera House to conduct that theatre alternately as an English playhouse and Italian opera. This aroused Collier's jealousy, who, two years later, got Swiney to exchange theatres with him. But again the Opera House proved unsuccessful, and, in 1712, Collier returned to Drury Lane and took the leading actors with him. In the shuffle that was going on continually at this time, Doggett was discarded, and another actor, Booth, was taken into partnership at the patent house. The unfortunate Swiney, who had served as a hand-ball for others' games, failed at Vanbrugh's Opera House and was forced to abscond early in 1713. As for old Christopher Rich, "he would still hold out, notwithstanding his being so miserably maim'd. . . . He had no more regard to Blows, than a blind Cock of the Game; he might be beaten, but would never yield, the Patent was still in his possession, and the Broad-Seal to it visibly as fresh as ever." [1] But Rich did not live to avenge himself upon his enemies. He had bought and fitted up the Lincoln's-Inn-Fields Theatre against

[1] Cibber, *Apology*, p. 337.

the time when he might hope for better favor
from the crown. But he died a few weeks before
the opening of that theatre under his son, John
Rich, to whom the patents descended and who
opened the new Lincoln's-Inn-Fields Theatre in
1714, probably on the supposition that those
documents were valid and that Queen Anne's
silencing mandate ceased with her death.

One other circumstance, essential to the later
development of our subject, belongs to this period.
This was the conflict over the patent granted to
Sir Richard Steele in the first year of the reign
of George I. The patent was for the lifetime of
Steele, plus three years, the three years having
been included for the purpose of giving Steele's
executors time to settle his estate. The names of
Wilks, Cibber, and Booth were in Steele's patent
which, it would seem, was a continuation of Collier's license, which in turn had superseded Rich's
patent. From 1714 to 1719, theatrical affairs
ran smoothly enough. But, in the latter year,
the Lord Chamberlain (then the Duke of Newcastle) affected to receive some sort of umbrage
from Colley Cibber, one of the shareholders in
Steele's patent, and forbade that gentleman to
perform at Drury Lane. This action was but
the preliminary to the one that followed, declaring the patent forfeited. It is not my purpose to
enter into all the details which culminated in

this event — some of these, at least, belong to the
history of politics; it is sufficient here to point
out those facts affecting the theory and practice
of theatrical monoply. Steele appealed his case
to the Lord Chamberlain, but was forbidden
by that official to write, speak, or correspond
with him in any manner whatever. Steele then
raised the plea that his patent was a freehold,
and had been so adjudged by the Solicitor-General and Sir Edward Northey, another eminent
lawyer, when the document was passing. The
same legal authorities are quoted as favoring
the opinion that the grants of Charles II in
nowise limited succeeding sovereigns in similar
matters. In other words, Steele maintained that
his patent was of the same legal value as those
of Killigrew and Davenant, except as to time,
the equivalent of which, he claimed, he might
have had for the asking. The highest legal authorities of the day, F. Pemberton, Sir Edward
Northey, and Sir Thomas Parker, are cited as
supporting the view that, though the operation of
the patents granted by Charles II might continue
after his death, no prohibition on acting plays
in London or Westminster could be effectual
beyond the life of the king issuing it. But all
resistance was in vain. Every argument brought
forward by Steele in support of his patent, as opposed to the original patents granted by Charles

II, only armed the King so much the more in exercising his prerogative, which he did on January 23, 1719–20 in an order revoking Steele's patent, and another discharging the performers.[1]

A review of Steele's case, together with Rich's ejectment in 1709, brings out the very evident conclusion that, irrespective of the political jugglery which characterized the period, the crown saw the necessity, and acted accordingly, of bringing theatrical amusements in London under the jurisdiction of the Lord Chamberlain. As to the question of patent rights, based on the grants to Killigrew and Davenant, neither King William, Queen Anne, nor George I hesitated to issue licenses and patents regardless of the action of any former sovereign. Even the patentees themselves, with the single exception of Steele, never once questioned the crown prerogative in theatrical matters. Christopher Rich alone seemed to appreciate the value of the old patents, and while he silently obeyed the mandate of Anne to close Drury Lane Theatre, he held fast to his patents

[1] Steele supported his cause before the public in a two-page sheet, issued twice a week, over the pseudonymn of " Sir John Edgar." Later, his defense was published in pamphlet form as "The State of the Case between the Lord Chamberlain of His Majesty's Household, and the Governor of the Royal Company of Comedians, with the Opinions of Pemberton, Northey, and Parker, concerning the Theatre." Pp. 31, London, 1720. See also *Dramatic Censor* for 1811, cols. 115 ff.

and passed them on to his son. After events proved Rich the most far-seeing manager who appeared during the first half-century of the history of the monopoly. And as regards that same monopoly, it is well to note here that not once during the period thus far reviewed do we hear a single voice in support of a theatrical monopoly. Drury Lane itself, the home of the monopoly, after the ejection of Rich, was managed under a temporary license for twenty-one years, which expired and was renewed in 1732. It was during this period (1711–1732) that Drury Lane, under the expert management of Wilks, Cibber, and Booth, was the most prosperous. It was during this period, too, that the theatrical situation in London was affected by new elements which led to the climax of 1737.

CHAPTER II

THE RISE OF THE HAYMARKET AND GOODMAN'S
FIELDS THEATRES, AND THEIR EFFECTS ON
THE QUESTION OF PATENT RIGHTS

THE first half-century of the Patent Theatres
in London constitutes an epoch in the history of the monopoly, characterized by a lack of
competition in the theatrical business — outside
that between the two houses, of course — and by
an almost constant exercise of the crown prerogative over the patentees. The public were interested in the theatres chiefly as means for their
amusement. However, from about 1720, a new
turn is given to theatricals in London, a turn
which, for a time, threatened to submerge both
the patent houses, but, instead, culminated in establishing the monopoly more firmly than ever
before. Numerous causes might be adduced to
explain this phenomenon. Two of these stand
out in strong contrast to the rest. The immense
success of Cibber and his colleagues in managing Drury Lane called the attention of shrewd
business men to the commercial side of supply-
ing the public taste with theatrical novelties.
Furthermore, as has been suggested already, the

strong hand of the crown over the patentees, on numerous occasions, led men interested in the matter to have a contempt for the patents issued by Charles II. And, in the second place, the rising spirit of satire had an instantaneous effect on the stage. There is no avenue so inviting to the satirist as the drama, for the very gossipy nature of such performances assures for them a large public. The development of competition in theatricals and the rapidly growing tendency to satirize political and social foibles reinforced each other, and thus increased the demand for more theatres. Within a decade after 1720, London boasted half-a-dozen theatres, and every street had its theatrical booth where performances similar to those at the other theatres might be seen.[1] This new phase of the problem forced the patentees to adopt a fixed policy of action against the "minors" (for so the independent theatres were called), and precipitated parliamentary interference in theatrical exhibitions.

It was in 1720 that a carpenter by the name

[1] In a single number of the *Grub Street Journal* (August 27, 1730), no less than five theatrical booths are advertised. One of these advertisements runs as follows: "At Mr. Penkerthman and Mr. W. Giffard's great Theatrical Booth, is acted a new Droll, called *Wat Tyler and Jack Straw*, in which are presented my Lord Mayor, four Mobbs, and a great deal of hollowing, singing and dancing."

of Potter began the erection of a new theatre in the Haymarket, nearly opposite to the Opera House built by Vanbrugh. It does not appear that Potter intended to start a rival company to the patentees; he seems to have built his new theatre as a mere speculation, hoping to let it for occasional dramatic exhibitions. It is difficult to determine the exact date when Potter opened his Little Theatre in the Haymarket (so called to distinguish it from the Opera House); but the first play-bill collected by Genest for this theatre is as follows: " At the new Theatre over against The Opera House in the Haymarket, December 12, 1723, will be presented a new Comedy called the Female Fop — to be performed by persons, who never yet appeared in public." Cheap operas, burlesques, and farces formed the usual programme at the Little Theatre during its early years, and these performances became more and more pointed and pronounced in their satiric and burlesque elements. *Penelope*, a burlesque opera in three acts, was brought out at the Haymarket in 1728. The next year, *Patron*, or *Statesman's Opera*, was produced there, as was also the *Beggar's Wedding*, suggestive of Gay's famous *Opera* of the year before. Probably, the most popular of the satires put on at the Haymarket in 1729 was *Hurlothrumbo*. This took London by storm, had a phenomenal run of over thirty nights, and was discontinued only because the season was at an end.[1] It swept over England, was enacted with great applause at the chief cities, — and the suspected political satire made it none the less popular.

The following season (1730), *Tom Thumb* made his *début;* and, the same year, *Rival Father* (from Corneille's *Death of Achilles*), *Female Parson, Merry Masqueraders*, and other farces and burlesques of similar character came out at the Haymarket. The taste of the theatre-going public and the tendency of the London stage in 1730 are indicated by the foregoing list of plays; for although the Little Theatre may have been the greatest sinner of the lot, it was not alone, as will soon appear, in catering to an ever-increasing depraved public demand for highly seasoned dramatic exhibitions. In 1731, Chetwood took his *Generous Freemason* to the Haymarket Theatre (it had been acted the year before at Oates and Fielding's booth),[2] and it is probable that Fielding's *Letter Writer* was acted there the same year.

The condition into which the stage was rapidly drifting could not long continue without a crisis. The climax to be reached needed only a master

[1] *Fog's Weekly Journal*, July 5, 1729.
[2] *Grub Street Journal*, August 27, 1730.

in satire. By 1731, the necessity for placing a check on unbridled scurrility on the stage had become evident. It was during the summer of that year that the then but recently popular *Hurlothrumbo* was placed under the ban. In "Fog's Weekly Journal" for August 28, 1731, we read the signs of the time: "The Players of the Little Theatre in the Haymarket last Week printed their Bills for acting a celebrated piece call'd *Hurlothrumbo*, but were prevented by certain Constables, who came to seize them by Virtue of a Warrant or Warrants from the Justices of Westminster; so that this seditious Play will be acted no more, and, if it be true, that the silly Character of Lord Flame is meant as a Satyr upon any body, it was prudent to prevent it." The following year a histori-tragi-comi-ballad opera, entitled *Restauration of King Charles the Second*, or *The Life and Death of Oliver Cromwell*, was forbidden to be acted at the Haymarket. But the limit of this satiric rage in the London theatres had not yet run its course, and before the sudden reaction of 1737 new elements were added to the situation, tending to hasten and to complicate the solution.

Hitherto, the London theatres had been confined to the West End, that is, within the limits of the city proper. In 1729, a new theatre was added to the list; and this business venture

was made in the East End. In the "Coffee-House
Morning Post" of the 24th of September, 1729,
an announcement appeared to the effect that "a
Gentleman well-skilled in the Management of
a Theatre, has obtained Letters Patent to erect
one in *Ayliffe-Street*, in *Goodman's Fields*, by
Way of Subscription, and that the Undertaking
meets with Approbation." On the 30th of the
same month, the "Daily Post" informed the
public that "it appears that only seven or eight
Persons have applied to the Justices against
Erecting the said Theatre, but that there has
been no meeting about it." The gentleman
"well-skilled" was Thomas Odell; but if his
"undertaking" met with "approbation" at the
time of the advertisement in the "Morning Post,"
there must have been a violent reversal of public opinion within a few weeks, for, "on Tuesday
Night last [October 7, 1729]," reports "Fog's
Weekly Journal" for October 11, 1729, "the
Justices of the Peace, Gentlemen, and principal
Inhabitants in Goodman's Fields, and Places adjacent, had a General Meeting at the Hoop and
Grapes in the Minories, to concert Measures to
put a Stop to the further Progress of the New
Theatre, intended to be erected in Ayliffe-Street."
This protest bears the signatures of "Sam. Cow-
per and Sam Sadleir, clerks to the Justices for
the Tower Division." Their opposition to the

proposed new theatre was based on the grounds that, being " so near several publick Offices, and the *Thames*, where so much Business is negotiated, and carried on for the support of Trade and Navigation, will draw away Tradesmen's Servants and others from their lawful Callings, and corrupt their Manners, and also occasion great numbers of loose, idle and disorderly Persons, as Street-Robbers and Common Night-Walkers, so to infest the Streets, that it will be very dangerous for his Majesty's Subjects to pass the same." [1]

In a similar strain, the Lord Mayor was appealed to, to suppress the Goodman's Fields playhouse, for, it was apprehended, the cost of that theatre to the kingdom would be found to be " a great deal above *Three Hundred Thousand Pounds* a year by the loss . . . in the work and labour of the Artificers and other Spectators that fill it." [2] From the pulpit Arthur Bedford, chaplain to Hoxton Hospital, and preacher of

[1] *Gazette* for October 14, 1729. Appended to Arthur Bedford's " A Sermon Preached in the Parish Church of St. Butolph's in the City of London, November 30, 1729."

[2] From a letter by a citizen to Sir Richard Brocas, Lord Mayor of London, 1730, referred to in " An Extract from a MS. by Oldys," and commented on in a marginal note to an original (1708) copy of Downes's *Roscius Anglicanus.* See Joseph Knight's Preface (xxxiii) to his facsimile reprint of Downes's book.

afternoon Sunday sermons at St. Butolph's, Aldgate, hurled his invectives against Odell's project. The charges brought by Bedford against the stage remind one of the upbraidings of the Puritans a century before. He accused the dramatists and the theatres of profaning the name of God; of inciting duels and murders; of inducing idleness among the youth by alluring them away from their work " again and again; " of fostering adultery and whoredom;[1] of paving the road to thievery and outlawry (a thrust at the *Beggar's Opera*); and of breeding a contempt for all religion.

Odell does not seem to have been deterred by these railings; for all authorities agree that he completed his theatre, gathered a company of actors, and began theatrical performances. The exact date of the opening, however, is uncertain. There is every indication that the Goodman's Fields Theatre was extremely successful from the outset; so much so, indeed, that the clamor against it was greater after it opened than before. The evils apprehended before the erection of the theatre seemed to have multiplied fourfold after the opening, and it became evident that some-

[1] Bedford cites the play *Gibraltar* in which the following appears : " Whores are dog cheap here in London. For a man may slip into the play-house Passage, and pick up half-a-dozen for half-a-crown."

thing must be done to appease its opponents. But the situation was unique. Goodman's Fields lay outside the jurisdiction of the Lord Mayor and Aldermen of London, and there was no precedent, at least in the memory of men then living, for dealing with the case. In an attempt, therefore, to bring the matter to a head, on the 28th of April, 1730, the Lord Mayor and Aldermen petitioned the crown to silence Goodman's Fields Theatre, alleging the objections, moral and industrial, already presented. To this appeal his Majesty gave his promise to issue the required order.[1] The next day Odell waited on the King at court and appealed for leave to continue his performances at the theatre as usual; but his request was denied.[2] Thus forced out of his undertaking, Odell secured a piece of ground near Tottenham Court Road and began to erect a new playhouse.[3]

But the silencing mandate of the King was of short duration, and if Odell had been possessed of the temerity of his manager, Henry Giffard, he might have continued his operations at the Goodman's Fields Theatre without

[1] *St. James Evening Post*, April 30, 1730. Quoted in *Grub Street Journal*, May 7, 1730.

[2] *Post Boy*, April 30, 1730. Quoted in *Grub Street Journal*, May 7, 1730.

[3] *St. James Evening Post*, July 30, 1730. Quoted in *Grub Street Journal*, August 6, 1730.

other molestation than the maledictions of the
preachers and tradesmen. Giffard, for his age
(b. 1699), had had considerable experience: at
seventeen, he was a clerk in the South Sea Company; at twenty, he took to the stage, played at
Bath awhile, then joined Rich's Lincoln's-Inn-
Fields company, thence to Dublin where he rose
to the management of the theatre. Soon after
Odell launched on his Goodman's Fields venture,
he admitted Giffard, and, because of the latter's
superior training in the business, turned over the
management of the theatre to him.[1] When Odell
was driven, as he thought, to seek new fields for
his speculations, Giffard remained at his post in
Goodman's Fields and awaited his opportunity.
The year after the silencing order, Giffard took
the theatre on his own account, remodeled it,
refurnished it with costumes and scenes, and
opened on the 27th of September, 1731, with
George Barnwell.[2] The old clamors against the
playhouse were at once revived with redoubled
fury. "The street where it is built," wails the
"Universal Spectator" (April 12, 1732), "was
formerly inhabited by Silk-Throwsters, Riband-
Weavers, etc, who employ'd the industrious

[1] This account of Giffard, up to his joining Odell, is made
up from Chetwood's narrative, *A General History of the Stage*,
etc. p. 166.

[2] *Fog's Weekly Journal*, No. 149, September 11, 1731.

poor; immediately on setting up this Playhouse, the rents were raised, and now there is a Bunch of Grapes hanging almost at every door, besides an adjacent bagnio or two; . . ." But Giffard continued in peaceful security, nothing disturbed, until 1737, when the Goodman's Fields Theatre was effectually closed.

The question whether Giffard built a new theatre distinct from the one erected by Odell, and, if he did, where it was located, has been in much doubt and confusion. Most, if not quite all, of the authorities on the subject are of opinion that Giffard, after Odell's ejection, did build another theatre; but they all are at sea as to the location of one or other of the supposed two theatres in Goodman's Fields. The misconception respecting the matter has probably grown out of one of Chetwood's numerous incorrect statements. The statement is this: " In 1733 Giffard caused to be built an intire new, beautiful, convenient Theatre, by the same architect as that of Covent Garden." The other eighteenth century writers correct Chetwood as to the date, 1732 being more in favor with them; but none of these designates the site of Giffard's theatre. The painstaking Genest is disturbed by such indefiniteness, and seeks relief in the assumption that there were two theatres in Goodman's Fields, and conjectures that Odell's was in Leman Street, Giffard's

in Ayliffe Street.[1] One other evidence gives
color to the theory that Giffard built a new theatre. "The Gentleman's Magazine" for October,
1732 (p. 1028), in giving an account of the
opening night at Goodman's Fields, speaks of
the house as a "new Theatre," and gives a de-
tailed description of its interior.

The probabilities are, however, that there was
only one theatre in Goodman's Fields at the time
under discussion, that it was built by Odell in
Ayliffe Street, and later was remodeled or rebuilt by Giffard. The evidences for this conclusion are numerous. The advertisement in the
"Coffee-House Morning Post," September 24,
1729, distinctly mentions Ayliffe Street as the
site of the proposed new theatre. That this was
Odell's theatre is plain, for Giffard was not then
in London, and no authority places Giffard's con-
jectural new theatre before 1732. Furthermore,
we know that Giffard did remodel the Odell theatre in 1731, if we may rely on the statement
made in " Fog's Weekly Journal," September 11,
1731, and it is improbable that he should build
" an intire, new, beautiful, convenient Theatre "
between the closing of the season 1731–32 and
the opening in the following autumn. As to the
reference in " The Gentleman's Magazine " to
" the new Theatre in Goodman's Fields," Odell's

[1] Genest, *Some Account of the English Stage*, iv, 196.

theatre was still new, and the refurbishings made
during the summer would justify the description.
Again, in the " Weekly Miscellany," March 8,
1735, there is a remonstrance against a proposed
new theatre near the centre of the city, and in the
course of the complaints reference is made to
the silencing of Odell's theatre ; " but it still continues despite the order," emphatically declares
the remonstrant. As a final proof that Giffard
did not build a second theatre, one needs only
to recall that when John Rich moved into his
new Covent Garden Theatre (1733), Giffard
was induced to rent Rich's Lincoln's-Inn-Fields
house, whither he removed in the spring of 1736
(but soon returned to Goodman's Fields). If
Giffard had but recently completed a new theatre of his own in Goodman's Fields, it is not
likely that he would leave it so soon for the
vacated theatre in Lincoln's-Inn-Fields.

But a question of greater importance to our
subject relates to Giffard's tenure at Goodman's
Fields Theatre. It would seem that Odell opened
the theatre under some sort of royal authority,
and it was the withdrawal of that authority which
caused him to abandon his venture. This, however, he did not do without a vehement protest.[1]
Yet there can be no doubt that he acknowledged
the authority of the crown in the matter. As to

[1] Knight's Preface to Downes's *Roscius Anglicanus*, p. xxxiii.

Giffard, the case is quite different. Public opinion was as strong against him as against Odell; nevertheless, he continued to operate the Goodman's Fields Theatre for years unmolested, and without any visible authority other than his own audacity. Still, not only does it appear that it was the common opinion of the time that Giffard's course in acting plays without a license was not unlawful, but, also, the doubt was frequently expressed whether the crown prerogative itself extended so far as to silence playhouse managers not holding their privileges from the crown.[1] This is the key to an understanding of theatrical affairs in London from 1720 to 1737, distinctly marking the period off from the first fifty years of the patent theatres. It means that, for the first time since 1660, crown prerogative in matters of public amusement, so far as protection was concerned, was placed below the authority of independent theatre managers. It means that those interested in the theatre as a business had discovered that patent rights were inferior to independent speculation; for experience had proved that the crown might silence what it had created. Hence, the bold competition which sprang up from about 1729 onwards; a competition which placed the patentees on a par with

[1] Cibber, *Apology*, p. 228; *Weekly Miscellany*, March 8, 1735; *London Magazine*, March, 1735.

any adventurer who desired to enter the field. An extravagant abuse of this newly discovered toleration led to the stringent measure of 1737.

Before taking up the immediate causes which brought about the Licensing Act, it will be necessary to examine the doings of the patentees themselves. In 1733, John Rich removed from Lincoln's-Inn-Fields to his new Covent Garden Theatre, which he opened under one of the two original patents, still in his possession. About the same time, Booth, one of the owners of Drury Lane Theatre, died, and his widow, Wilks, and Colley Cibber disposed of the theatre to John Highmore, Esquire.[1] Giffard of Goodman's Fields seems to have been admitted by Highmore to a one sixth share in the concern, because of his successful experience.[2] Highmore was a gentleman of leisure and sport, but was unsuited to the business of managing a theatre. For, almost immediately after he assumed control of Drury Lane, he fell out with his actors, who accused him of tyranny and revolted from his standard. The fact of the matter is that Theophilus Cibber, son of Colley, was incensed because his father did not pass the control of the theatre on to him instead of disposing of it to

[1] *Daily Post*, March 27, 1732-33. Quoted in *Grub Street Journal*, March 29, 1733.

[2] *Grub Street Journal*, October 11, 1733.

Highmore, and so determined to wreck the new manager. Exorbitant demands were made on Highmore, among others that he should share the profits with the actors. This the proprietor, somewhat stiff-necked, flatly refused to do: he felt that twelve guineas per week each for the season was as much as the actors were worth to him. No doubt, prejudice was created against Highmore from the circumstance of his holding in his single possession the shares of the three former patentees. And, moreover, the contention raised by Theophilus, that a theatre would be better managed by actors than by private speculators, had its weight in the controversy; for had not the halcyon days of Drury been under the management of Cibber, Wilks, and Booth? But Highmore was adamant; even the threats of the actors to take forcible control of the theatre did not move him. Thereupon, in May, 1733, the younger Cibber led a revolt against the new manager, and secured the Little Theatre in the Haymarket for his disaffected company. The elder Cibber used his influence to secure a patent for his son; but this was denied, and the revolters continued the season at the Haymarket without authority.[1]

---

[1] *Grub Street Journal*, June 7, 14, July 2, 1733; Cibber, *Apology*, pp. 228 ff.; Victor, *History of the Theatres of London and Dublin*, i, 20 ff.; Genest, *English Stage*, iii, 400–406.

Charles Macklin, the Irish comedian, at first joined the seceders, but thought better of it and returned to Highmore. He was the only actor of note to remain at Drury Lane, and, just as Colley Cibber had found his opportunity to rise in his profession by the revolt of Betterton, years before, so now Macklin took the current when it served and placed himself in a position from which he could not be stirred when the revolters returned to Drury Lane in the following March. But it was impossible for the "very middling company" at Drury Lane to compete with the old actors at the Haymarket, and, almost from the outset of the contest, Highmore found his weekly expenses far to exceed his receipts. At first he had thought to depend on the interference of the Lord Chamberlain in his behalf, but that member of the King's household could not be induced to venture in the case at all. Finally, on the 30th of October, 1733, overtures with the actors at the Haymarket were attempted, in which Highmore succeeded in enlisting Rich of Covent Garden — for some of the actors at the latter theatre seem to have taken advantage of the occasion to join the Haymarket revolters. A letter from the patentees was addressed to " Mr. John Mills and the other persons acting at the Haymarket, but lately belonging to Drury Lane and Covent Garden." This superscription was adopted, no doubt, for the purpose of slighting Theophilus Cibber, the ringleader of the seceding company. In this letter the patentees expressed a hope that an amicable understanding might be reached between the contending parties, but added that, if the actors persisted in their separation, " which is greatly prejudiced to us, we shall be necessitated (tho' contrary to our inclinations) to proceed in such a manner as the law directs, for supporting the royal patents under which we act." [1] The letter was returned unopened. It was then readdressed to " Mr. Theophilus Cibber," who at once answered in a haughty note that " he had been advised that his action was legal, that he knew it to be reasonable, and that he declined to change his present condition for servitude."

Seeing that all negotiations for peace were of no avail, the Vagrant Act of 12 Queen Anne was resorted to by the patentees to test the legality of acting plays without a license, or, in other words, to test the power of theatrical monopoly rights. Accordingly, on the fifth day of November, 1733, at the instigation of Rich of Covent Garden and Highmore of Drury Lane, Mills of the Haymarket company and Giffard of Goodman's Fields were summoned to appear

[1] This letter and the answer by Cibber appeared in the public prints at the time.   Genest copies them, iii, 404, 405.

before Sir Thomas Clarges, justice of the peace
for Middlesex, to show why their respective
companies should not be convicted as vagrants
(within the meaning of 12 Anne) for acting without patents. Both sides were represented by a
strong array of counsel, after hearing which "the
Justices were pleased to dismiss both the companies honorably, without making any order
against either of them."[1]

The patentees refused to abide by this decision. Learned counsel advised them to seize on
the person of one of the leading players at the
Little Theatre, by virtue of a warrant of a justice of the peace, and commit him to prison as
a vagrant. Accordingly, one Harper was arrested by the constables and hurried off to Bride-
well. Ample preparations were made on both
sides to test the act of 12 Anne; and on the
28th of November, 1733, Harper's cause came
up for hearing in the King's Bench. Once more,
to the chagrin of the patentees, the case went
against them, and Harper was dismissed. Colley Cibber, who was present at this trial, gives
the following reason for Harper's acquittal:[2]
"When the Legality of this Commitment was
disputed in *Westminster-Hall*, by all I could
observe, from the learned Pleadings on both

---

[1] *Grub Street Journal*, November 3, 1733.
[2] *Apology*, p. 229.

Sides (for I had the Curiosity to hear them) it did not appear to me, that the Comedian, so committed, was within the Description of the said Act, he being a Housekeeper, and having a Vote for the *Westminster* Members of Parliament. He was discharged accordingly, and conducted through the Hall with the Congratulations of the Crowds that attended, and wish'd well to his Cause." Victor dissents from this opinion, averring that housekeeping was no defense against vagrancy, insinuating that this was a mere ruse to hoodwink poor Highmore ; for it would seem that there was a concerted plot to ruin the new manager by the very ones who had most to thank him for. Victor's discussion of this point is sufficiently important to quote in full. "I doubt not," he says,[1] "but my Reader has had Penetration enough to see the notorious Blunder committed here; tho' Mr Cibber either did not, or would not see it, though he observes the learned Pleadings entirely turned on that single Point, *Harper's being a Housekeeper;* I well remember when I heard the Event of this Trial, and on what a scandalous Error all their boasted Triumph was founded, I could not help suspecting the Integrity of the Person who conducted this Affair; because, if the *Housekeeper, who paid Scot and Lot*, could not be deemed

[1] *History of the Theatres of London and Dublin,* i, 23–25.

a Vagrant, the natural Question then follows,
Why was Harper singled out? A Man known for
many Years to be a Housekeeper in the Parish of
St Paul's, Covent Garden; when there were several more Eminent Comedians in that Company,
that constantly acted at both our Fairs, and were
not Housekeepers! But the Dice were thrown,
and the poor new Manager devoted to Ruin."
In a footnote to the foregoing argument, the
author, referring to the legal grounds on which
Harper was dismissed (as reported by Cibber),
says, "I have been well informed, Mr. Cibber
was mistaken in his Observation on the Pleadings in Court at that Trial, that so far from the
Housekeeper being a protection from the vagrant Act, a learned Councellor asserted, that
it was in the Power of the greatest Subject in
England to be guilty of an Act of Vagrancy;
and that the only point to be disputed there was,
whether Harper's performing in the Haymarket
Theatre was committing that Act?"

Only on personal grounds can we explain
Cibber's friendly attitude towards an avowed
enemy of patent rights, for he may usually be
found arrayed on the side of the theatrical monopoly. At any rate, soon after the close of
Harper's trial, Highmore sold out his interest in
the Drury Lane Theatre to Charles Fleetwood,
Esquire, to whose standard the revolters soon

returned, after they had closed their season at the Haymarket on the 9th of March, 1734, opening at Drury Lane on the 12th of the same month.[1] The circumstance of Cibber's revolt and Harper's trial brings out the fact that the patentees had determined to adopt some policy whereby they might defend the rights claimed by them under the grants of Charles II. It shows, also, that there was a growing practical opposition to the theatrical monopoly, which the King's officers seemed unable to brook, either because the legal aspects of the question were indistinctly understood, or because of the popular outcry against all appearance of servitude. It is not sufficient to account for the result of the two trials in this case on the grounds of Highmore's aristocratic hauteur; Theophilus Cibber's notoriously contemptible character was enough to turn that scale. The fact is, as was frequently iterated during the period, that the patents were no longer held in high regard, and the crown prerogative in theatrical amusements was openly doubted. Had not the revolt of 1733 directly affected the treasuries of the patent

[1] According to Victor (i, 26), Fleetwood purchased the whole of the Drury Lane patent; according to Cibber (*Apology*, p. 231), only five sixths of it. The latter is probably correct, as it appears that Giffard was still a partner at Drury Lane in August, 1735. (Genest, iii, 406, 471, 472.)

houses, it is doubtful whether their managers
would have thought of attempting to enforce
the Vagrant Act.

If the victory won in the Harper case had
been turned to the best account by the promoters of independent theatres, it is barely possible that the struggle of a century's duration to
free the metropolis from the worst features of a
theatrical monopoly might have been averted.
But something like an overweening audacity
was bred by the result of that trial, and what
before had been but the doubtful assertion of
free competition became now an avowed license
for all sorts of extravagances. Henry Fielding,
who for some years had been writing farces and
burlesques for the stage, saw the opportunity
which the outcome of the revolters' trial and
the success of the Goodman's Fields Theatre
opened to him to launch out on a theatrical venture on his own account. Some time after the
return of the seceders to Drury Lane, Fielding
organized his famous Great Mogul Company
and took possession of the Little Haymarket
Theatre, where he brought out his three-act comedy, *Don Quixote in England*, which had been
begun for the Drury Lane stage.[1] During the

[1] Genest, iii, 435. For an account of Fielding's Haymarket
Theatre and the Act of 1737, see Cibber's *Apology*, p. 231 ; Victor, i, 26, 66 ff ; Genest, iii, 406 ff ; Dibdin, iv, 709 ff ; Baker's

season of 1736, the political satire, *Pasquin*, had a run of fifty nights at the Haymarket. The next year, a number of Fielding's satires and burlesques were put on; *Tumble-down Dick, or Phaeton in the Suds*, was written to ridicule theatrical entertainments of the times in general, and, in particular, *The Fall of Phaeton*, which was acted at Drury Lane, March 1, 1736. Not only was Drury Lane satirized in the piece, but also the management of Covent Garden; in the dedication Fielding returned his compliments to Mr. John Lun (*i. e.* John Rich) for the latter's *Marforio*, a satire on *Pasquin*. In the "Historical Register for 1736," Fielding combined theatrical and political satire. "Quidam" was supposed to take off Sir Robert Walpole; the ridiculous contention between Mrs. Clive and Mrs. Cibber for the part of "Polly" was alluded to in the second act; and Colley Cibber's presumptuous alterations of Shakespeare's plays were unmercifully, but justly, scored.

Fielding's fire proved entirely too hot for the ranks against which it was aimed. Furthermore, no discriminations were made in the exposition of corruption, — the Prime Minister was placed

Biographia Dramatica, p. xii, and vol. ii, 138; *Life of Quin*, ch. v (London, 1766); *Prompter; Grub Street Journal; Gentleman's Magazine; Town and Country Magazine; London Magazine; Common Sense*, 1737; *Craftsman*, 1737; *Historical MSS. Commission.*

on a level with Harlequin of Covent Garden.
Most offensive of all, his satires and burlesques
hit too near the mark of truth to be long with-
stood unflinchingly. The report of the Secret
Committee, appointed by the government to investigate the criticisms of the satires, revealed
the fact that Fielding had not exaggerated.[1] At
any rate, some means had to be devised to put a
stop to this satiric license, which might degenerate into licentiousness at any time. The appearance of *The Golden Rump* gave the opportunity
to the goverment for interfering with the abuse
into which the theatre was rapidly drifting. This
was a two-act farce, containing the most pointed
sarcasm on the King and his ministers. The
author was unknown, the piece never appeared
in print; but a suspicion was current at the
time that it had been composed at the dictation
of Walpole himself, as the most direct way of
silencing Fielding and other political satirists
of the day.[2] This view is strengthened by subsequent events connected with the history of the
piece. The little farce was sent to Giffard of
Goodman's Fields, who had, it was thought,
made Sir Robert his enemy by representing

[1] J. Ralph, *The Case of our Present Theatrical Disputes*, p.
43, London, 1743.

[2] See *Town and Country Magazine* for October, 1787, p.
467.

pieces on his stage inimical to the character and interests of the minister. If the satire was sent to Giffard to entrap him into acting it, the snare did not work, for he at once forwarded a copy to Walpole, who laid it before the King. The result of this episode was a recommendation to Parliament to pass a bill to regulate and restrict the stage. This was the famous Licensing Act, or, as Genest characterizes it, the "gagging bill for the stage." It passed Parliament June 21, 1737, and is of such importance as to require separate treatment.

CHAPTER III

THE LICENSING ACT; THE CAUSES PRODUCING IT,
AND THE ATTEMPTS TO REGULATE THE STAGE
BEFORE THE PASSAGE OF THAT ACT

"To Henry F–d–g then are we indebted for the licencing act, and
the theatrical power that is now lodged in the licenser." — *Life of Mr.
James Quin*, London, 1766, ch. v, p. 27.

THE above quotation contains the statement
of a belief which was universally current
in the eighteenth century, and has continued
down to our time. Colley Cibber is, in a large
degree, responsible for this opinion, for writers
have followed his account of the transactions of
the period under consideration. But it is well
known that Cibber had cause for prejudice
against Fielding, since the latter had lampooned
the Cibber family pretty severely in the "Historical Register for 1736;" and hence, though
the "Apology" is generally fair, in this particular case allowance must be made for the vindictive spirit in which the account is written.
Cibber nowhere deigns to mention Fielding by
name, but alludes to him as "a broken wit."
"This enterprising Person," so runs the spite-
ful narrative in the "Apology," "this enterpris-

ing Person, I say (whom I do not chuse to name,
unless it could be to his Advantage, or that it
were of Importance) had Sense enough to know
that the best Plays, with bad Actors, would
turn but to a very poor Account; and therefore
found it necessary to give the Publick some
Pieces of an extraordinary Kind, the Poetry of
which he conceiv'd ought to be so strong, that
the greatest Dunce of an Actor could not spoil
it: He knew too, that as he was in haste to get
Money, it would take up less time to be in-
trepidly abusive, than decently entertaining ;
that, to draw the Mob after him, he must rake
the Channel, and pelt their Superiors ; that, to
show himself somebody, he must come up to
Juvenal's Advice, and stand the Consequence:

> *Aude aliquid brevibus Gyaris, & carcere dignum*
> *Si vis esse aliquis* — Juv. Sat. I.

Such then, was the mettlesome Modesty he
set out with ; upon this Principle he produc'd
several frank, and free Farces, that seem'd to
knock all Distinctions of Mankind on the Head:
Religion, Laws, Government, Priests, Judges, and
Ministers, were all laid flat, at the Feet of this
Herculean Satyrist! This *Drawcansir* in Wit,
that spared neither Friend nor Foe! who, to
make his Poetical Fame immortal, like another
Erostratus, set Fire to his Stage, by writing up
to an Act of Parliament to demolish it. I shall

not give the particular Strokes of his Ingenuity
a Chance to be remembered, by reciting them ;
it may be enough to say, in general Terms, they
were so openly flagrant, that the Wisdom of the
Legislature thought it high time, to take a proper
Notice of them." Victor, writing a few years
after the " Apology " was penned, Baker, Dibdin,
and subsequent students of the stage. substan-
tially agree with Cibber that Fielding's satires
were the cause of the Licensing Act.

While no one will doubt that the severity of
Fielding's satires was the occasion for precipitat-
ing the action of the government in restricting the
stage, to say that Henry Fielding was solely responsible for that Act of Parliament — without
materially modifying the statement — would be
rash, to say the least. For the tendencies at
work at the time, which called forth the biting
sarcasm of the great satirist, would, ultimately,
have brought about the regulation of the stage,
irrespective of Fielding's influence. It is my
purpose in this chapter to trace those tendencies,
as well as the attempts made to counteract them,
prior to the Licensing Act.

It is not easy, nor always possible, to point to
a definite beginning of a tendency of thought,
for the psychology of " movements " is too elu-
sive to be tabulated in statistical form. But it is
safe to say that the political tracts and pam-

phlets of the time, the satires and burlesques, criticising government, had their origin in the opposition to the policy and methods of the Whig Ministry of Sir Robert Walpole. The means sometimes used by that great statesman to maintain his hold on King and Commons, however praiseworthy the end aimed at, would have been, at any period of modern England, the target for political foes ; while the more serious mistakes (such as the methods employed in the attempt to pass the Excise Bill, 1733) were the occasions of a perfect volley of scathing abuse. Even within the ranks of the Whigs themselves, the Walpole Ministry was not always safe from attacks of the severest kind. Indeed, the great financier and advocate of peace could trace his final downfall to internal dissensions in his own party, as much as, or more than, to the strength of the Tories.

It was the most natural thing imaginable for the stage to make stock of the political foibles of the period, and the *Beggar's Opera* marks the beginning of that species of dramatic satire which reached its climax in Henry Fielding and the Licensing Act.[1] Soon after the accession

[1] In the *Craftsman*, No. 569 (May 28, 1737), appears an essay alleging that the satirical attacks on the government began in " Pamphlets, Poems, Journals," and afterwards " Prostituted the Stage." See also *Gentleman's Magazine*, May, 1737.

of George II, Gay's burlesque was brought out
(January 29, 1728). It was immediately as-
sailed as " the most venemous *allegorical libel*
against the Government that hath appeared for
many years. . . . The satirical strokes upon *Ministers*, *Courtiers*, and *great Men*, in general,
abound in every Part of this most insolent
Performance." [1] In adition to the charge of
" seditious design," contained in this farce, it
was said to encourage street robberies.[2]

The success of the *Beggar's Opera* [3] induced
Colley Cibber to attempt something of the same
nature, and, the next year, *Love in a Riddle*
appeared, only to be roundly damned. " It was
then generally thought," writes the biographer
of Quin, "that his [*i. e.* Cibber's] jealousy of
Gay, and the high opinion he entertained of his
new piece, had operated so strongly, as to make
him set every engine in motion to get the sequel
of the *Beggar's Opera*, called *Polly*, suppressed,
in order to engross the town entirely to *Love*

---

[1] *Craftsman*, No. 85, February 17, 1727–28.

[2] *Ibid*. No. 87.

[3] The *Beggar's Opera* was so successful that a company
actually ventured to Jamaica with it, where they are reported
to have taken in 370 pistoles (about $1450) at the door the first
night. The climate of the island, however, was so insalubrious
that "within the space of two months they buried their third
Polly, and two of their men." — Chetwood, *History of the Stage*,
pp. 40, 41.

in a Riddle." This bit of gossip may, or may not, be true ; but, at any rate, the Lord Chamberlain absolutely prohibited *Polly* from being presented, after it had been rehearsed and was just ready to come out.

This method of political satire, which began in pamphlets and journals, became so popular that the plays of the day contained repeated invectives against men of high position and authority in the state ; so much so, indeed, that some, who otherwise were in favor of a free stage, felt the necessity of some sort of censorship, and went so far as to propose the appointment of a committee to expurgate objectionable passages from dramatic pieces.[1]

Other complaints than that the theatres were going too far in their abuse of government were brought against the stage. " Avarice, Insolence, and Stupidity " were epithets applied to the Cibber-Booth-Wilks management of Drury Lane, in their treatment of dramatic writers ; and Rich of the other patent house escaped but little better. Of the latter it was asserted that " poets . . . must submit to have their work mangled by a Tumbler who can't spell, and truckle to the *ipse dixit* of an assuming ignorant *Harlequin.* The Vanity of *W——ks*, the Pertness of *C——r*, and the Arrogance of

[1] *Craftsman*, No. 140.

B——h,[1] they have found united in one single
Fellow without any of the good Qualities of the
other to atone for them." [2]

Such treatment as this, it was claimed, deterred the best writers from offering their productions to the stage, thereby leaving that
function to low-grade dramatists, who lowered
public taste and the dignity of the profession.
Once more, as in the early days of competition
between the patent houses, the legitimate drama
was allowed to decline, and pantomime, puppet-
show, and operas with their "sing-song concerts" without sense or plot, were substituted
instead. Aaron Hill, editor of the "Prompter,"
waged an incessant warfare against the managers of theatres for permitting and fostering
buffoonery in the place of the regular drama.
In addition to banishing common sense from
the stage, the managers were accused of don-
ning "party coloured caps" in their competition,
while "in respect of the French Harlequin at the
Little Theatre in the Haymarket," the national
drama was sure to suffer, if the middle gentry
and their children persisted in following the lead

1 Wilks, Cibber, and Booth.

2 "Tag-Rhime" in *Daily Courant* for February 26, 1732.
Quoted in *Gentleman's Magazine*, February, 1732. See also
Grub Street Journal, Nos. 112 and 115. In the latter, "Prosai-
cus" defends Rich, and insinuates that "Tag-Rhime" was
associated with the Drury Lane interests.

of "people of Quality" in learning French for the purpose of understanding such foolery.[1] The degeneracy and immorality of the English stage, due to "selfish management of actors, vicious performances, and a debauched public taste," was the subject of contempt and scorn for more than one moralist. "All our theatres put together," breaks out one of these, "could not furnish out one perfect company."[2] The silencing of some of the theatres was declared to be the only means left to protect public morals and save the dramatic art. Speculation in amusements had developed into "theatrical madness," and it was "high time that the stage should be opposed" by parliamentary interference.

As early as 1732, the evil tendencies into which the theatres were drifting and the necessity for regulating them were pointed out. The reason alleged for the deplorable condition was that theatres had been allowed to be conducted at random without regard to the merit or qualification of theatrical managers. It was this open trade in theatricals which had substituted farce and pantomime for Shakespeare and Otway.[3] The author of " A Proposal for the Regulation

[1] *Prompter*, No. 13, December 9, 1734.

[2] *Universal Spectator*, No. 340, April 12, 1735. Quoted in *Gentleman's Magazine*, April, 1735.

[3] *A Proposal for the Regulation of the Stage*, an essay, p. 21. London, 1732.

of the Stage" did not spare either of the patentees from the arraignment. The essayist,
while disavowing any aim to dispossess the two
houses (Drury Lane and Covent Garden) of their
patents, advocated the erection of a new theatre
"on a quite different establishment." "Theirs
[the patentees'] is confined to their own advantage, this [the essayist's proposed theatre] is
calculated for the good of the publick, for the
encouragement of learning, the improvement of
politness, and the honour of the age." All the
details of the plan of this proposed new theatre
are set forth at length, from the raising of the
funds to the writing and dressing of the plays
for representation. The main idea of the plan
was that a national theatre should not be run
by private speculators, as were the two patent
houses and the other theatres, but solely for the
purpose of encouraging the dramatic and histrionic arts. The plan is of the greatest significance
as being the earliest of its kind and as containing the germ of the third theatre arguments of
the next century. By third theatre is meant,
of course, a third theatre under the protection of
government.

Other schemes for the relief of the dramatic
situation were not wanting. In the summer of
1733, Exeter 'Change was advertised for sale,
and it was suggested that the building be pur-

chased and maintained by endowment as a theatrical college to "encourage virtue, discountenance vice, advance education, and be the means of perfecting theatrical entertainments . . . ," so that "foreigners would not find our theatres, which should be fountains of wit, fountains of folly." [1]

But nothing came of these plans, and the vices complained of continued. It was the opinion of most men that nothing short of parliamentary action could remedy the evils then possessing the theatres in London, and, early in 1733, a bill for that purpose was introduced into the lower house. In a letter from the Hon. Charles Howard to Lord Carlisle, dated May 24, 1733, mention is made of such a bill in the House of Commons "to regulate the playhouses." On its first reading, there was "a debate of about two hours upon it, but no Division," [2] and nothing came of this attempt.

A far more vigorous effort was made to check the current when, on the 5th of March, 1735, Sir John Barnard asked leave to bring a bill into the House of Commons to restrain the number and scandalous abuses of the London playhouses.

[1] *Grub Street Journal*, July 5, 1733 ; *Gentleman's Magazine*, July, 1733.

[2] *Historical MSS. Com.* Report XIV[6], p. 115. I have found this mentioned in no other place.

He represented, in particular, the mischief done by them to the metropolis "by corrupting of youth, encouraging vice, and debauchery, and greatly prejudicing industry and trade." The immediate occasion of Barnard's bill was the projection of a new theatre in St. Martin's le Grand.[1] When Barnard's motion was read, it was reported that many in the House "seemed to smile." However, Sir John was seconded by a number of gentlemen, including Sir Robert Walpole; and although the motion was "at first received with a sort of disdain," at length its supporters were numerous, and "it was spoke for both by young and old."

The speech of James Erskine, on this occasion, is especially interesting. The half dozen London playhouses, he declared, had brought a change for the worse to the British temper, "which, though cheerful and facetious formerly, yet was sedate and solid; but now so extravagantly addicted to lewd and idle diversions, that the number of Play-Houses in London was double to that in Paris; so that now we exceed in levity our fluttering, fiddling masters the French," whence came these follies "and many other im-

---

[1] Aaron Hill scouted this idea, thinking it to be only a stratagem of one of the patentees to alarm and incense the magistrates to destroy the lesser establishments. *Prompter*, No. liv, May 13, 1735.

pertinencies." Mr. Erskine greatly deplored the fact that " Italian eunuchs and signoras should have set salaries equal to those of the Lords of the Treasury and Judges of England, besides the vast gains which these animals make by presents . . . so that they carry away with them sums sufficient to purchase estates in their own country, where their wisdom for it is as much esteemed, as our vanity and foolish extravagance laughed at and despised." The speech had the desired effect, and leave was given to bring in a bill " for the restraining the number of Houses for playing Interludes, and for the better regulating common Players."

A month later (April 3), the bill was read for the first time and ordered to its second reading. But it was not destined to reach its final reading without serious obstacles. One clause in the bill provided that " no person or persons shall act, represent, or perform any tragedy, comedy, opera, play, farce, or other entertainment of the Stage, for gain, hire, or reward, other than, and except such person or persons in whom the right of property in and to the said Letters Patent, granted as aforesaid, to the said Thomas Killigrue, Sir William Davenant, Robert Wilks, Colley Cibber, and Barton Booth . . . is vested, and their respective deputies or servants, during the continuance of the process and privi-

leges of them by their several Letters Patents
respectively granted." The injustice of this part
of the bill to actors appeared in "The Case of
the Comedians of the Theatres Royal Drury
Lane and Covent Garden." This, it was pointed
out, would subject actors to the arbitrary will
of any one happening to own one of the patents,
reducing them to the hard terms and indignity
of being bought and sold as oxen. To remedy
this evil, should the bill become a law, a board
of arbitration was proposed, to act as an impartial court in all disputes between the patentees and the actors. It was thought wholly
unfair to authors and actors alike to place the
maintenance of the stage within the control of
caprice, or the possible ignorance of any one who
might look upon a theatrical patent merely as
a proper security in which to invest his money.[1]
If this complaint was new in 1735, it was to be
heard many times and oft before the evil feared
was corrected. It is noteworthy, this modern
view put forward in 1735, that the *profession*
of the actors was an investment as much to be
protected as the rights of the patentees.

A "vagrant" amendment, and others, also

[1] *Prompter*, No. xlv, April 15, 1735. Hill was in favor of
stage regulation, but he denied that restricting the number of
playhouses would at all correct the evil. The regulation, he
thought, should be of the management. Subsequent events
proved Hill a level-headed critic.

brought vigorous objections to the bill ; but its
doom was sealed in the proposal to insert a
clause to confirm (if not to enlarge) the power
of the Lord Chamberlain over the players. This
was carrying the question of restriction farther
than the promoters of the bill were willing to go.
The power of the Lord Chamberlain was thought
too great already, or at least it had been too
widely exercised on occasion (notably in prohibiting *Polly* and *Calista* from being acted). It
was therefore deemed advisable to postpone the
attempt to pass a bill such as that originally
contemplated, rather than to establish by law a
power which might be exercised in an arbitrary
manner, accompanied, it might be, by mischievous results. For this reason, the bill was suddenly withdrawn on the 30th of April (1735),
and the whole question left open for discussion
and for settlement at some future time.[1]

It was at this juncture that Henry Fielding
saw his opportunity, and, taking advantage of
the foibles about him in state and society, applied his genius to them with a success scarcely
dreamed of. And here it should be observed
that the great satirist had no special motives
against government ; he used the materials he

[1] The proceedings on Barnard's Bill are reported in Cobbett's *Parliamentary History of England*, vol. ix, cols. 944–
948. See also *Parliamentary Register*, vol. ix, p. 93.

found ready-made for the exercise of his talent and for his business interests. The low condition of the London stage itself, quite as much as the subject-matter of his political satires, accounts for his success at the Little Theatre in the Haymarket ; and this fact, which was then, and is still, generally overlooked, was clearly recognized by the best critic of the time. " The very great Run *Pasquin* has already had, and is still like to have," declares the acute editor of the " Prompter " (No. xlvii), " is the severest Blow that cou'd be given to our Theatres, and the strongest Confirmation of an Opinion I have ventured *singly*, to advance, viz, *That the Stage may* (and as it may, ought to) *be supported without Pantomime*." While the patent houses, with all necessary facilities for acting the legitimate drama, were competing in spectacle and dumb show, " a Gentleman, under the disadvantage of a very bad House, with scarce an Actor, and at very little Expense, by the single Power of *Satire, Wit*, and *Common Sense*, has been able to run a play on for 24 Nights, which is now but beginning to *rise* in the Opinion of the Town." *Pasquin* reached fifty nights before it was taken off. Hill saw that the work of Fielding was sure to bring about a speedy reorganization of the whole theatrical business in London. and he encouraged the effort with all his might.

His main objection to the satires was that they were not plain enough, that they should be more " in the *Carreggio Manner*."

As might be expected, it was Fielding's scurrilous attacks upon the follies of government on which men's opinions differed. Some maintained that a system of *lettres de cachet* and the Bastile should be practiced in England against those who dared question the affairs of state. To which it was retorted by the thorough-blood Briton : " What do you intend by mentioning these ? I hope not to threaten us nor to insinuate that nothing will make it *necessary* to introduce such damned Engines of Tyranny among us." [1] Men of the latter turn of mind believed that satire on government had a beneficial effect, and, though they would not contend that all government was a farce to be satirized, nevertheless, they asserted that greatness combined with meanness is the essence of burlesque.

But there was a third interest at stake in the controversy, namely, the question of decency and morality. So long as vice and corruption merely were satirized, men might argue till the crack of doom on the question of liberty and tyranny ; but so soon as society's sense of re-

[1] Correspondence in *Gazetteer* for May 7, 1737, and *Common Sense* for May 21, 1737 ; quoted in *London Magazine* for May, 1737.

spectability was offended by the *method* of satire, it was time to close the discussion and erect
the proper safeguards. And this is exactly what
happened ; as soon as the novelty of burlesque
itself wore off, the low public taste had to be
stimulated, and the manner, the language, of
satire was degraded for the purpose. In unprin-
cipled and irresponsible hands — and free competition had realized this possibility by 1737 —
there was no limit to this tendency. " Satyr
without scurrility," says one of the speakers in
*A Dialogue between the most Eminent Players
in the Shades*, " never failed of a warm Reception, but of late such an Inundation of Immorality, Scandal, and unbounded Licentiousness
had overwhelmed it, that loudly called upon the
Legislature for Reformation." [1] When this stage
was reached,[2] the remedy was at hand, sure and

---

[1] *Theatrical Correspondence in Death. An Epistle from Mrs.
Oldfield, in the Shades, to Mrs. Br . . ceg . . dle, upon Earth ;
Containing a Dialogue between the Most Eminent Players in the
Shades, upon the late Stage Desertion.* London, 1743.

[2] " They [*i. e.* the satirists] proceeded so far at last, that
a *Farce* was actually in Rehearsal, at one of our Theatres, in
which the *same excellent Person* [in the Government] was to
have been introduced on the stage, as we are informed, with
a *Pair of Scales* in one Hand, to Scandalize his Office and
lugging up his Breeches, to reflect upon his Politeness. But this
Abominable Design was happily discovered by the *Vigilance* of
Another great Personage, . . . who . . . is determined to take
Vengeance . . . by putting an effectual Restraint upon the

severe, but more far-reaching in its effects, probably, than was intended at the time.

Consequently, a bill was prepared (in all probability at the suggestion of the Prime Minister), bearing certain resemblances to Sir John Barnard's bill, as amended, and hurried through the House of Commons at a time when but few members were present. The main provisions of the bill were simple and direct. It prohibited, under penalty of £50, the acting for " hire, gain, or reward " of any play or theatrical performance of any kind soever not previously sanctioned by letters patent from the crown, or licensed by the Lord Chamberlain. All theatres were to be restricted to the city of Westminster and the liberties thereof, and to the place where the royal family happened, at any time, to reside. Copies of all plays to be acted must be placed in the hands of the Lord Chamberlain at least a fortnight before being represented.

In a letter from Colonel Cope to Edmund Weston, dated May 28, 1737, among other interesting things is a curious side-light on the Licensing Bill. It runs as follows: " Mr. Horace Walpole is expected in London from Norfolk this night. The Parliament, 'tis thought, will sett about a fortnight after the Holydays,

Stage." *Craftsman*, No. 569, May 28, 1737 ; *Gentleman's Magazine*, May, 1737.

in which time The Scotch Bill may be passed in
case the North Brittains are not strong enough
to throw it out before, for as they divided 99
against 140 odd, on the early or late day for the
consideration of the Bill, 'tis imagined they will
come pretty near in the Progress of the Bill, by
many of the Majority going out of Town & such,
as the Master, Mr. Pulteny and others, I am
told, not designing to attend it, they were acci-
dentally in the division for the Comitment of the
Only Bill by waiting to flame & exclaim about
the Playhouse Bill, I mean Mr. Pulteny for the
Master was strong for the suppression of Playhouses &c. and said that tho' it was a thin house,
yet he thought if those Gentlemen who were ab-
sent, as had been urged, differ in opinion with
him and be against the bill, he thought they were
better employed in looking after their own affairs,
upon which Pulteny did roast him most violently, & said a man who made so great a figure
in his Profession in another place, might better
keep to that place, then fell upon Winnington
without mercy, and spared not Sr. Robt nor Sr
Wm Yonge urging that this restraint upon the
Writers for the Stage, was a certain preamble to
the taking away the Liberty of the Press in general, told a story, that Charles ye 2nd seeing a
man in the pillory, asked the crime, 'Twas libelling Lord Clarendon, odds fish ! cries the king,

why did not the Fool go on libelling of me, he must now certainly suffer for libelling this great man. Ye Bill will pass & no Playhouse be allowed but in the Liberties of Westminster, & these to be licenc'd & under the direction of the Lord Chamberlain." [1]

One of the first objections raised to the bill was the almost unlimited power which it vested in the Lord Chamberlain. The discouragement it would cast on dramatic art by forcing writers to cater to the Lord Chamberlain's taste was also pointed out. Again, it was asserted that, if it was the licentiousness and immorality of the stage at which the bill aimed, it was unnecessary, as the law already provided for the prosecution of libelers and immoral persons. Furthermore, an occasional abuse of liberty, it was thought, could be better tolerated than the fettering of liberty itself. [2]

In Parliament, Pulteny, leader of the " Patriots," was, of course, opposed to any bill sanctioned by Walpole. But it was Lord Chesterfield who attacked most vigorously and effectively the illiberal features of the Licensing Act. He called attention to the precipitancy with which it had

[1] *Tenth Report of the Royal Commission on Historical Manuscripts*, i, 266, 267.

[2] *London Magazine*, June, 1737 ; *Common Sense*, No. 18, June 4, 1737 ; *Gentleman's Magazine*, June, 1737 ; *Craftsman*, June 4, 1737.

passed the House of Commons; he pointed out
that, to enforce what was claimed as the main
idea of the bill, — the suppression of licentiousness, — the press itself must be bridled. If a play
were rejected from the stage, was it not human nature to be curious about what had been forbidden?
And if the press were restricted, as well attack
liberty outright. The power vested by the bill
in the Lord Chamberlain was declared to be
greater than that intrusted to the King himself.
Finally, the bill was unnecessary, as the abuses
which its promoters claimed it was intended to
restrain were already provided for by law.[1] These
were the main points of Lord Chesterfield's arguments against the measure.

But all objections were in vain, and the Licensing Act passed on the 21st of June, 1737, and
became a law three days later. A number of interests had been involved in its passage, and,
undoubtedly, the smarts from the lash of satire
which had been inflicted on government, and particularly on Walpole, were the immediate forces
carrying the bill through. But there can be little doubt that along with this ran the jealousy
of the patentees for the managers of independent theatres. These had robbed Drury Lane of
its leading actors on one occasion, and had taken

[1] *Gentleman's Magazine*, July, 1737 ; *London Magazine*,
August, 1737.

away the audiences of both Drury Lane and
Covent Garden on numerous occasions ; all of
which made it indispensable for the existence of
the latter that the former should be exterminated.
If the sole aim of the act had been to free the
stage from abuse and to protect society, why
were the patent houses excepted ? For certainly
they were the first offenders. Or, why was not
some such plan adopted as that advocated by
Aaron Hill, namely, to permit only the legitimate
drama to be acted in the unlicensed (or unpa-
tented) theatres, thereby forcing theatrical competition out of the domain of buffoonery and
pantomime to a higher level ? [1]

The underlying cause of animosity toward the
unlicensed theatres was scarcely covered over by
the political arguments in favor of protection to
the state. Cibber, after dwelling for some pages
on the political necessity of the Licensing Act,
lets slip another argument for it. "And now
we have seen the Consequence of what many
People are apt to contend for, Variety of Playhouses! How was it possible so many could hon-
estly subsist, on what was fit to be seen ? Their
extraordinary Number, of course, reduc'd them
to live upon the Gratification of such Hearers,
as they knew would be best pleased with pub-

---

[1] *Prompter*, liv, May 16, 1735. This editorial contains the
best criticism of the theatrical situation I have found.

lick Offence; and publick Offence, of what kind
soever, will always be a good Reason for making
Laws to restrain it." The logic of "of course" is
not at first apparent, nor is the force any more patent of the following conclusion, which assumes
that, since new plays must be written to support
a number of theatres, therefore, such plays must
be disgracefully bad. But to resume Cibber's
discussion. "To conclude, let us now consider
this Law, in a quite different Light; let us leave
the political Part of it quite out of the Question;
What Advantage could either the Spectators
of Plays, or the Masters of Play-houses have
gain'd by its having never been made? How
could the same Stock of Plays supply four Theatres, which (without such additional Entertainments, as a Nation of common Sense ought
to be ashamed of) could not well support two?
Satiety must have been the natural Consequence,
of the same Plays being twice as often repeated,
as now they need be; and Satiety puts an End
to all Tastes, that the Mind of Man can delight
in." [1]

In the foregoing discussion I have attempted
to bring together all the essential evidences
showing the causes, immediate and remote, of
the Licensing Act, as well as to explain the difference in status of the theatrical question in

[1] Cibber's *Apology*, pp. 241, 242.

London before and after the passage of that act. If I have succeeded in this, it will appear that the Vagrant Act of 12 Queen Anne, which had been passed to meet local and temporary conditions, had fallen into disuse, and with it the control of the crown over theatrical amusements. This is clearly seen in the rise of the Haymarket and Goodman's Fields Theatres in defiance of that law, and in the results of the contests between the manager of Drury Lane and the actors in 1733, especially the decision in the case of the Patentees *vs.* Harper. The preamble to the act itself plainly expresses, in general terms, this fact, that the act was made for the express purpose of amending and *making more effectual* the Vagrant Act of 12 Queen Anne, as relates to common players of interludes. In other words, the Licensing Act restored the crown prerogative respecting plays and players, and brought into one legal focus what had already been sanctioned by common law. No alteration was made in the fact; simply, the fact was placed in the light of an enforcing and enforceable legal form. This being the case, it would hardly seem requisite to point out again that no individual can be held responsible for the act of 1737; or, that the real need of such a law lay in the necessity of centralizing responsibility for the abuse of privileges in matters theatrical. That the meaning and intent of the act was perverted to the use of selfish and tyrannical ends has nothing to do with the discussion in hand.

With the passage of the Licensing Act, a practical policy was crystallized in a moment for the patentees, and the government was committed to the support of that policy. It marks the first distinct definition of the position of the government relative to theatrical amusements, and outlines the defense of that position. The magnified occasion which gave it birth soon passed from sight, and the underlying real significance appeared. All the ground gained for a free stage since the days of Charles II was lost in the twinkling of an eye, and the monopoly was sealed more certainly than ever before. More certainly, because the real meaning of theatrical monopoly was better understood than ever before. Disorganization distinguishes theatrical disturbances before 1737; with the Licensing Act, the lines were clearly drawn, and the struggle on both sides gradually fell into settled order and plan. But it was more than a century before the advocates of freedom in theatrical affairs in London were able to put to rest the obnoxious Licensing Act of 1737.[1]

---

[1] The new law made necessary the appointment of a new official, an examiner, or licenser of stage plays, who acted under the immediate authority of the Lord Chamberlain.

Relative to the first appointment to this office, Genest says
(*English Stage*, iii, 522) , " In February, 1738, according to the
Manuscript in the British Museum, or in April, according to
Chalmers, William Chetwynd was sworn in Licenser of the
stage (under the Lord Chamberlain) with a salary of £400 a
year. " Odell, founder of the Goodman's Fields Theatre, was
made deputy licenser.

CHAPTER IV

THE immediate effect of the Licensing Act was the closing of the Goodman's Fields Theatre, and also the Little Theatre in the Haymarket; and two manuscript tragedies the ensuing season were prohibited by the licenser of plays. One of these was *Gustava Vasa* (by Henry Brooke), and, as was predicted by Lord Chesterfield, the proscription was followed by a numerous subscription and wide circulation of the tragedy. Victor says of this circumstance, "I am certain he [Brooke] cleared above a Thousand Pounds by that Subscription; so much incensed were the Public at this first Instance of the Power of a Licencer." The other piece was *Edward and Eleanora*, a play founded on an apocryphal episode in the life of Edward I. This was printed in 1739, and, like *Gustava Vasa*, was supported by subscription. It was written by James Thomson, author of "The Seasons." The unpopularity of the act reached its climax when a company of French strollers were licensed to exhibit at the theatre lately occupied

by Fielding. The advertisement of these performers was headed in bold letters, " BY AU-
THORITY ! " but they soon discovered that there
was an authority above that of mere sound, as
evinced by public clamor which developed into
a riot, effectually putting a stop to the performance.[1] The obnoxious law itself was quite as
much as the public were willing to stand; its
enforcement by means of permitting to a foreign
troupe — and that a French troupe — the liberty
which had been denied Englishmen, was considered a sufficient justification for the violence of
the incensed audience.

Matters stood thus for a year or two, when it
occurred to the enemies of the new " gagging law "
that a practical evasion might be devised. Our
old friend Giffard was ringleader to the scheme,
which was simply to get around the " for gain,
hire, or reward " clause of the Licensing Act, and
on the 15th of October, 1740, he caused to be
published the following announcement : " At the
late Theatre in Ayliffe Street — A Concert of
Vocal and Instrumental Musick in 2 Parts —
Between the Parts of the Concert will be presented *gratis* a Comedy, called The Stratagem —
By Persons for their diversion." Three days

---

[1] The play was a three-act Comedy, *The Plague of Riches*,
and was advertised for October 9, 1738. *Gentleman's Magazine*,
October, 1738. See also Victor, i, 53.

later, *Venice Preserved* was given, and performances appeared more or less regularly on the
Goodman's Fields stage throughout the season,
which closed on May 7, 1741.

That Giffard was unmolested in his operations
at the Goodman's Fields Theatre in 1740–41
does not appear to be due to the fact that he
evaded, or thought he was evading, the act of
1737, though, no doubt, it was that which em-
boldened him to make the attempt. It would
seem, rather, that for abetting Sir Robert Walpole, by delivering to him the *Golden Rump*,
Giffard had earned the good-will of the Premier,
who now took the opportunity to express his grati-
tude to the manager by winking at the infraction
of the law passed at his own request. As a further reason why Giffard was uninterrupted in his
movements, it was said that since he confined
himself to the plays of Shakespeare " and a few
deceased poets of eminence," he avoided running
counter to the interests of the patent houses.[1]

But the time was near at hand when these
reasons, if ever potent, were insufficient to defend
Giffard from the envy of the patentees. When
the young David Garrick, with a brief appren-

---

[1] *Town and Country Magazine*, October, 1787. It was reported that Walpole ordered a gratuity of £600 to be tendered
Giffard for his 'zeal for government,' but that it was never
given. See also Baker, *Biographia Dramatica*, ii, 139.

ticeship in one of the country theatres, first appeared in London, little attention was bestowed on him. Neither of the managers of the patent houses, it was said, offered him any encouragement when he applied to them. It is to the credit and honor of Henry Giffard that the greatest actor who has yet appeared on the English stage had an introduction to a London audience. On the 19th of October, 1741, Garrick appeared, for the first time on a London stage, at Goodman's Fields Theatre, in *Richard Third*. That theatre had not been noted, hitherto, for the excellence of its performers, and so the first night was not distinguished by a large, or otherwise exceptional, audience. But the genius of Garrick brought with it a revolution in the histrionic art, from a sing-song, affected declamation to a representation of nature ; and by dint of this genius the character of the audiences at Goodman's Fields was almost immediately metamorphosed. The young actor's fame spread throughout every part of the town with the greatest rapidity ; and Goodman's Fields Theatre, which had been confined to the inhabitants of the city, became the resort of the polite, and was honored with the notice of all ranks and orders of people.[1]

From a business point of view, Garrick's en-

---

[1] Baker, *Biographia Dramatica*, Introduction, p. xlii ; Davies, *Memoirs of Garrick*, 3d ed., i, 42–50.

gagement at Goodman's Fields swelled the cof-
fers at that theatre, and, in an inverse ratio,
diminished those of the patent houses. The patentees became alarmed at the turn affairs were
taking, and determined no longer to brook the
success, at their expense, of Giffard's house.
Uniting their efforts, and securing the coöperation of Sir John Barnard (mover of the
Playhouse Bill of 1735), then one of the chief
magistrates of London, they threatened Giffard
and Garrick with the Licensing Act. Thus in-
timidated, Garrick made terms with Fleetwood
of Drury Lane and joined the company at the
patent house at a salary of £500. Giffard was
finally compelled to shut the Goodman's Fields
Theatre, and soon afterwards he engaged at
Drury Lane.[1] The whole transaction illustrates
not only the efficiency of the act of 1737, but
it also discovers the fact that the patentees intended that the law should not remain a dead
letter so long as it could be enforced to serve
their ends.

Although the patent rights of the two old the-

[1] With the exception of a brief occupancy of Lincoln's-Inn-
Fields, in the spring of 1743, this ended Giffard's career as a
theatre manager. While in charge of Goodman's Fields, he
had revived *All's Well*, *Winter's Tale*, *Henry V*, and *King
Arthur*, introduced Garrick to London, and also brought out
two of the actor's own pieces, *The Lying Valet*, a farce, and
Lethe, a satire. Genest, iv, 47–49.

atres seemed thus secure from external foes, they
were not secure from internal discords. Feeling
too acutely the independence furnished by a
legal safeguard, Fleetwood of Drury Lane took
advantage of the situation to treat his actors in
a niggardly fashion, refusing them their salaries,
and otherwise showing them professional dis-
courtesies. Led by Garrick and Macklin (who
had been acting-manager of Drury Lane since
the revolt of 1733), ten of the performers formed
a compact to oppose the obstinacy and insolence
of the manager. Hoping to enlist the sympathy
of the Lord Chamberlain in their cause, as Betterton had done in 1695, the seceding actors
applied for a license to set up a theatrical company at the Little Theatre in the Haymarket.
But to their amazement the Duke of Grafton
(then Lord Chamberlain) treated their suit with
manifest coolness; he probably remembered the
unjust and despicable attempts of Theophilus
Cibber to ruin the prospects of Highmore, ten
years before, and so refused to grant a license.
This contingency was entirely unlooked-for, and,
although there can be but little doubt that the
revolters were all pledged to accede to no terms
proposed by Fleetwood, rather than bring disaster on so many by holding out, Garrick hastily
beat a retreat and signed a treaty of peace with
the Drury Lane manager. The action of Garrick

on this occasion, though excused on the grounds
of judgment and prudence, was bitterly attacked
by Macklin, and was the cause of a long and
caustic war of pamphlets. Macklin, true to his
nature and the principle which led him to take
his stand against Fleetwood, in the first instance,
remained fixed in his determination to continue
the warfare. As a consequence, when the compromise was patched up between the other actors
and the patentee, Macklin found himself out of
the company, likewise out of employment. However, the old veteran was a fighter, and did not
long remain idle. Though excluded from Drury
Lane, he gathered a company of young actors at
the Little Theatre in the Haymarket, and, with
the ostensible purpose of instructing them in the
art of acting, opened the theatre on February
6, 1744, with a concert, followed by *Othello*.
Once more the letter of the law was evaded. As
explained by the play-bill, " No money will be
taken at the doors, nor any person admitted,
but by printed tickets which will be delivered
by Mr. Macklin at his home in Bow Street, C.
G." Among this heterogeneous company of raw
recruits was a name which was destined, in its
way, to become famous. In the title rôle of
Othello Samuel Foote made his first appearance
on a London stage.[1]

[1] Cooke, *Memoirs of Macklin*, pp. 133–148 ; Davies, *Memoirs*

For all Macklin's wrath at Garrick, and the avowals of eternal enmity between Fleetwood and Macklin, the latter was, with the opening of the season of 1744–45, once more back at Drury Lane in his favorite character of Shylock. The occasional Prologue, spoken by Macklin at this time, was so full of humble contrition for his recent offense, that it must have caused merriment to all lovers of comedy. Theophilus Cibber was left at the Haymarket to succeed to the management, and his purpose, or devise, may best be explained in his own words, quoted from his " Serio-Comic Apology : " —

" *As I am advised by the Learned in the Laws of the Land, that no Act of Parliament deems Acting* Malum in se, I shall not be afraid, for the better Instruction of my Pupils, the more to embolden them to a Stage, to permit them frequently . . . publickly to rehearse several Pieces of our most celebrated Authors ; and that the Town may be the Judges of the Progress they make in their Studies, those *Rehearsals (with proper Habits, Decorations, &c.)* will be exhibited *Gratis*."

It was announced that money would be taken for the concerts only, an emphasis being laid on the *free* " publick Rehearsals." The musical pro-

of Garrick, Am. ed., vol. i, ch. viii ; *Gentleman's Magazine*, October–December, 1743.

gramme was to be rendered from about four to seven in the afternoon, after which the doors would be closed, to open immediately for the *gratis* performance. There needed no powers of divination to see through this thin veil of deception, and it was the more readily rent because Theophilus Cibber was in very bad odor with the patentees, and with the public in general. Soon after the appearance of the above announcement, a Justice of the Peace notified Cibber that an application was in process of making to prevent his scheme. Theophilus persisted that he had a right to earn his bread, if, in so doing, he were in no wise violating the laws of the land. To test the case, he manifested a willingness to have his cause tried in the King's Bench; but he was informed that his "school" was a mere sham, that the law distinctly required a license of him, and that if he failed to secure one, he was liable to prosecution as a vagabond. The pressure was too strong for Cibber, and, after a week of quibbling, "down dropped the Academy," and the monopoly once more proved to be invulnerable. Cibber thereupon threw up the business and got employment with Rich at Covent Garden where he appeared in the playbills among the actors in the *Relapse*, advertised for January 2, 1745. Mrs. Charke (Colley Cibber's daughter) completed, without molestation, the few remaining performances announced by Cibber.[1]

The revolt of 1743, following so closely upon the passage of the Licensing Act, called for the expression of public opinion in no equivocal terms. Although the result of the controversy was a positive victory for the defenders of patent rights in theatres, certain criticisms were raised relative to the legality of the patents themselves, which placed the holders of those documents in a most uncomfortable position.[2] The whole cause of the disgraceful contest was entered into at length, and the results of numerous " impartial examens " were published to the town in that convenient and popular medium, the printed pamphlet. It was readily seen that the new law had not reached all the evils connected with the theatres, for, it was conceived, the competitive warfare carried on between the two patent houses was, in reality, at the bottom of the disputes of 1743. " When each Playhouse labours to have

[1] Genest, iv, 171. Soon after the occurrences related in the foregoing paragraph, Fleetwood was under the necessity of selling, or mortgaging, his license at Drury Lane to two brokers, Green and Amber (1745). Lacey, the actor, joined the venture, and, in a short time, became the sole proprietor. In 1747, Garrick was admitted to partnership, and the Drury Lane license was renewed to Lacey and Garrick conjointly.

[2] While Drury Lane continued to be governed by a *license* instead of a *patent*, it was during the whole of the eighteenth century, and later, considered a " patent " house.

all," argues one, " and strives to have more good
Sense, better Singers and finer Dancers than the
other, the natural Consequence must be that the
Town will reap Satisfaction from neither, especially if there be a deficiency of Prudence in
the Management of both. . . . The Misfortune
is, that the Managers are Brokers only,[1] and
bid for the Town," with the result that both the
public and the actors must suffer. To obviate the
difficulties arising from such a senseless competition, it was suggested by J. Ralph, in " The
Case of the Present Theatrical Disputes," that
one of the theatres should appropriate tragedy,
while the other might cater to the public taste for
comedy. The serious and disgraceful controversy
which had been foisted on the public, it was
apprehended by the author of " An Impartial
Examen of the Present Contests between the
Town and the Manager," was due to rival actors
and unnecessary jealousies, fostered by the manager himself ; and to the paying of salaries un-
justified by merit or the financial condition of
Fleetwood,— all for the purpose of destroying the
competition of the house in Covent Garden. Such
unbusiness-like extravagance resulted in putting
on cheap and poorly " dressed " entertainments,
and forced the conclusion that the immediate difficulty was due to incapable management.

[1] See note on p. 81.

The abuse of the Licensing Act, as enforced
in the contests of 1743, did not escape the most
scathing denunciation. All that had been feared
from its unequal operation had come to pass.
"The Actors are a People from the highest to
the Lowest," breaks forth "Mr. Neither-side"
in his "Impartial Examen," "the most to be
pitied of his Majesty's Subjects; because the last
Theatrical Act of Parliament has made them the
only Slaves in the Nation: All other Degrees of
People have Liberty to try to get a Livlihood
in the Profession they were bred to ; and I hope
from the ill use of Power the two Theatrical
Managers have made, to see this ensuing Sessions that Act repealed, . . . "

" This Act of Parliament was so lately made,
and the Cause of it so well known, viz. the scandalous Licentiousness of an abusive Wit, &c, that
one may venture to say it is made use of, at present, for a quite contrary Purpose than it was
first intended. The Innocent only have suffer'd
by it! . . . As it was not, I'm confident, design'd meerly to promote a Monopoly of Theatrical Diversions for two People, who, in many
Points, have shewn themselves unequal to the
Station they are in, I will hope some Amend-
ments will at least be made in it, or such explanation of it, as seems now palpably necessary:
As it stands, let any one make Interest privately,

with any Justice of Peace, they can even disturb any Persons who really *give* their Performance of a Play ; and as their Commitment is in Execution, the Person oppress'd must first undergo the Punishment, and may afterwards try whether 'tis legal : An odd Circumstance, in a free Country, according to an old Phrase — *to Hang 'em first, and Try afterwards*." This is so just an interpretation of the practical meaning of the Licensing Act, that I have been tempted to quote it at length. If the writer of the pamphlet could have known that the act was to continue unaltered to near the middle of the nineteenth century, he would have had cause to exclaim.

But the real difficulty lay, as some were wise enough to see, in the very principle of patent rights, the perpetuity of which depended on the bolstering-up of an unjust law. It was boldly questioned whether by virtue of any grant, patent, or license, a theatrical manager had the right to turn the public interest to private ends. The manager of a theatre, it was declared, was as answerable for the public taste, as a prime minister for a well-ordered government ; and, it was thought, any abuse of the privileges contained in a patent should be deemed sufficient grounds for the forfeiture of the grant. The treatment of the actors by Fleetwood was an instance of abuse of privilege ; the use of a public commodity (for such was theatrical amusement considered) for private ends was another. To avoid, in future, any recurrence of the disputes of 1743, it was proposed to regulate the national theatres in such a way as to insure their management for the public good. The difficulties attending such an attempt at reformation were anticipated. To quote again from Ralph's pamphlet, " The parties concerned may not submit to such a new regulation; . . . the Managers will insist upon their Patents, which flow from the mere Grace and Favour of the Crown; and the Players on their respective Merits, . . . to value that same Merit of theirs at what rate they shall think fit. But alas! can they imagine, that the Crown itself will ever suffer a Patent to stand in the way of public good, . . . or, have more regard for the private interest of a Manager, than for that of the Community. No, No, this is never to be feared, and besides, if even such were the case, there are ordinary, and extraordinary ways of coming at Patents, and of rendering them void, when they are visibly abused." Some years before, the editor of the " Prompter " (No. cxvii) had summarized, in brief terms, the exigencies which might (and did) overtake the theatrical patents: " Had those Patents . . . determin'd with the *Lives* of their *Grantees*, Had they been limited (as certainly they ought to have been) to the *Personal* claims of those Gentlemen, in Right of whose *Genius* they were granted, the Power *reverting* continually to the Crown, Care would still have been taken, to bestow it afresh, with View to the Original Motive, the *Merit* of the Hand it went into. . . . But *Hereditary Right* to be WITTY, being a false, and unmaintainable *Title*, the EDICTS for *Perpetuating* JUDGMENT, *fell* (in the literal sense of the Word) to be *stock-jobb'd*, into incapable Hands: Whence a mercenary Disposition to *make the most* of their Bargain, became the chief Point of Sight, to those *Buyers* of an Opportunity to expose their own Ignorance."

But such arguments and pleas were now futile, for, although the episode of the secession of 1743 reduced Fleetwood to bankruptcy, which forced him out of the management of Drury Lane, the theatrical monopoly came out of the conflict unscathed and securer than ever. Henceforward, the matter of theatrical privileges was at the disposal of the patentees, or, rather, what seemed to them the same thing, the Lord Chamberlain. If any one desired to entertain the public with a performance falling within the meaning of the Licensing Act,[1] the custom was soon established

---

[1] The list was inclusive, comprehending "interludes, tragedies, comedies, operas, plays, farces, or other entertainments of the stage."

of first gaining the consent of the patentees, and, afterwards, the license of the Lord Chamberlain. On rare occasions this order was not observed, but the greatest care was exercised that the patent houses be kept free from the annoyance and danger of outside competition.

For many years after the events just recorded, no serious attempt was made to break over the barriers erected about the theatrical business in London. In the spring and summer of 1747, the eccentric Samuel Foote, who made his first appearance as an actor in Macklin's "school" during the revolt of 1743, began his "Dish of Chocolate" and "Dish of Tea" diversions at the Little Theatre in the Haymarket.[1] The next year he varied the programme with what he pleased to call "An Auction of Pictures," which he continued in 1749. A few years later (1755), the Lord Chamberlain (then Duke of Devonshire) took pity on the wretched condition of the disreputable Theophilus Cibber, and, for a brief period during the summer, permitted him to open the Little Theatre for performances. Genest[2] quotes Cibber's advertisement as follows : "At the new theatre in the Haymarket, with authority by Bayes' new raised company of comedians."

[1] *General Advertiser* for April 22, 1747 ; quoted by Genest, iv, 225.

[2] *English Stage*, iv, 424.

The regular drama was presented at these performances. On September 28, 1759, *The Busy Body* was given at the Haymarket for Mrs. Charke's benefit, and the next year Foote's farce, *The Minor*, came out there. But in 1761, a man with a dog-show forestalled Foote in securing the Haymarket Theatre, and so Foote and Murphy were suffered to open Drury Lane as a summer theatre. Every summer for the next four years, as we learn from the old play-bill collector, Foote was at the Haymarket, bringing out his own characteristic productions — *Minor, Orators, Mayor of Garratt*, and others.

But little significance can be attached to these summer amusements of Foote's at the Haymarket from 1747 to 1756, for they were so unique that many of them fell outside the definition of theatrical performances proper, and scarcely any of them could be regarded as competing with the exhibitions at the patent houses. It was in view of this fact, and particularly since Foote's entertainments were given in the summer season, that they were tolerated. However, essential results sometimes develop from apparently inconsiderable beginnings. In February, 1766, Foote made a visit to Lord Mexborough, in Hants. A number of gentlemen of distinction were there at the time, among others the Duke of York, and, knowing Foote's reputation for repartee, they bantered him on the subject of his horsemanship. In a spirit of braggadocio, he was induced to mount the Duke's horse, a most spirited animal, but he was scarcely seated in the saddle when he was thrown with such terrific violence as to break one of his legs in two places. Everything known to the surgery of the day was done to save the limb, but to no avail, and amputation was finally resorted to.[1] The Duke of York keenly felt his responsibility in this sad affair, and did what he could to compensate Foote for his loss. Using his influence in the proper quarter, the Duke succeeded in obtaining for Foote a patent for a theatre in the city and liberties of Westminster, with the privilege of performing dramatic entertainments there from May 15 to September 15 (inclusive) during the period of his natural life.[2] Foote's biographer (Cooke) says that he purchased the old premises in the Haymarket and erected a new theatre on the same ground ; but it is altogether likely that he merely improved and occupied the old theatre built by Potter.[3]

The patent thus granted to Foote created a

[1] The accident happened on February 3, 1766. Mention is made of it in the *Gentleman's Magazine* for February, 1766.

[2] *Gentleman's Magazine*, July, 1766. " Wed. 9 [July], 1766. " A Patent Passed the Great Seal, to Samuel Foote Esqr. only."

[3] Baker, *Biographia Dramatica*, Introduction, xlv ; *London Magazine*, May, 1767 ; *Public Advertiser*, July 24, 1766.

third *royal* theatre, though, it will be observed,
it was to Foote *solely*, and was to continue
merely for the lifetime of the original grantee.
Furthermore, it was to operate during the summer season only, and hence could not be construed as interfering with the privileges claimed
by the monopoly. Foote began performing at
the Haymarket under his patent soon after it
had passed the Great Seal. During his second
season (1767), a circumstance arose which threatened the success of Foote's establishment. Barry,
"the greatest of Romeos," returned from Ireland, where he had been acting, in July, 1766,
and, together with Mrs. Dancer (who later became Mrs. Barry), Mr. Lee, and others, rented
the Opera House, built by Vanbrugh in the
Haymarket, and began playing Shakespeare to
enthusiastic audiences. The rivalry proving too
dangerous to the Little Theatre, Foote put a
stop to it in the most effectual (and modern)
fashion, by securing the leading actors of the
opposing company and taking them into his own
employ.[1] This move necessitated a change of
program at Foote's theatre: in order to give
opportunity to the talents of Barry and Dancer,
for the remainder of the season the legitimate
drama, including *Lear*, *Venice Preserved*, etc.,
appeared pretty regularly, in place of the usual

[1] Cooke, *Memoirs of Macklin*, 2d edition, 164–169.

fare of comedy and farce. But at the opening
of the winter season of 1767, Garrick, who was
at the helm at Drury Lane, shrewdly put a stop
to these successes by taking Barry and Dancer
into the patent company.

Nothing further, for some years, occurred to
alter or in any way affect the theatrical situation
in London as it appears at the opening of the
season of 1768. Garrick was still at Drury
Lane. John Rich had died in 1761, and was
succeeded at Covent Garden by his son-in-law,
Beard, who, in 1767, sold out to Colman,
Harris, Powell, and Rutherford. On the 30th of
May, 1768, Foote brought out his famous *Devil
upon Two Sticks*. In the course of the dialogue,
towards the conclusion of the piece, occurs the
following interesting passage which contains
certain strictures on the patentees worth quoting.
The Devil has just recommended Harriet and
Invoice to go on the stage, but adds that he can
be of no service in getting them employment
either at Drury Lane or Covent Garden.

"*Invoice*. No? I thought, Sir, you told me
just now, that the several arts of the Drama
were under your direction.

"*Devil*. So they were formerly; but now they
are directed by the Genius of Insipidity: he
has entered into partnership with the Managers
of both houses, and they have set up a kind of

circulating library, for the vending of dialogue
novels, — I dare not go near the new house, for
the Demon of Power, who gave me this lameness,
has possessed the pates, and sowed discord
among the mock monarchs there; and what one
receives the other rejects,[1] — and as to the other
house, the manager has great merit in himself,
with skill to discern and candour to allow it in
others; but I can be of no use in making your
bargain, for in that he would be too many for
the cunningest Devil amongst us.[2]

"*Invoice*. I have heard of a new playhouse in
the Haymarket.

"*Devil*. What, Foote's? Oh, that's an eccentric, narrow establishment: however, it may do
for a *coup d'essai* and prove no bad foundation
for a future engagement."

In February, 1773, Foote announced his
"Primitive Puppet Show," and before the middle of April had given it seventeen times. *The
Sentimental Comedy* was also acted at the Haymarket before the 15th of May, and as late as
the 18th of September. Other pieces were performed out of the season limit of the patent, but
the jealous eyes of the patentees, especially of
Garrick, were on the movements of the freak at

[1] Referring to the notorious quarrels of the managers at
Covent Garden.

[2] A hit, of course, at Garrick's close-fisted business characteristic.

the Haymarket, and any irregularities there, in the way of stretching privileges, were almost always "by permission" and usually for some performer's benefit. As an example of the extreme vigilance exercised by the patentees, in May, 1776, when Foote opened the Haymarket for the summer season, he shut it again at once because Drury Lane had not yet closed. Finally, in 1777, Foote sold his patent to George Colman (the elder), who at once disposed of his share in the Covent Garden management and devoted his attention to his new purchase.[1] But it should be observed that the tenure under which Coleman managed the Haymarket Theatre was not, as is usually supposed, the same as that by which Foote claimed privileges. Colman held by virtue of an *annual* license, issued by the Lord Chamberlain;[2] and, although the Little Theatre continued to be called a royal theatre, probably because of its origin, it was in reality on the same precarious footing as the other theatrical concerns which, later, made their appearance.

The circumstance noted in the foregoing paragraph, of the Drury Lane Theatre keeping its

[1] Foote was to receive £1600 per annum during his life; Coleman was to receive, in addition to the theatre and wardrobe, all of Foote's unpublished pieces. As Foote died soon after this transaction, Colman, it would seem, made rather a good bargain. Oulton, *History of Theatres of London*, i, 57.

[2] Colman, *Random Records*, i, 235.

door open in 1776 until after the 15th of May,
that is, until after the opening of the Haymarket
season, was not, as might appear on a casual
observation, purely fortuitous. It really marks
the beginning of a new policy adopted by the
patentees to counteract the growing popularity
of the summer theatre. For some time, Garrick
had manifested a jealousy of Foote's success,
and, on occasion, had become even apprehensive.
For example, when Foote advertised his "Puppet Show" in 1773, Garrick was noticeably ner-
vous until he knew just what Foote intended
to do. As early as 1767, the success of Barry
and Dancer at the Haymarket aroused the envy
of the Drury Lane manager. The successors of
Garrick were no less vigilant. Now, the patents
granted to Killigrew and Davenant contained
no restrictions respecting the length of the theatrical season; custom alone had fixed the limits.
Foote's patent did restrict him to a definite
period, beyond which he dared not go without
"permission;" while, if the patentees were so
disposed, there was nothing to prevent them from
encroaching, *ad libitum*, on the season of the
summer theatre. That such a course was the
deliberate plan of the Drury Lane managers is
proved by subsequent events. The elder Colman opened his first season at the Haymarket
at the usual time, May 15; and, just as Foote

had done the preceding year, closed it again until the 28th of May, when he reopened the house for three performances a week until June 11, after which, for the remainder of the season, the Haymarket was open six nights each week. The younger Colman in his *Random Records* has explained the irregularity of the performances at the Haymarket in 1777 as follows: —

" The closing of the Theatre directly after the opening on the 15th of May . . . is easily accounted for, by the attempt to enter into a competition with the two great Winter Houses; — The Proprietors of which were not yet preparing to shut their doors for the summer. Empty benches at the Haymarket were the consequence of this experiment; — and no wonder, when so weak a rivalry, in an incipient scheme, was set up against the attractions at Drury Lane and Covent Garden."

The charitable, or innocent, way in which this explanation is put shows clearly that the right of the patentees to continue their performances into the summer was not qestioned, at that time, by the manager of the Haymarket. It may indicate, also, that the real motive of the patentees in extending their season was scarcely understood by the proprietor of the summer house. But a continued repetition of the tactics was sure to induce the suspicion that the action of

the patent houses was the result of a precon-
certed plan. Again in 1779, Colman felt under
the necessity of deferring the commencement
of his season until May 31, because the actors
on whom he was dependent were engaged at one
or other of the " great " houses, and the latter
continued their performances until the last of
May.[1] These belated openings of the Haymarket
continued without interruption or active opposition until the season of 1787, when the manager
made a vigorous attempt to run his establishment without regard to the programmes at the
winter theatres. But the Haymarket manager
utterly failed in his aggressive policy. Two years
later (1789), Colman again put on a bold front,
this time adopting the maxim that "the devil
can be fought only with fire," and competed with
Covent Garden in the character of the performances put on at the Haymarket, by reducing the
Miser to three acts.[2]

By this time the meaning of the contest between the patentees and the manager of the
Little Theatre in the Haymarket had become
perfectly apparent. The struggle had gradually
assumed such proportions that it was a question
whether the monopoly would allow any theatrical

[1] Oulton, *History of Theatres of London*, etc. (2 vols.), i, 82,
164.

[2] *London Chronicle*, May 26, 1789.

diversions in London, except those under the immediate control of the patentees themselves. But the mode of extermination adopted by the winter theatres could not be conducted without some compensatory losses. "The winter managers," comments the editor of *Town and Country Magazine* for June, 1789, " make approaches every season towards continuing their houses open during the summer season — but in our opinion they must always lose in the experiment as a recess is necessary to excite curiosity." However, it appears at first sight that the contest was too unequal to cause serious damage to the two old houses. But the struggle had hardly yet commenced, and it was too early to predict results. Meantime, an episode of peculiar interest had occurred to absorb the attention of the London public, and to turn aside, for the moment, the warfare between the patentees and the Little Theatre in the Haymarket. Before resuming the latter subject, it may be well to take account of the curious incident alluded to.[2]

[1] The following chronology may be of service in keeping straight the events of the next few years : In 1774, Lacey died, leaving Garrick sole proprietor of Drury Lane ; in 1776, Garrick sold out to Thomas Sheridan, Linley, and Ford ; in 1777, the elder Colman purchased the Haymarket, leaving Harris and Powell at Covent Garden. In 1779, Garrick died. R. B. Sheridan succeeded Thomas at Drury Lane soon after the transfer of 1776.

CHAPTER V

BACK in the days when the inimitable Foote was amusing the public with that new species of theatrical entertainment called "A Dish of Tea," there was in that eccentric comedian's train of admirers a lad who was destined to all the buffets, with but little of the glory, of the actor's lot. This was John Palmer, "Plausible Jack," a kind-hearted, irresponsible, lack-judgment, devil-may-care sort of a fellow, who, as usual with such characters, laid the consequences of his own follies at the door of his fellow creatures, or to the account of fate.

Palmer had a predilection for the stage, if for anything, from early youth; and, by one of the many chances which marked his course through life, was turned into that profession. Nor was he by any means devoid of all the elements belonging to the histrionic art, although he received rebuffs, time and again, on his applying to Garrick, "the great little man." However, after a checkered career as an itinerant actor among the provincial theatres, Palmer finally secured an

engagement with Foote, on the opening of the
Haymarket under the patent in 1767, and, soon
after, succeeded in getting a minor part in the
Drury Lane company. With the Haymarket
under Colman, and Drury Lane under Sheridan, Linley, and Ford, Palmer became a regular
performer at both theatres, and rose to a respectable position in the leading comic characters. As
the original Joseph Surface, he may be said to
have fairly secured his reputation as an actor.[1]

But John Palmer could endure success no
better than poverty and obscurity. No sooner
had he been established on his comedian's throne
than schemes of a wilder ambition than he had
yet dreamed of took possession of him. He would
build and manage a theatre of his own in the
metropolis! To this venture he had probably
been impelled by the injudicious advice of
friends. The plan was to go to the East End
of the city and there erect a theatre, for which
purpose the audacious Palmer secured a sufficient loan; and on the 26th of December, 1785,
the first stone of the new structure was laid by
the projector himself. The occasion was the
scene of a grand procession, and the ceremonies
at the laying of the corner-stone went off with

[1] For contemporaneous accounts of the life of John Palmer,
see *The General Magazine* for January, February, and March,
1788. Also *The Monthly Visitor* for December, 1798.

a great flourish.[1] In a receptacle prepared for the purpose, the following inscription was deposited, after it had been read first by the Recorder of Maidstone : —

" The Inscription on this Scroll is intend-
ed to convey
The following Information, —
That
On Monday the 26th day of December,
In the year of our Lord 1785,
And
In the 26th year of the Reign
Of our most Gracious Sovereign
GEORGE THE THIRD,
The first stone of a Building,
Intended for a Place of Public Entertain-
ment,
was laid by
JOHN PALMER, COMEDIAN,
In the presence of a numerous Party of
Friends to the Undertaking;
JOHN WILMOT, Esq, being the Architect
and Builder,
The Ground selected for the Purpose
Being situated within the Liberty
OF
HIS MAJESTY'S FORTRESS and
PALACE
OF the TOWER of LONDON
It has been resolved, that in honour of the Mag-
istrates, the Military Officers, and Inhabitants of the
said fortress and palace, the edifice, when erected,
shall be called,
THE ROYALTY THEATRE.
Sanctioned by authority, and liberally patronized
by subscription."

[1] *Town and Country Magazine* for July, 1787. Oulton, i, 167–196.

This was the beginning of the Royalty Theatre, auspicious enough, indeed, but the sequel proved that the attempt fell on evil days. It was about a year and a half from the breaking of the ground in Wellclose Square until the new theatre was completed. From all accounts the structure, both exterior and interior, was the most beautiful and most convenient of the London theatres, at the time it was built. It was 120 feet in length, 56 feet in breadth; and, by accurate computation, was capable of seating 2594 persons.[1]

Several days before the announced opening of the new theatre, a "house-warming" was indulged in by the manager, the subscribers, and friends to the undertaking, all of whom were invited by card, after the most approved fashion. By seven o'clock of the appointed evening (Saturday, June 9, 1787), a "brilliant audience were assembled." The house was crowded from pit to gallery, many having to be turned away for lack of room. The building was brightly illuminated, and when the curtain went up, discovering to the admiring gaze of the spectators the magnificence of decoration and the convenience of arrangement, the highest praise was called forth from those present.

To entertain and gratify the invited guests, a

---

[1] For a complete description of the Royalty Theatre, see *Gentleman's Magazine* for June, 1787. See also *General Magazine* for same date, i, p. 49.

number of scenes (painted by Dixon) were exhibited, "which, by judges of the art, are allowed to be capitally executed," while some vocal pieces were rendered with "exquisite taste." Delpini, who had been secured for the occasion, created some amusement by a burlesque air, humorously accompanied on the guitar. At this juncture Mr. Palmer entered the orchestra amidst applause from every part of the theatre; "which continuing long and violent, he stood on the seat appropriated to the band, and several times bowed in return for the flattering distinction." After refreshments had been served, the assemblage, which consisted of "some of the most respectable families in the vicinage, the magistrates, and several persons of eminence in the city," began to disperse; but first, "by mutual smiles, testified the pleasure which so elegant a spectacle had afforded them."[1] The opening of the Royalty for regular theatrical performances was announced for June 20, 1787.

During all the time, be it observed, that Palmer had been pursuing his Royalty scheme, he had been engaged at Drury Lane in the winter season, and at the Haymarket during the summer. On just what legal authority, or in what capacity, Palmer intended to conduct his new theatre, he had kept scrupulously to himself,

[1] *London Chronicle*, Monday, June 11, 1787.

either evading or dissimulating when questioned on this point, but leaving the impression that he felt perfectly secure in his movements. A few days prior to the advertised opening of the Royalty, Messrs. Harris, Linley, and Colman, managers of Covent Garden, Drury Lane, and the Haymarket, respectively, caused to be published in the newspapers of the day extracts from the various Vagrant and Vagabond acts, and accompanied these with a joint resolution to enforce the same against Palmer should he attempt to open his theatre in defiance of those statutes.[1] This action caused the leading performers, engaged for the Royalty, to decline to enter into any transactions that might make them liable to prosecution and fine for acting for " hire, gain, or reward." However, Palmer went forward with his preparations for the opening, but was under the necessity of announcing that the proceeds of the evening would be devoted to the benefit of the London Hospital.

On the evening of June 20, 1787, the Royalty Theatre was thrown open to the public to witness the first performance. The house was crowded and the competition for places was very marked. When the curtain arose (at seven o'clock), some

---

[1] *General Magazine*, June, 1787; Oulton, i, 167–196. It is curious to note that, in the face of a common enemy, the three Royal Theatres buried all differences among themselves.

little disturbance was caused by a few persons
calling for Palmer's patent. The suave manager
came forward and after appealing to the audience
not to give cause of complaint to his enemies
by boisterous conduct, delivered an address (written by Arthur Murphy), containing the following lines in reference to the opposition of the
patent theatres to the new Royalty : —

> "Yet some there are who would our scheme annoy;
> 'Tis a monopoly they would enjoy.
> Th' Haymarket, Covent Garden and Old Drury
> Send forth their edicts ' full of sound and fury.'
> Three jarring States [1] are leagu'd in jealous fit,
> And they — whom *wit* maintains — *wage* war on *wit*.
> But wit, like day-light, nothing should restrain,
> The same in Goodman's-fields and Drury-lane.
> And if the Drama list on Virtue's side,
> Say — can the moral be diffus'd too wide!
> If the sun gild yon *West* with golden ray,
> The *East* [2] may feel the beam of rising day.
> Like gen'rous rivals let all parties boast
> One only struggle — Who shall please you most ;
> Fines and imprisonment no more proclaim,
> But praise the soil from which our Garrick came." [3]

This was followed by the representation of *As
You Like It*, and an after-piece, *Miss in Her*

[1] Alluding to the strifes of the patentees, and the war of
encroachments between the winter houses and the Haymarket.

[2] The Royalty Theatre was situated in the East End of
London ; the royal theatres at the West End.

[3] Garrick made his first appearance in London at Goodman's
Fields, near the site of the Royalty.

Teens. At the close of the performance, Palmer
made his appearance before the audience and
addressed them on the subject of the founding
of the new theatre and of the "jealous opposition" of the old theatres. At this time, he made
public the authority on which he had founded the
hopes of the Royalty. He had, he said, deemed
the license of the Governor of the Tower, and the
Magistrates of the Hamlets attached to its jurisdiction, sufficient sanction for the acting of plays
in that district. He complained bitterly of the
action of the three managers in waiting till the
last moment, after he had gone to the expense
of erecting and furnishing the theatre, before
raising any objections to the project. The attitude of Mr. Colman was characterized as particularly unfair, for, said Palmer, "in the course
of the last summer, when I performed at the
Little Theatre in the Haymarket, Mr. Colman
wrote a Prologue, which I spoke on my benefit
night, and among others, were the following
lines : [1] —

> " For me whose utmost aim is your delight,
> Accept the humble off'ring of this night ;
> To please, wherever plac'd, be still my care,
> At Drury, Haymarket, or *Wellclose-Square.*"

" As Mr. Colman knew the plan I had then in

[1] In Prologue to the Comedy of *Tit for Tat.* See *European Magazine*, September, 1786.

view, it was fair to conclude that he did not
meditate an opposition."

Of the Covent Garden manager, Palmer alleged that he had given his consent in writing
for one of his actors, Quick, to engage at the
Royalty. That the patentee should now be found
in active opposition to the new theatre was sufficient cause for astonishment and chagrin; while
the enforcement of an act of Parliament against
one attempting to represent a moral exhibition
was a hardship and an injustice. "Tumblers
and Dancing Dogs might appear unmolested before you: but the other performers and myself,
standing forward to exhibit a moral play, is
deemed a crime." The address closed with the
announcement that the theatre would be shut
until a species of entertainment could be provided that would not subject the manager to
danger.[1]

This address aroused the sympathy of the
public in Palmer's behalf, and had the immediate effect of bringing on a paper warfare; for
the managers, whose characters had been ex-
posed to public view in a contemptible light, felt
it incumbent on themselves to explain their atti-

[1] For accounts of the opening night, see *European Magazine*
for June, 1787; *Town and Country Magazine* for July, 1787;
General Magazine, June, 1787; *London Chronicle*, June 22,
1787.

tudes. In answer to the charge of duplicity, the
elder Colman authorized the editor of the "London Chronicle" (June 23, 1787) to say, that
before the lines referred to in the Prologue by
Palmer were either spoken or written, not only
was the Royalty Theatre well under way, but
also that he (Colman) had been assured by
Palmer that the latter's plans in no wise contained anything that would interfere with the
interests of the Haymarket Theatre; that, indeed, the chief object of the undertaking was to
engage the public attention for the winter season; that to these assurances Palmer added a
ready concurrence to a proposed renewal of his
engagement at the Haymarket Theatre, but that
instead of carrying this proposal into effect
he had evaded the matter of reëngaging with
Colman until February (1787), when the latter
notified him that if he did not make an immediate engagement, he would be considered as
having withdrawn himself from the company in
the Haymarket; and, finally, under pressure of
this ultimatum, Palmer had signed an agreement
for the summer season of 1787, though apparently offended at the lack of confidence evinced
by Colman on the occasion.

Harris of Covent Garden likewise felt himself in the position of self-defense, and, in a
public letter, answered Palmer's allegations. He

explained that it was hardly within the jurisdiction of the patentees to notify any one of the existence of a law so notorious as the Vagrant and Vagabond Act; that as to the lateness of the notice served on Palmer that he would be prosecuted if he attempted to open the Royalty, Palmer himself was to blame for that, since he kept the source of his authority a secret until the Monday preceding the 20th of June; and that the opposition of the patentees could be justified on the ground of protection to their "legal monopoly." As to the correspondence with Quick, referred to by Palmer, Harris quoted the same letter, showing that he had made no active opposition to the Covent Garden performers engaging at the Royalty Theatre.[1]

Palmer returned to the attack in a full-page letter to the " London Chronicle " (June 26, 1787). Harris was the main target for the Royalty manager's invectives. As to the " legal monopoly " being in danger of the rivalry of a new theatre, Palmer asserted that he had formerly proposed to the managers of the winter houses, that if they would abandon their prosecutions and acquiesce in the opening of the Royalty Theatre, he (Palmer) would agree to shut his theatre the day prior to the commencement of the winter theatres, and that Harris had treated this

[1] *London Chronicle*, June 22, 1787.

proposal with disdain. "Protected in a *legal monopoly*, he would not yield, even when yielding might have redounded to the credit of his liberality, and could not by any means have been detrimental to his present property, or eventual interest. So much for the spirit of rivalry, which, in the true Turkish stile, actuates Mr. Harris to bear no brother near the throne."

Relative to Harris's denial of "active opposition," Palmer insinuated that the Covent Garden manager went among the different performers, dissuading them, "and by every species of menace endeavored to deter them from appearing on Mr. Palmer's boards;" that the same person was "closeted with Sir Sampson Wright, in deliberation on the methods to be taken to prevent Mr. Palmer from performing;" that he prepared "the only magistrate for the Tower Royalty, in the mode by which he could conduct himself to suppress and ultimately ruin Mr. Palmer;" that he encouraged informers, and "had the information in style ready cut and dried;" and that in the very letter from Harris to Quick, there was a threat to prosecute as "rogues and vagabonds" those actors engaging with Palmer. All of this seemed to Palmer to bear the marks of "active opposition." [1]

[1] The quarrel was taken up by the pamphleteer: *A Review of the Present Contest between the Managers*, favoring the

These recriminations, when reduced to their lowest terms, that is, divorced from the personal element, may be simplified to the bare statement that Palmer, in attempting to open the Royalty Theatre, was violating what had come to be the leading clause of the Licensing Act; and that the patentees were determined to defend the advantageous position which that act gave them. The incident is the first flagant example of utter defiance of that act, during the first half century of its operation ; for the contest which had sprung up between the Little Theatre and the patent houses had not grown out of any palpable infraction of the written statute. How Palmer could have been allured into the self-deception of believing that his scheme had even a fair chance of success, is beyond the power of understanding. He must have known that the mandate of the Governor of the Tower was inferior to an Act of Parliament, else why did he guard the secret of his authority? If he placed his dependence on the moral support of public opinion, it would seem that he should have waited until that public opinion had been tested, before making a material sacrifice of himself and his friends. Furthermore, the least appreciation of

Royalty, was refuted by *A Very Plain State of the Case*, or, *The Royalty Theatre* versus *the Theatres Royal*, — probably by Colman.

the meaning of the theatrical events of his own
times would have assured him that the patentees
would be " actively opposed " to any and all
efforts to break through the walls of their " legal
monopoly." It was sheer waste of time to accuse
the patent managers of duplicity and illiberality ;
as Harris asserted in his open correspondence,
he was simply following the instinct of self-
preservation, a line of conduct which Palmer
himself would have adopted could he have
changed positions with any one of the patentees.
The fact is, that in Palmer's whole procedure in
the Royalty affair, audacity strove with lack of
judgment and foresight for mastery.

The next morning after the opening (and closing) of the Royalty, Palmer assembled his crest-
fallen company in the green-room of the theatre
and delivered himself of the following characteristic speech :

" LADIES AND GENTLEMEN,

" The combination formed against my new undertaking may have occasioned you to suppose
yourselves deserted. I am the injured party, and
as a proof that I wish to be considered exclusively in that light, I mean to do everything in
my power to take care of you. I have engaged
you respectively at certain salaries. The house
is now shut, and you cannot be of use to me ;

but God forbid that you should be sufferers by the combination against me! Until the theatre shall open, which will be soon, I will allow each of you half the amount of your salaries; and when the theatre opens, should not one of you be of service to me in the capacity of an actor, or an actress, you shall all receive your salaries, for the continuance of the season. My friend is not here, but I can answer for him in point of liberality. God bless you all. I feel myself bound to protect you as parts of *my* family." [1]

In less than two weeks from the abortive attempt to open the Royal Theatre with the regular drama, on the 3d of July, Palmer re-opened the house with exhibitions similar in character to the performances at Sadler's Wells, Astley's, and other places of amusements in which " theatrical entertainments," as generally understood by the Licensing Act, were not included. Such performances comprised burlettas, dances, pantomimes, and the like, in contradistinction to the regular drama, of which the patentees claimed a " legal monopoly." Palmer prefaced the evening's entertainment with an

[1] *London Chronicle*, June 23, 1787. "My friend" probably refers to Dr. Jackson, who was indorsing Palmer's scheme. Jackson is the supposed author of *Sodom and Onan*, a scurrilous attack on Foote.

occasion address, written on the subject of the opposition made to the Royalty Theatre by the patentees and Colman. This was followed by a musical pastoral, *The Birthday*, or *Arcadian Contest*, and a new dance called *The Triumph of Cupid*. The evening closed with a panto-mime, *Hobson's Choice*, or *Thespis in Distress*, a hit at the patent houses, and well received.[1] This bill, with additional and occasional varia-tions, was repeated a number of times with con-siderable success, meriting the approbation of theatre critics.[2]

Indeed, so successful was the irrepressible Palmer with his singing, dancing, and dumb-show exhibitions, that, even with this reduced order of performance, the jealousy and anger of the patentees were aroused anew, and every action at the Royalty was scrutinized in the hope that some violation of the Licensing Act might be detected. Threats were made that any attempt to speak in a pantomimic performance would be interpreted as dialogue, and prosecuted as representing the regular drama ! By some indiscretion, it seems that one of the performers in a dumb-show uttered a word or two. The ex-ecution of the managers' threats began when the

[1] *London Chronicle*, July 4, 1787.
[2] *London Chronicle*, August 15, 1787 ; *European Magazine*, vol. xii, 63.

elder Bannister [1] and the younger Palmer were, in consequence of informations, convicted as vagrants in Justice Staples's court and committed for fourteen days. The case, however, having been transferred to the court of James Robinson, William Robinson, and Richard Brooke, Justices of the Peace for the Tower Hamlets, the prisoners were discharged on bail.[2]

But the affair was not to end here. The action of the second justice's court, in reversing the decision of the first, was something more than professional discourtesy; it was a conflict of authority within the same district, which demanded a hearing in Westminster Hall. The case dragged on for months. On the first day of February, 1788, we find the following record: "In the Court of King's Bench a second rule was made absolute against two magistrates of the Tower Hamlets, for having illegally discharged some performers of the Royalty Theatre, who were committed by another magistrate in that district for performing in plays and interludes, contrary to an express Act of Parliament." [3] Not until May (22d) of the following

---

[1] Charles Bannister, Sr., refused to abandon Palmer when the rest of the company left him at the time when the three managers threatened them first, *i. e.* before June 20, 1787.

[2] *Town and Country Magazine*, August, 1787.

[3] *Gentleman's Magazine*, March, 1788.

year were these offending justices brought up
for judgment, when Justice Ashurst pronounced
the sentence of the court upon them, which was,
that each of the defendants should pay a fine of
£100 and be imprisoned until it was paid.[1]

Meantime, Palmer continued his operations
at the Royalty. When opportunity afforded, he
advertised his complaint against the relentless-
ness of the patentees. In an Occasional Address,
delivered at the Royalty in the autumn of 1787,
occur the following lines : [2] —

> " Behold the Comic Muse, a dire event ;
> Lost to the Stage — by Act of Parliament —
> Then wonder not good folks, or think it strange,
> That I, long tongue-tied, hazard *now* a change.
> For who could this same dumb-show hear, and feel
> The flatt'ring transports which such scenes reveal."

And again, the following month (December,
1787),—

> " But not for me th' immortal bard to quote :
> Three modern managers claim all he wrote,
> Else Henry's wars and Agincourt we'd show
> And bid with kindred warmth your bosoms glow." [3]

Palmer's appeals to the popular mind had their
effect, and aroused much sympathy in his cause.
Measured by the rules of abstract justice, there

[1] *Gentleman's Magazine*, vol. lix, pt. i, p. 463.

[2] *European Magazine*, November, 1787.

[3] *Ibid.*, December, 1787.

can be little doubt that the course pursued
against him by the inexorable patentees was
mean and unfair, and this is especially true of
the unrelenting spite which characterized the attacks on Palmer after the latter had been forced
to abandon the idea of a regular theatre. The
real injustice and absurdity of the prosecution
of the Royalty performers did not escape censure. "Does it not imply some little inconsist-
ency in a well-regulated State, for one subject to
be punished as a rogue and vagabond for doing
that in publick, which another, perhaps the first
peer in the realm, is proud to do with applause
within the walls of his own house!"[1] On the
other hand it is quite as certain that, by his
own questionable conduct, Palmer lost much
compassion, which otherwise might have been
his due, and injured the cause for which the
Royalty movement stands. The circumstance of
his reëngagement with Colman for the summer
of 1787 has already been mentioned. His treatment of the Drury Lane management is still
more blameworthy. Palmer was engaged to act
at that theatre for the season of 1787–88, which
was to have opened on September 15 with *The
School for Scandal*. Palmer gave no warning

[1] *Gentleman's Magazine*, March, 1788. The allusion, "first
peer," etc., is to private theatricals, which were much in vogue
at this time.

that he was not to be depended on, until the day
immediately preceding the one advertised for the
opening, and then precipitately sent in his resig-
nation from the company. Unprovided with a
Joseph Surface, the managers were under the
necessity of withdrawing their bill, until they
could supply the deficiency. This called for an
explanation from Palmer to the public. In a
letter published in the prints of the day, he excused himself by saying that he had been " illib-
erally treated by the Managers of the Winter
Theatres," that he had been " insulted individually," that his brethren had been stigmatized
in general, and that for these reasons he had
convened his subscribers and " had submitted
implicitly to their opinion and advice; they
honourably concurred with him in sentiment,
that he had been extremely abused, and accorded with his proposal of quitting Drury Lane
Theatre." For the delay in sending in his resig-
nation, Palmer put up the unintelligible excuse,
" the hurry in which I have been kept for some
days past, by the respect I owe to the public."
In his indignation, he pointed to the appellations
of " Vagrant, Rogue, and Vagabond " which had
been applied to him " for some months past ; "
and then broke out into the exclamation, " Do
the Managers of Drury Lane imagine that I
can, with any propriety, appear on their boards ?"

But Palmer was always acting, both on and off the stage, and so well did " Plausible Jack " succeed in his profession that the public was more than once fooled. To protect himself from the censure which was sure to follow his reprehensible conduct in waiting until the last day before the opening of Drury Lane before notifying the management of his withdrawal from the bills, in a blustering spirit of magnanimity, he offered to appear in his part as advertised, knowing full well that the proposal would be rejected. Palmer, by contemptible means, thus scored one point in revenge.[1]

Undaunted by his failure to open the Royalty for the regular drama, or by the incessant attacks of the patentees on the success of his pantomime shows, Palmer petitioned Parliament at its next sitting for leave to bring in a bill to enable His Majesty to license the Royalty Theatre. This petition was accompanied by another, signed by five thousand inhabitants of Middlesex, in favor of Palmer's theatre. But the peculiar course adopted by Palmer in conducting his scheme from the beginning began now to tell against him. The very member (Mr. M. A. Taylor) who pre-

---

[1] For the correspondence connected with this incident, see *European Magazine* for September, 1787. *The Town and Country Magazine* for October, 1787, severely reprimands Palmer for his conduct in this affair.

sented the petition apologized to the House for so
doing, while the opposition to the motion showed
the hostility which Palmer had aroused in ig-
noring the Licensing Act. Mr. Anstruther, in
speaking against the petition, called attention to
the fact that Palmer, "after having for twelve
months trampled upon the law of the country, applied with a very bad grace to Parliament for an
Act to license his theatre. Now that the arm of
the law had reached him, he applied for a law
to sanction his proceedings; but, prior to this,
he had set the law at defiance. The pretence
that he thought the license of the Constable of
the Tower would enable him legally to give dramatic entertainments, was barely a pretence; for
every man who could *read* might learn, that the
King himself, much less the Constable of the
Tower, could not exercise powers which were restrained by a positive Act of Parliament."[1] The
motion was, of course, lost (February 8, 1788),
and thus ended Palmer's attempt to establish the
Royalty Theatre. It would, naturally, be supposed that the contest had left him the inveter-
ate enemy of the three managers, but to our
great surprise we read in the "London Chronicle" for June 11, 1788, that he was once
more at the Little Theatre in the Haymarket,
where he "was welcomed back to that stage on

[1] *Gentleman's Magazine* for May, 1788; *Parl. Reg.*, xxiii, 159.

which he has ever exhibited his talents to the best advantage, with most gratifying tokens of favour and affection." The hatchet was buried and the pipe of peace smoked with Drury Lane also, and Palmer renewed his engagement at the patent house, where he was warmly congratulated.[1]

The legal aspects arising out of the episode of the attempted founding of the Royalty Theatre have been brought out in the course of the narrative and need not be repeated here. That the patentees aimed to stretch the Licensing Act to its utmost limit in aiding their own designs was manifest in every point in their opposition. It was clear that they interpreted the Act of 1737 as meaning to legalize their monopoly, and that they intended to use the advantage for all it could be made to produce. It was barely possible, that, in their zeal, they went even too far for the safety of their own position.

The contest brought out, also, the necessity of some modification of the Act of 1737. This fact appeared in a startling form when, in the House of Commons, Anstruther pointed out that not even the king could license a theatre in opposi-

---

[1] Oulton, in his *History of the Theatres of London*, i, 167–196, has collected a great deal of valuable contemporaneous material on the Royalty for 1787.

tion to the Act of Parliament. That act included Westminster only,[1] and, evidently, the
time was near at hand when this limitation
would prove too narrow.

Finally, and of the greatest importance, public
attention, in a wide sense, for the first time
since the passage of the Licensing Act, was
called to the glaring absurdities and gross in-
justices attaching to that act when operated for
purely private ends, in defiance of the public
desire. It clearly appeared that the predictions
of Aaron Hill, over half a century before, had
come to pass, namely, that a monopoly of the
legitimate drama must ultimately lead to a
lowering in tone of theatrical performances.
This was the essential complaint of Palmer
against the opposition of the patentees, and the
public had had the first lesson in its truthfulness; time alone would prove how well it had
been learned.

It may not be out of place here to mention
the main facts connected with the stormy history
of the Royalty Theatre from 1787 to its final
destruction in 1826. It opened and closed under
numerous managers, and, together with the
usual cheap order of performances and the

[1] On petition a number of cities and towns had obtained, at
various times, acts of Parliament relieving them, in part,
from the restrictions of the Licensing Act.

frequent persecutions by the patentees, it eked
out but a half-existence, at best. After Palmer
abandoned his scheme, a bookseller, named
Steele, came into possession of the Royalty, but
he soon surrendered the management to Wewit-
zer, the actor. Then, for a time, Macready,
father of William Charles, gave some dignity to
the place. In 1803, Mrs. Steele and Astley, the
amphitheatre king, applied to the Wellclose
magistrates for, and were granted, a license to
perform interludes at the Royalty. By 1807, it
had again changed hands, and, in 1813, another
Palmer tried his fortune with it. It was about
this time that the name of the theatre was changed
to "The East London," though the old name, also,
stuck to it. Rae, of the Drury Lane company,
attempted to raise the theatre into respectability
in 1819, but fate seemed to have marked it
from the beginning. In 1826, the Royalty was
burned to the ground. It was immediately rebuilt as "The Royal Brunswick," and opened
on February 25, 1828. Three days later, during
a rehearsal of *Guy Mannering*, the theatre
collapsed, killing fifteen and injuring a score
more.

On the site of the Royalty and Royal Brunswick now (1905) stands the Sailors' Home, and
the only vestiges remaining to suggest that here
was once a place of theatrical amusements, are

the curb-stone posts bearing the inscription,
" R. B. T." [1]

[1] For contemporaneous accounts of the Royalty, 1787–1828,
the student is referred to the following: *General Magazine*,
September, 1788, June, 1789, April, 1790 ; *Town and Country
Magazine*, November, 1789 ; *Monthly Visitor*, November, 1797,
February and April, 1798, March, 1799 ; *Morning Chronicle*,
October 7, 1802, October 25, 1807 ; *London Chronicle*, October
6, 1803, October 5, 1819 ; *Reasoner*, July, 1813 ; *Literary Chronicle
and Weekly Review*, December 18, 1819 ; *New Monthly
Magazine*, April, 1827 ; *Britannic Magazine*, x, p. 70.

CHAPTER VI

TO appreciate the delusion under which Palmer
and his advisers attempted to establish a
theatre in London for the regular drama, it is
necessary to glance at the various parliamentary
acts in force during the last half of the eighteenth century. The old Vagrant Act of Queen
Anne, which descended from the Rogue, Vagabond, and Sturdy Beggar Act of 39 Elizabeth,
had continued through the century unrepealed,
and had been reinforced by the Licensing Act
of 1737. These acts were primarily for the same
purpose, to protect morality and defend the
peace; though the Licensing Act aimed, also,
to secure government from the scurrilous abuse
of satiric invective. We have seen how both
these laws became, in time, interpreted in the
narrow sense of forming the legal safeguard to
the patent monopoly. Had no other laws than
these existed, regulating the theatre, Palmer's
stupidity in violating them had been wholly in-
excusable, for the practice of half a century had

clearly established the fact that the patentees had succeeded in turning the Licensing Act strictly to their own account.

But there was another act of Parliament, passed in the 25 George II (fifteen years after the Licensing Act), which is responsible for misleading Palmer. This law was enacted to meet the police demands of certain places of amusement, and Sadler's Wells in particular. The "Wells," as a resort, may be traced back into the period of the Commonwealth. By 1727, the place had regular performances of dancing, singing, rope-walking, and so forth. The extravagances of the next few years in theatricals, treated in an earlier chapter, extended to Sadler's Wells, shortly reducing it to one of the most disreputable dens of thieves, robbers, and licentiousness in, or about, London. In 1744, information was laid before the grand jury against the proprietors for keeping a disorderly and disreputable house. To put a stop to these evils at the Wells, and kindred places, in 1752 (25 George II), Parliament passed " An Act for the better preventing Thefts and Robberies, and for regulating Places of public Entertainment, and punishing Persons keeping disorderly Houses." [1]

After reciting the deplorable state of morals, fostered by places of public entertainment, the

[1] *Statutes at Large*, vii, p. 43.

act provides for the licensing of such places at the discretion of the magistrates in their quarter sessions of the peace. The act was an experiment to be tried for three years, and was to extend to London and Westminster (and within twenty miles thereof). Any person found keeping a "house, room, or garden" for public entertainment, without such license from the Justices of the Peace, was to suffer the penalty of one hundred pounds fine, and "be otherwise punishable as the law directs in cases of disorderly houses." No charge was to be made for issuing licenses for the purposes aforesaid. Drury Lane, Covent Garden, and the King's Theatre in the Haymarket were exempt from the act.

At the expiration of this law governing the licensing of public places of entertainments, its operation had proved so beneficial that it was renewed and made perpetual.[1] It was under this act that Palmer thought to open the Royalty Theatre. As it made no pretense of including the regular drama within its provisions, it is plain why the performance of Shakespeare's plays "for hire, gain, or reward" was adjudged illegal, and the theatre closed. When it opened again on the 3d of July (1787), and for a good portion of the remainder of its history, it was by authority of the 25 George II, as outlined above.

[1] 28 George II, cap. 19 (1755).

The attempt of Palmer to establish a theatre in London in spite of the patent houses and their "legal monopoly" was, to all appearances, a miserable failure. But the public interest which it elicited in the question of exclusive privileges in matters relating to the general good was an incalculable victory on the side of an unrestricted stage. The immediate result of the conflict was a complete demonstration of the security of the patentees within their stronghold; but, at the same time, it was also made clear that the passive acquiescence of the preceding half century had changed to an active and determined opposition to the theatrical monopoly.

The effort made in the Royalty venture was the signal for other places of amusement to sue for an extension of privileges. On the 10th of March, 1788, a bill was presented to the House of Commons, and passed its first reading, to enable His Majesty to grant letters patent for the licensing of certain entertainments at Sadler's Wells. At this time, the patentees were fortunate in having a representative in Parliament who was both interested in the welfare of the theatrical monopoly, and also capable of defending it. Richard Brinsley Sheridan had been associated with the management of Drury Lane since the exit of Garrick, and a worthy successor he was of the great actor's jealous watchful-

ness over the patent rights of the theatre. When
the Sadler's Wells bill was introduced, Sheridan
(who had represented Strafford since 1780)
placed himself on record as regards his attitude
towards all attempted encroachments on the
"legal monopoly." He was the first on the floor
after the reading of the bill, and his speech on
this occasion characterizes the policy of the patentees for the next quarter of a century.

At the outset of his remarks, Sheridan stated
that he had consented to the first reading of the
bill in order that the house might fully appreciate what was demanded of them. To protect the
proprietors (Arnold and Wroughton) of Sadler's
Wells from loss to their investment, no one, said
Sheridan, would go farther than himself. And
here he took occasion to draw a contrast between
the method adopted by the proprietors of Sadler's Wells in seeking a legal existence, and that
of Palmer in attempting to establish the Royalty
Theatre. " That was a scheme set up upon false
pretences, and supported by a conspiracy of Justices of the Peace, to defeat the law. . . . The
present application came forward in a decent
manner." But this was only a bit of plaster applied in advance of the lashing that was to follow. Further signs of magnanimity, in dealing
with Sadler's Wells, were manifested by the
Drury Lane manager. He desired the pending

application to be liberally treated, that the "legal monopolists might not stand on their rights too strictly." The wily orator had ever been, and he trusted "he ever should be an enemy to anything like oppression in any matter great or small." As to the matter under consideration, he confessed that the apprehension of others interested in certain rights, supposed to be infringed by the Sadler's Wells bill, went farther than his own. But, notwithstanding Sheridan's apparent friendliness toward the petitioners from Sadler's Wells, he saw certain cogent reasons why the bill should be rejected. The cause, stated in the application, he alleged, was at variance with the truth. It was there asserted that the proprietors of the winter houses "had lately instituted suits at law not only against the last newly erected theatre [meaning the Royalty], but intended to commence suits and prosecutions against all others indiscriminately." Sheridan assured the House that this charge was wholly unfounded. Another misleading statement in the application was discovered by the patentee. Seemingly, the proprietors of Sadler's Wells asked only to be legally empowered to continue their performances as usual. What they really asked for, as interpreted by Sheridan, was a monopoly. Now, admitted Sheridan, if Parliament desired to grant a monopoly for a certain class of performances,

it could do so, of course ; but he strongly objected to giving parliamentary sanction to a concern which, according to its own testimony, had
been guilty of violating the privileges of its license. What the Sadler's Wells proprietors
were actually seeking, asserted Sheridan, was a
legal safeguard to protect them in their illegal
practices. The allusion is, of course, to the encroachment at the Wells on the regular drama.
It would be embarrassing, thought the advocate
for the patent houses, to say to other applicants
for licenses to exhibit performances similar to
those at Sadler's Wells, that, inasmuch as the
latter place of amusement had been the first to
transgress the law, it should have a monopoly in
that line.

Sheridan assumed, without argument, that, in
case the House saw fit to grant the application
for a Sadler's Wells bill, it would be so altered
"that no part of the new powers would be suffered
to entrench on the rights of the Winter theatres,
either as to season or the species of performance."
He alluded to the fact that the petition for the
bill had been before the House "for nearly two
months," insinuating there had been a special
purpose on the part of the promoters for waiting
till near the season for opening Sadler's Wells
before bringing it up. On account, therefore, of
the nature of the application, Sheridan moved a

postponement of the second reading until April 4. The purpose of this motion was, of course, to delay the further consideration of the bill until after the time for the usual opening of the Wells.

In answer to Sheridan, his opponent, Sir H. Mackworth, denied that a monopoly was aimed at by the bill, or that any attempt was made by it to infringe the rights of the patentees. Neither was it needful to suppose that, by granting Sadler's Wells a license to continue harmless performances, such as they had been used to do, a precedent would be thus established compelling Parliament to grant similar licenses to all applicants. Sheridan, however, enlisted the influence of Charles James Fox, and the second reading of the Sadler's Wells bill was postponed, as moved by Sheridan, by a vote of 48 to 39.[1]

It was with comparative ease that Sheridan seemed to defeat the Sadler's Wells bill, but the matter was not to drop here. Mainwaring, the original mover of the bill, immediately framed another of a more general and far-reaching nature, looking towards an amendment and explanation of the theatrical laws then in force. The motion to bring in this bill, which was known as the Interlude Bill, was made on the 8th of April, 1788, and, as outlined by one of the clauses of

[1] *Parliamentary History of England*, vol. xxviii, cols. 159–163 ; *Gentleman's Magazine*, August, 1788.

the bill, it was clearly intended to attain the same
end as the Sadler's Wells bill. The motion was
agreed to by the House without opposition. A
week later, a petition came up from the Royalty
Theatre, praying to have a similar clause to that
of Sadler's Wells inserted in the Interlude Bill.[1]
The Speaker of the House declared the Royalty
petition out of order. The Sadler's Wells petition
to be annexed to the bill, he said, had been presented within the time limit [2] allowed to petitioners for private bills; the Royalty had come
in too late to have its merits examined. Poor
Palmer's petition was, thereupon, referred to a
committee, but not until a staunch supporter of
fair play and an unshackled stage had expressed
surprise at the prejudice exhibited towards
the Royalty. This advocate (M. A. Taylor, the
original mover of the Royalty bill) went farther, and asked the reason why Drury Lane and
Covent Garden should have a monopoly to the
exclusion of all other places of amusement. He
insisted that a theatre in Whitechapel could not
injure the " great " houses, and that that part of
town (the locality of the Royalty) ought to be
indulged as well as the West End.

[1] *Parliamentary Register*, xxiii, 458, 459, 497 ; *Gentleman's
Magazine*, September, October, 1788.

[2] At this (5th) Session, the 8th of February was fixed as
the last day for receiving petitions for private bills. *Gentleman's
Magazine*, May, 1788 ; *London Chronicle*, February, 1788.

Fox contended that there was already a sufficient number of places of amusement, and that
any increase of these would destroy the perfection of those already established. As to the proprietors of Sadler's Wells, they had long been
acting from allowed prescriptive right, he said,
and were more entitled to the indulgence prayed
for in the petition than the proprietors of the
Royalty Theatre, who had no such grounds to
proceed on and no claim to favor.

The Royalty petition was infectious. On the
25th of April, a memorial from the proprietors
of the Royal Circus was presented to Parliament,
praying for a clause in its favor. But the ruling which had been applied to the Royalty petition was repeated, and the House proceeded to
the third reading. At this juncture, one of the
members (Mr. Hussey) thought to "feel the pulse
of the House," as he expressed it, by offering a
rider to the bill in the form of a clause intended
to relax the rigor of the then existing acts of Parliament relative to strolling players. As the law
stood, it was in the power of any malicious or
interested person to apprehend traveling comedians, and have the vagrant clause enforced upon
them. The amendment which was now sprung
upon the House, proposed to give to the quarter
sessions, and to the quarter sessions only, the
power to grant licenses to any company of come-

dians to act plays for forty nights, in the course
of a year, in any town or city in the realm ; provided, the said town or city should be specified,
and not to be at a less distance than thirty miles
from London, nor than fifteen miles from any
place in which there should be a patent theatre.

The motion was, of course, overruled, as it
contained matter entirely new ; whereupon, the
mover intimated his intention of forming it into
a bill. The original motion having passed the
House of Commons, the bill was sent to the
Lords for their concurrence. When on the 5th
of May (1788), the bill came up for consideration in the upper house, a determined opposition
appeared to the clause making it "lawful for the
proprietors of Sadler's Wells to continue exhibiting performances of singing, dancing, pantomime, and music, and other entertainments
which have been exhibited there, etc." It did
not escape the managers of the other minor
theatres [1] that if this clause, unmodified, were
left in the bill, not only would Sadler's Wells
secure thereby a legal monopoly of that species
of amusement (singing, dancing, etc.) which had

[1] The term "minor theatre" was, at first, intended to include those establishments not permitted to represent the regular drama, *i. e.* all except the two patent houses. The distinction continued even after the regular drama had crept into
the smaller theatres.

hitherto been open to all the lesser places of entertainment, but also that the indefinite privilege contained in "other entertainments which have been exhibited there," practically insured to Sadler's Wells the lawful presentation of other forms of theatrical performances than those permitted by custom or statute; for it appears that the proprietors of the Wells had, on occasion, stretched their licensed privileges. In the examination of the bill in the House of Lords, the proprietors of Astley's, the Royal Circus, and the Royalty were represented by counsel. For Astley, it was claimed that the magistrates of Surrey had licensed his house of amusement for ten successive years, a fact which seemed to indicate the respectability of the place, and that the proposed bill would operate to ruin the establishment. Witnesses from Sadler's Wells were here introduced, who deposed that that place of entertainment had been conducted for upwards of fifty years, and that very large sums had been expended on it. But it was not certain that these expenditures had been made since the restrictions of the 25 George II (1752).

The Lords were convinced of the partiality of the bill, and, therefore, considered an amendment to include the Royalty, the Royal Grove (Astley's), and the Royal Circus. The proprietors of the patent theatres and the Haymarket arose in alarm at this and forthwith petitioned the Lords against the proposed amendment. The Duke of Richmond shrewdly observed that counsel for the patentees had spoken strongly against three of the minor establishments, but had failed to say one word against Sadler's Wells. Why the latter concern should receive greater indulgence than the others on the same footing, the Duke was unable to conceive. It was admitted that all four of the minor theatres had been guilty of violating the statutes regulating those places, but Sadler's Wells had been a law-breaker for a much longer period than the rest.[1] That the winter houses and the Haymarket wished to monopolize the whole business of dramatic entertainment was no reason why the inhabitants of one part of the town, as well as those of another part, should not enjoy the amusements of a theatre. This allusion was to the Royalty Theatre; and in answer to the opposers of that theatre, who complained that the passages to the place were thronged by persons of immoral character, it was retorted that Drury Lane and Covent Garden were subject to the same criticism.

The position taken by the Duke of Richmond

[1] This allusion, no doubt, applies more particularly to 25 George II (regarding morals) than to any violation of the Licensing Act.

fairly voiced the attitude of the Lords. The bill, as amended, passed the House without a division, and was returned to the Commons. But the interests of the patentees were strongly represented there, and, on the 25th of June (1788), the amended bill was rejected. This was the formal conclusion of the attempt of Palmer to obtain parliamentary protection for the Royalty, though, as related in a former chapter, his hopes had been virtually blasted some time previous to the fate of the Interlude Bill.[1]

But the time was at hand when all parties were agreed that the Licensing Act should be amended. This was evident from the discussions on the Interlude Bill; and had that bill been stripped of its special features, which were tacked to it in the interest of private individuals, it would have passed. Now that the real objections to the bill had been pointed out in both houses of Parliament, nothing remained but to draw up a measure free from those objections. This was accordingly done in " An Act to enable Justices of the Peace to license Theatrical Representations occasionally ; under

---

[1] For the history of the Interlude Bill, see *Parliamentary Register*, xxiii, 458, 497; xxiv, 116 ; *Gentleman's Magazine*, June, September, October, 1788; *London Chronicle*, May 6, June 23, 26, 1788.

the Restrictions therein contained," which passed both houses.[1] The preamble to this act states that its purpose was to exempt England, as a whole, from the narrow restrictions of the 10 George II (Licensing Act). The bill grew immediately out of the Hussey amendment to the Interlude Bill, and gave to Justices of the Peace authority to license (on petition) such theatrical performances as were presented at the patent theatres in Westminster, at any place, city, or town, within the magistrates' jurisdiction, for a period not to exceed sixty days which should fall within the limits of the four months to be specified in the license. It was further provided, that no place licensed under the provisions of this act should be within twenty miles of London, Westminster, or Edinburgh.

There were now three distinct general laws of Parliament governing the theatres of the realm, besides numerous special acts applying only to certain large cities. By the act of 28 George III, it was intended to recognize the main provisions of the Licensing Act relating to the patent houses; to leave the magistrates free, within a radius of twenty miles from the metropolis, to license places of public entertainment, according to the 25 George II; and, at the same time, to give to the remainder of the

[1] *Statutes at Large*, 28 George III, cap. xxx.

kingdom, lying outside the magic circle, the opportunity for theatrical amusements enjoyed by the inhabitants of Westminster. Thus legislation stood, respecting the theatres, at the close of the eighteenth century : the Lord Chamberlain was chief authority in Westminster, the home of the patent theatres ; magistrates in London and Westminster, and within twenty miles thereof, might license certain species of theatrical amusements ; magistrates outside the twenty miles circle could authorize the regular drama for a limited period each year ; while special legislation in the case of individual cities permitted the same privileges (in the particular cities named in the special acts) as those enjoyed by the two patent houses in the metropolis. [1]

No more complicated or cumbrous legislation regulating the theatres of England (or anywhere) could be imagined. The purpose of the various laws was to give to the whole realm the privileges enjoyed by London ; but these acts were so palpably partial in their operation that that alone was sure, in time, to call for a reorganization of the whole system. Furthermore,

[1] Patents outside of London were issued as follows : Manchester, 1775, 1796 ; Newcastle, 1787 ; Bath, 1797 ; Chester, 1798, 1819 ; Bristol, 1799 ; Kingston, and York, 1803 ; Liverpool, Birmingham, and Margate, 1807 ; Edinburgh, 1809.

there was an overlapping of jurisdictions provided by these various acts of legislation, which was calculated to cause trouble ; while the indefinite restrictions relative to the kinds of entertainments that might be exhibited under authority of the magistrates' license (25 George II) contained the germ which was destined to work the destruction of the whole artificial theatrical organization. All these discrepancies and contradictions were the result of the attempt to keep inviolable the rights of the patent theatres, and when the readjustment to a rational basis should come, it must necessarily be at the sacrifice of the monopoly.

CHAPTER VII

THE period of twenty years succeeding the
Royalty episode marks a transition in theatrical affairs in London, hitherto unexampled in
the number and importance of events. One thing
was certain, the good times consequent on the
undisturbed quiet of exclusive privileges were
past forever. The managers of the "great"
houses felt the necessity of bracing their position
in every imaginable direction, and the stupendous efforts which they made to prove their long-established security reacted, in time, to pull down
their enormous defenses about their own heads.
Sheridan conceived the plan of meeting the
growing demands of an increasing metropolis by
demolishing the old Drury Lane Theatre, [1] and
erecting in its stead a much larger and more
magnificent edifice. The execution of this design

---

[1] The following statistics relative to Drury Lane Theatre
may be of interest: built 1662; burnt 1672; rebuilt 1674;
enlarged 1763; pulled down 1791; rebuilt, reopened 1794;
burnt 1809; rebuilt 1812.

was commenced in 1789. Sheridan secured the
Opera House in the Haymarket [1] for the patent
company while the new Drury Lane Theatre was
in course of construction. But huge difficulties
stood in the way of the great patentee. The new
structure was scarcely well on its way, when
suddenly all operations on it were arrested. The
subscribers had discovered that *there was no
patent for Drury Lane Theatre*, and they refused to pay their subscriptions to support a
concern of such dubious tenure. It has been
pointed out more than once in the course of this
investigation that, when the patents were united
in 1682, they passed into the hands of the successor to Davenant, and, presumably, were in-
herited by John Rich in 1714. By the same
order of conjecture, both the patents became the
property of Beard, son-in-law to John Rich,
on the death of the latter (1761), and, in the
transfer of 1767, were given over into the possession of the new managers, Colman, Harris,
Powell, and Rutherford. Of this quartette, Colman had gone over to the Haymarket (1777),

[1] This was the house built by Vanbrugh in 1704. It was
variously called The Opera House, the King's Theatre, and
Her Majesty's Theatre. It burnt in 1789, and the Drury Lane
company then moved to the Pantheon, in Oxford Street, until
the Opera House in the Haymarket was rebuilt (1791). The
Pantheon was first opened in 1772; converted into an Opera
House in 1784; burnt 1792.

Powell was dead (1769), and, at the time of the rebuilding of Drury Lane Theatre, Harris was practically the sole head in the management of Covent Garden.

The situation in which Sheridan found himself at this time (1792) was anything but enviable. Everything depended on the subscribers, and to maintain his hold upon their confidence, and purse-strings, it occurred to the ingenious Sheridan to get possession of the "dormant patent." Application, therefore, was made to Harris for the old Killigrew grant. The Covent Garden manager agreed to dispose of it for £15,000, and the document was at once deposited in the hands of a banker for the inspection and satisfaction of the Drury Lane subscribers. However, a new difficulty now arose to complicate matters. The transaction respecting the "dormant patent" coming to the knowledge of a Mr. White, who, by marrying the daughter of the then late Mr. Powell, possessed a considerable share (one fourth) in Covent Garden Theatre, White called on Harris and expressed his dissatisfaction at the proposed transfer of the old patent to Drury Lane. Harris was inclined to pay little heed to these objections, but White demonstrated his sincerity by obtaining from the Court of Chancery a prohibition of the sale of the patent, which was thereupon restored to Covent Garden.

It does not appear that White had any particular scruples against the Drury Lane management possessing the "dormant patent;" he simply insisted that, as a shareholder in the Covent Garden Theatre, he should be consulted in the matter under consideration, and he refused to sign the transfer of the patent to Sheridan unless he receive £5000. After considerable bickering, the sum of £20,000 was finally agreed on.[1]

Closely connected with this transaction runs another affecting our general problem, though apparently quite different. Since the troublous days in the reign of Queen Anne, the question of Italian opera had scarcely been a factor in the theatrical affairs of London. Among the schemes and counter-schemes of that period, it will be remembered, it was generally understood that Italian opera should be relegated exclusively to the Opera House in the Haymarket. This arrangement was undisturbed for years, except by the periodic attacks, in pamphlets and newspapers, on foreign actors and actresses. But in the theatrical disturbances of the last fifteen or twenty years of the eighteenth century, the opera ques-

[1] The history of this transaction appeared in the *London Chronicle* for July 30, and September 12, 1792. These two numbers of the *London Chronicle* contain the only mention I have ever seen of White's connection with the transfer of the patent to Sheridan. This throws entirely new light on the reason why Sheridan purchased the " dormant patent."

tion also was involved. The history of the opera controversy in London is long and interesting, but it is my object, in this connection, to touch on those points only which associate themselves naturally with the main pursuit.[1]

About 1781, the Opera House in the Haymarket (King's Theatre) became the property of William Taylor. Not long after this (1784), a building in Oxford Street, constructed in 1772, was converted into an opera house, which became the property of one O'Reilly in 1789. This was the Pantheon, and O'Reilly at once fitted it up for a class of entertainments similar to those represented at the King's Theatre in the Haymarket, that is to say, for Italian opera. On the 17th of June, 1789, Taylor's Opera House caught fire during a rehearsal, and burned. Taking advantage of the circumstance, O'Reilly, who was a politician, wielded his influence with the Lord Chamberlain, and secured a license for Italian opera at the Pantheon. A war was thus precipitated between the opera managers. Tay-

---

[1] For some of the material connected with the opera quarrels in London, see *A Concise Statement of Transactions and Circumstances respecting the King's Theatre in the Haymarket.* By W. Taylor. Pamphlet, pp. 46, London, 1791. Also, *The Opera Glass: exhibiting all the curious proceedings of the King's Theatre, &c.* By E. Waters, London, 1808. *Seven Years of the King's Theatre.* By John Ebers, London, 1828. *Outline for a General Opera Arrangement*, London, 1792.

lor was refused a license on the pretext that one for the same purpose had been granted to O'Reilly; and the question to decide was, who had the monopoly for Italian opera in London, — Taylor, whom precedent would sustain in his claim, or O'Reilly, who maintained his position by virtue of the Lord Chamberlain's license?

On December 31, 1790, a number of gentlemen, interested in the settlement of the dispute, met at Carlton House in the hopes of devising some means of reconciliation between the belligerents. A scheme of union of the two managements was proposed, the Opera House in the Haymarket (which was then rebuilding) alone to be used for operas, the Pantheon to be reserved for light and select entertainments of music and dancing. But the parties were too much at variance to reach a compromise, and the meeting broke up without having accomplished anything.[1] Meantime, the new Opera House in the Haymarket was pushed to its completion, and, as the new Drury Lane Theatre was barely commenced, Sheridan occupied the Opera House with the patent company, where he opened the season September 22, 1791.

The dispute between Taylor and O'Reilly was finally settled by the latter getting inextricably involved during the season of 1791, and by the

[1] *London Chronicle*, 4th, 8th, 17th January, 1791.

burning of the Pantheon the next year. Sheridan
was at this time (1792) negotiating for the
"dormant patent," and he now came forward in
the opera controversy, ostensibly for the purpose of definitely settling the point of the Italian
opera. The plan of settlement was known as
an *Outline for a General Opera Arrangement*,
and is a striking example of Sheridan's finesse.
In the first place, the Drury Lane manager appears as the chief representative of the interests
of the King's Theatre (Opera House in the
Haymarket), and general mediator between all
parties. The Pantheon was represented in the
Outline by William Sheldon, while Covent
Garden was not included in the committee that
framed the articles of settlement. This seems
the more strange inasmuch as Harris was still
in possession of both the patents of the monopoly. To secure for the proposed Arrangement
the dignity and support of high authority, the
approbation (in signature) of the Prince of
Wales and the Marquis of Salisbury, then Lord
Chamberlain, was obtained. The Duke of Bedford, owner of the ground on which Drury Lane
Theatre once stood, also entered his signature.

Shrewdness marks the entire thirty-one articles of the Outline. From a hasty examination
of these, it would seem that the main purpose
throughout was to settle once for all the vexed

question of the Italian opera; and, from the
attention given to Mr. Taylor's interests in the
settlement, that gentleman must have been highly
gratified with the Arrangement. A monopoly to
that species of entertainment was surrendered to
the Opera House in the Haymarket, and a clause
was inserted which contained a waiver of all
pretensions in that direction on the part of Drury
Lane and Covent Garden. To put at rest the
danger of the Pantheon rivalry, provision was
made for the dismantling of that Opera House
as soon as the new Opera House in the Haymarket should be ready for occupancy. In return
for such liberal concessions, Taylor was to assume
the indebtedness of the defunct Pantheon,
amounting to about £30,000. The management
of the Opera House, as proposed by the Outline,
was to be given to five noblemen who should be
named by the Prince of Wales, the Duke of Bedford, and the Marquis of Salisbury. To put it
plainly, the Outline was distinctly aimed at bringing the monopoly of the opera directly under
the influence of the Drury Lane management.

One other strategic stroke — the main one
for our purpose — should be observed in connection with the *Outline for a General Opera
Arrangement*. The matter of the "dormant patent" — Sheridan's chief concern at that time
— was thrust into the opera settlement, though

having absolutely nothing to do with it. To give
a semblance of propriety to the dragging into
the Outline of the "dormant patent," it was
agreed that the Opera House in the Haymarket
should contribute £5000 toward the purchase
of the patent from Harris, that document then
to be "annexed inseparably" to Drury Lane
Theatre. This assessment on the Opera House
happened to be the exact amount demanded by
White for his one-fourth interest in the "dormant patent," and it was levied at an opportune
time for the furtherance of Sheridan's plans. To
cover over the real meaning of this clause in
the Outline, another immediately follows, con-
firming and establishing the Opera House in the
monopoly of Italian opera; and this, in turn,
is succeeded by the provision to secure the management of the Opera House to the Prince of
Wales, the Duke of Bedford, and the Marquis
of Salisbury. These three clauses (6th, 7th, and
8th) of the Outline form a curious psycholog-
ical study, and together seem clearly to explain
Sheridan's motives.

The question of the "dormant patent" being
thus satisfactorily settled, as Sheridan thought,
work on the new Drury Lane Theatre progressed
without further serious interference.[1] The im-

1 It is significant that the new theatre was not opened under
the "dormant patent," but under a running license (21 years),

mense size of the new theatre is worthy of mention, as that was soon to become a factor in the struggle for a free stage. The building was 320 feet in length, 155 in width, and had a roof width of 118 feet. Covent Garden had anticipated Drury Lane in the matter of increased size, as it had been remodeled and enlarged only a short time before (1791). The influence of these changes in the size of the buildings on the theatrical problem was enormous and of constant recurrence. The subject will be treated more fully in another connection.

While the details of these larger and novel features of the patent theatres were in progress, the struggle for existence, on the one hand, and the war of extermination, on the other, between the Little Theatre in the Haymarket and the winter theatres, had been resumed. In 1792 (15th of June), an occasional Prelude entitled *Two Sides of the Gutter* [1] was presented at the Haymarket and contained a complaint of the unfair treatment by the patentees. It was intended, also, to satirize the size and gorgeous magnificence of

recently issued. It turned out later that Sheridan did not secure the patent in 1792, and the whole question reappeared in a later controversy, to be taken up in the next chapter.

[1] This was the sub-title, the chief title being *Poor Old Haymarket;* written by the younger Colman, who, since 1790, had been manager of the Haymarket, the elder Colman being incapacitated by hemiplegia (of which he died in 1794).

the new patent theatres.[1] It was during this
period that the Drury Lane Company, from time
to time, occupied the theatre in the Haymarket.
During the winter season of 1793–94 such was
the case. The new theatre in Drury Lane
was completed in March, 1794, and on the 12th
of the month received the patent company. A
play had been advertised the same evening at
the Haymarket, but, remarks Oulton,[2] as "*two*
theatres could not keep open under *one* patent,
the Little Theatre closed in a very abrupt manner." No better evidence of the completeness
of the monopoly could be conceived than this.
The futility of the effort to compete with the
winter theatres was more and more apparent to
Colman, and, for a number of years, with occasional brief intervals of exception, he practically
gave up the fight, and conformed his summer
season, not to the letter of his license, but to the
will of the patentees. At no time, be it remembered, during this rivalry, was the *right* of the
patent houses to encroach on the summer season
questioned; for it was freely acknowledged that
a patent contained authority above a license.
But the tyranny of exercising a legal power
for the sole purpose of crushing an inferior was

---

[1] *European Magazine,* June, 1792. See also *London Chronicle*
for June 15, 1790.

[2] *History of the Theatres of London,* ii, 135.

complained of bitterly, and, by degrees, the public sympathy was aroused on the side of the weaker party.

A climax was reached in 1802, when the winter theatres extended their season so far into the summer that the Haymarket was unable to open until the 26th of June. This determined Colman to put forward his best efforts to ignore the patent theatres altogether, and to open his theatre, for the future, on time. A short time before the close of the summer season of 1802, he had a notice posted in the green-room at the Haymarket, informing the actors that none of them need consider themselves as subject to engagement for the ensuing season, unless they could be in readiness to act for the period authorized by the license, that is, from the 15th of May to the 15th of September. And the day before the close of the season the play-bills contained the following announcement to the public :

" Circumstances have arisen for several years past, which have curtailed the term allotted to this theatre, for the representation of dramatic performances, of *more* than one fourth.

" As the justly due and customary *thanks*, at the conclusion of the *present season*, will be followed by reasons why this theatre will, in future, decidedly exercise its rights, during the *full period* which has long been graciously granted by

His Majesty, it is humbly hoped that the audience will show indulgence to the length of *the address*, which will, on this occasion, be submitted to their candour."

This advertisement had the desired effect of filling the theatre the next night (September 15) to its utmost capacity. At the close of the entertainment, Fawcett, Colman's acting manager, came to the front of the stage, and, after delivering the annual thanksgiving, read the promised address from the proprietor. As this contains an admirable summary of the relations existing between the Little Theatre and the patent houses, it should be quoted in full. The Address runs thus:

" When a Royal Patent was about to be granted to the late Mr. Foote, it was inquired, with that justice which characterizes the English throne, what annual extent of term might be allowed him, without injury to theatrical patents then existing in this metropolis. The proprietors of the winter theatres were interrogated on this point, and, in consequence of their documents, a patent was granted to Foote for his life, to open a theatre annually, from the 15th of May to the 15th of September, inclusive.

" Winter houses never closed precisely on the commencement of his term; but Foote was *unique*, and depended chiefly on his own writing, and his own acting. A licence was given to the Elder Colman, *for the same annual term*, on Foote's death ; but, aware that he could not, like his singularly gifted predecessor, depend on his own individual powers, he engaged a regular company of comedians, chiefly selected from the winter theatres, for whose assistance *he was obliged to wait till those theatres closed*. He ventured in every shape, very deeply on a limited privilege, which this mode of speculation rendered still *more* limited. The Younger Colman, our present proprietor, succeeded his father in this licence, but bought the *property* at the expense of several thousand pounds, and thus came into a theatre, where the custom of depending on the movements of the winter houses has now curtailed its short season by *nearly one third !*

"The object at length in view is, to remedy the evil without invidious and vain attempts to attack much more powerful theatres, who have an undoubted privilege of acting plays all the year round. The proprietor has no intention of tiring the public ear by a querulous appeal; he admits that others have the fullest right to make their property as productive as possible; he wishes merely to follow their example ; and solicits your support in his effort in establishing a company of actors totally independent of them.

There are but three houses permitted to give you regular batches of plays in London; and this house (by far the most humble) sees no reason when they will all be making their bread, on the 15th of next May; why even *three* of a trade should not perfectly agree.

"Should his arrangements succeed, which are even at this early period, actively forming, you will (on the reopening of the theatre) greet the return to London of some favourites, who, it is trusted, will find no diminution of your protection; you will witness new and rising merit, which it is your marked practice to foster. There is no theatrical town in the United Kingdom which will not be resorted to, in the hope of procuring you its choicest produce; and, in addition to other authors, you will be intreated, early in the season, to show your indulgence to the proprietor's further attempts at dramatic competition; whose pen he humbly hopes, notwithstanding the long duration of your encouragement, is not yet quite worn out in your service."[1]

Such was the ambitious "platform" of the Haymarket proprietor for the campaign of 1803, and every promise made therein was carried out punctually to the letter. Late in 1802, Colman

[1] *London Chronicle*, September 16, 1802. See also *European Magazine* for May, 1803.

writes to Elliston, the comedian, relative to engaging him for the season of 1803, and takes pains to impress his determination to open the theatre on time. " In short," he continues, " we must meet on the Haymarket ground next year for four months, or not at all. It is my intention to open the house on the 15th of May with an independent company . . ." [1] The Worcester theatre, Portsmouth, Weymouth, Bath, and York were levied on to furnish actors for this experiment,[2] and on Monday the 16th of May, 1803, the Haymarket Theatre opened free from any dependence on the patent houses for actors. If the attendance was any criterion, the venture was a success, for "the house was better attended than is usual on the first night." The play for the evening (*The Jew*) was prefaced by a dramatic sketch in one act, entitled *No Prelude*, in which Waldron appeared in the *rôle* of prompter, lamenting, in soliloquy, the hard lines in which the Haymarket had been placed, and reading a letter from Colman, whimsically explaining his theatrical expedients.   Elliston then came on as deputy-manager, and, in the dialogue which followed, the new actors who had been secured were discussed and the support of the public supplicated for them.

[1] Raymond's *Life of Robert William Elliston*, p. 78.

[2] *London Chronicle*, May 17, 1803.   Mathews was the chief recruit from York.

The effort proved successful, and the season at the Haymarket coincided, for the first time in years, with the limits of the license. Again, in 1804, the Little Theatre opened on time, though not quite so auspiciously as the year before, as Drury Lane did not close her doors until the 12th of June.[1] The summer season this year (1804) was pushed once more to September 15, and was pronounced "most successful." However, on the closing night, the audience showed some dissatisfaction, arising from the circumstance of one of the actors (a Mr. de Camp) being obliged to quit the theatre before the play was ended, in order to attend an engagement at the Drury Lane Theatre.[2] Early in the season a similar difficulty arose when two of Colman's actors, Bannister and R. Palmer, continued at Drury Lane, thereby crippling the Haymarket company for nearly two weeks. The sturdy resolution of Colman was thus checkmated at the very beginning of its operation, and the tactics displayed by the patentees in this particular season (1804) became the regular practice with them. The provinces were scoured by Colman for an independent company, only to have his best recruits at once transferred to one or the other of the patent houses; for it

---

[1] *London Chronicle*, June 13, 1804.

[2] *Ibid.*, September 18, 1804.

was the ambition of every actor who came up to London in those days to get an engagement at either of the two "great houses."

As a result of Colman's fruitless experiment, the Little Theatre in the Haymarket was for sale at the close of the season of 1804; and before the opening of the ensuing season, the property had changed hands, Messrs. Morris and Winston succeeding to the management.[1] But this change in the directorship of the theatre had no effect on the attitude of the patentees, who continued to advance their winter performances farther and farther into the summer season. In 1805, the Haymarket Theatre did not open until June 8, the reason being, according to the "London Chronicle," that the new partnership had been formed too late to begin sooner. The real reason of the delayed opening was that the winter houses pleased to keep open until late in June, Covent Garden not closing until the 15th of the month. From this on until after the burning of the patent houses, the Haymarket fell back into its old dependence on the winter

[1] *London Chronicle*, June 10, 17, 1805. Oulton has it (iii, 58) that one-half interest in the Haymarket was for sale and that Colman's brother-in-law, Morris, and Thomas Dibdin were supposed to be the purchasers, but that it turned out that Dibdin declined to enter into the transaction, being deterred, probably, on account of the encroachments of the winter houses. Colman still remained in the theatre as a shareholder.

houses for performers, with the practical admission that it was useless to oppose the "legal monopoly."

Meantime, new conditions were arising which were to tax the ingenuity of the patentees far more than any difficulty which had yet presented itself. The old opera controversy had reappeared in a new phase; for the Outline had not altered men's natures. The large theatres had gradually repudiated the legitimate drama; spectacle and dumb-show had proved better suited to their size. Especially did the new century bring with it a type of dramatic entertainment which, ever since, has succeeded in holding its own in competition with the regular drama. This new species was the melodrama which came into England with spectres of German castles, and nerve-racking scenes of the "Monk" Lewis order, together with the long train of modifications and variations of these which at once fascinated the minds of the rabble. The patent houses went with the current, but the movement was sure to call for a reaction on the part of sticklers for the legitimate drama. The patentees were bound to bear the brunt of the criticism when it should come, for, since the passage of the Licensing Act, they had stood as the champions of Shakespeare and Otway.

But the greatest change, immediately affect-

ing the question of patent rights, was in the
Lord Chamberlainship. When the Act of 1737
was under consideration, the monarchical power
vested in the Lord Chamberlain by that act was
pointed out; but the needs of the case seemed
to demand some fixed responsibility, and as for
the patentees, they favored the act because they
thought they saw in it their bulwark of defense
against opposition. And such had been the case
as proved by events. The Dukes of Grafton
and Devonshire, and the Marquis of Salisbury
had guarded the patents with a jealousy second
only to that of the patentees. But there was
scarcely anything in the Licensing Act to insure
the perpetuity of this guardianship. The office
and the law remained after the individual filling
it was no longer Lord Chamberlain. And now
the other side of the shield was to be turned to
view. Salisbury had joined Sheridan in his so-
called Opera Arrangement, — which was in reality a Drury Lane arrangement. But Salisbury
had been succeeded by the Earl of Dartmouth,
and the Earl of Dartmouth exercised the authority given him by the Licensing Act as he saw
fit, not as dictated by the patentees. The boom-
erang had returned.

The independence of the Earl of Dartmouth
in the capacity of Lord Chamberlain appears on
more than one occasion. In the summer of 1804

a series of concerts were given in London by
amateur native talent. These were so successful
that Henry Fulke Greville, Esq. (a retired
colonel in the army, whom we shall hear more
of later) became enthusiastic for an established
English opera.   He drew up a plan of his
scheme, and sent it, together with a letter (dated
July 27, 1804), urging action in the matter, to
the Earl of Dartmouth. It was proposed to secure the Pantheon in Oxford Street, and to induce the Lord Chamberlain to grant a license for
music and dancing twice a week (Monday and
Friday).   Greville argued that such a venture
must necessarily succeed, for, as it was intended
to employ only English singers, the national
vanity would be flattered, and the entertainments
would be popular. The difficulty of getting the
proprietors of the Pantheon to agree to a proposal to sell the building was anticipated : in
case of failure in that quarter, it was suggested
that a site in Albemarle Street might be had
where a suitable room for the purpose could be
erected.

Colonel Greville's plan went much further
than music and dancing.   After indicting the
patent houses for debasing the public morals
and literary taste, he boldly proposed to enact
the regular drama — " genuine comedy and approved good tragedy " — on two more days of

the week (Tuesday and Saturday). The house should be small, to hold not to exceed six hundred, and of the "600 persons attending these nights amusements," prognosticated the sanguine Colonel, "I will venture to assert not twenty would otherwise have attended the public theatres; but granting the whole number was drawn from the theatres, what right and title have these establishments to a monopoly of the whole town?" The Lord Chamberlain apprehended "a great deal of trouble would be made by the proprietors of the three winter playhouses" (evidently including the Haymarket), should they attempt to carry out Greville's proposed scheme. This was granted by the Colonel, who insisted on the question "whether improvement and utility are to be prevented shooting forth to maturity because the individual interests of three patentees whose affairs are most flourishing are to be in some measure rivalled." Greville had conversed on the subject with Braham (the tenor), he said, and that gentleman had fallen in with the suggestion to establish a new theatre. The purpose and result of such a venture were summed up by Colonel Greville in the hope that, "if His Majesty would grant a patent or even a licence, I am sure society might reap very considerable benefit, from a greater encouragement being administered to the exertion of talent supported by refinement and taste." [1]

Lord Dartmouth was unwilling to take the step of declaring the patents null and void by using his authority to set up a rival theatre for the regular drama in the precincts of Westminster, and even the license for music and dancing was not issued for some time after the correspondence just quoted. For all his enthusiasm and progressiveness, Colonel Greville was not destined to inaugurate the English opera in London. Nevertheless, his proposal in 1804 marks the first effort in that direction, and his audacious plan to erect a third theatre for the regular drama is the first *legal* attempt to break through the monopoly.[2] It is of further interest to note that, though Lord Dartmouth could not be induced to grant a license for " genuine comedy and approved good tragedy," he was not unfriendly to a discussion of the points at issue. That he did not lean towards the theatrical monopoly is apparent from another incident. Early in 1807 he was petitioned in behalf of James Grant Raymond, Robert Palmer, and

[1] *Historical MSS. Commission*, Report XV, pp. 284–286.

[2] I am aware, of course, that Dr. Arnold, the musical composer, attempted to secure a license in 1794 for the Lyceum, which he had recently purchased and fitted up for a theatre. But this was for musical entertainments.   The patentees prevented the license.

others, who alleged that the proprietors of the Haymarket were guilty of partiality against the winter performers. The attitude of Lord Dartmouth in his answer to this petition is unmistakable. The signatures are denounced as forgeries, and, if real, to be only performers of minor ability, " some of them the mere refuse of the London Theatres." To the complaints in the memorial Lord Dartmouth's retort was sharp and decisive : " The grievances under which the petition[er]s appear to labour (if they ever did exist) exist no longer : but the fact is that the Winter London performers were *never* aggrieved by the Summer Theatre, while the Summer Theatre has been long struggling to prevent itself from sinking under the power of its Winter neighbors." Instead of the Haymarket refusing to receive the performers from the patent houses (as asserted by the petition), it was a well-known fact, retorted the Lord Chamberlain, that the Little Theatre was forced to depend on the winter houses for its company of performers.[1]

If any doubt remained as to the Earl of Dartmouth's views respecting the patent houses, it was soon removed by his practical interpretation of that clause in the Licensing Act which vested the power to grant theatrical licenses in the Lord Chamberlain alone. He had not felt that he

[1] *Historical MSS. Commission*, Report XIII[4], 503, 504.

dared openly to violate the patents granted by
Charles II, but leaving the patentees in the enjoyment of their monopoly of the regular drama,
he turned to exercise the authority secured to
him over the irregular drama. Some of the various places of amusement had for years been suffered to exhibit a variety of musical performances, dances, and pantomimes. These were,
as has already been pointed out, Sadler's Wells,
Astley's, Royal Circus, and Royalty. To these
should be added the Sans Souci, in Leicester
Square, a little " band-box of a theatre," built by
Charles Dibdin and opened by him on the 13th
of October, 1792, with an entertainment called
The Quissars, " in the course of which he introduced one-and-twenty new songs." [1] All of these
had continued down into the nineteenth century
without molestation (except in the case of the Royalty), for they could scarcely be said to compete
or interfere with the monopoly.   Lord Dartmouth's friendliness towards these smaller concerns now (1807) produced a perfect inundation
of applications for theatrical licenses.   In the
" Morning Chronicle " for November 16, 1807,
appears the following article on the subject:

" NEW THEATRES

" A new Theatre, the San Pareil, was opened
on Saturday night [Nov. 14].   It is under the

[1] *London Chronicle*, October 15, 1792.

direction of *Monsieur Giroux*, whose young and elegant daughters perform at it, and which is designed to form a Nursery for the Opera and other Theatres. It is a beautiful little place, almost opposite the Adelphi, in the Strand.

"Another Theatre, to be called the *Minor* Theatre, situate in Catherine-street, is to be opened this night [Nov. 16, 1807]. There are several others in a state of forwardness, which are all to start as rivals to the great Theatres.

" The theatre, in Argyll-street; [1]

" A theatre, in Tottenham Court-road ;

" A Theatre, in Berwick-street ;

" A Theatre, in Leicester-fields [the Sans Souci] ;

" Two Theatres, at the Lyceum, in the strand ;

" The Pavilion, in Wych-street ;

"Besides Sadler's Wells, the Royal Amphitheatre, the Circus, and the Royalty.

" In addition to all which, we understand that application has been made to the Lord Chamberlain to grant a licence for a New Opera.

" Paris must hide its head."

This marks the first great stirring of practical opposition to the patent houses. But even now, the action of the Lord Chamberlain in granting licenses to the lesser establishments for enter-

[1] The Argyll Street Institution decided to wait another season, pending the difficulties of the King's Theatre.

tainments outside the regular drama need not
have produced any serious rivalry to the "great
houses," had not the latter seen fit to accept the
challenge and to abandon the ground appropriated to their exclusive use by the monopoly. As
it turned out, they took alarm at the innovation
and audacity of the Lord Chamberlain in pre-
suming to grant a license without their consent
and approval, and were resolved to chastise the
upstart offenders. Thus was inaugurated the
war between the majors and minors, which was
not to cease until the monopoly itself was no
more. It was given out on "undoubted authority" that the proprietors of the winter theatres
had resolved " to put an immediate stop to the
encroachments made on their property, under
the authority of the Lord Chamberlain." Counsel were employed, who gave the decided opinion that the patents were explicit and absolute
as to what theatres should exist in Westminster, and that any attempt on the part of the
Lord Chamberlain to license any other place
for theatrical representations, without the consent of the patentees, was an infringement on
those patents, and, hence, was illegal. " Certain it is," continued the argument for the
monopoly, " that from the day the first royal
patent was granted to Old Drury, through the
whole of Mr. Garrick's time, and ever since,

until the chamberlainship of Lord Salisbury,
the uniform practice at the Chamberlain's Office, was to refuse even to listen to an application for a single night, though for a charity
benefit, unless the party applying brought with
them the previous consent in writing of the
Proprietors of the established Theatres."

So much for the legal claim of protection to
the patents. In addition to this, the patentees
referred to their title in equity, averring that,
even if the right were with the Lord Chamberlain,
nevertheless he was "bound by positive covenant"
not to license any new concern for dramatic
exhibitions. And here the underlying motives
of the *Outline for a General Opera Arrangement* came to the surface. That was the "covenant," the result of "a long discussion and
arbitration, recognizing and guaranteeing the
exclusive rights of the three established Theatres," which, it was pointed out with an air of
injured right and dignity, had been signed by the
Marquis of Salisbury, and had been honored
by the concurrence of his Royal Highness the
Prince of Wales himself. On the faith of that
settlement, "so guaranteed," the proprietors of
Drury Lane had, they protested, laid out a considerable sum for the "dormant patent," the
King's Theatre (Opera House) had "contributed
thirty thousand pounds on recovering its licence

. . .; and finally this deed formed the whole
foundation for the rebuilding of Drury Lane
Theatre, in which undertaking a property not
less than three hundred thousand pounds have
been embarked, and all in the confidence and
on the faith of this arrangement, secured under
such high authority."

Threat was made by the patentees, that, should
the proprietors of the Opera House (King's
Theatre in the Haymarket) not succeed in settling their wrangles, they would resort to the
" dormant patent " for the benefit of the winter
houses, " which patent is at present only withheld
from being operative through respect to the
established Opera House, and the terms of the
agreement before referred to." The defense of
the patentees included also a proposed petition
to the Crown.[1]

This statement of the patentees' demand, that
the Lord Chamberlain restrict the duties of his
office in such manner as to insure the inviolability of the monopoly, fairly defines the contest
which was soon to wax fierce and strong. According to the position taken by the monopoly
owners, the patents issued by Charles II to

[1] The outline of the patentees' position in the controversy
with Lord Dartmouth was printed in the *Morning Chronicle* for
November 21, 1807. See also *European Magazine* for November, 1807 ; and *The Cabinet* for December, 1807.

Killigrew and Davenant took precedence over
all subsequent acts of Parliament, and the latter
were effective only as interpreted by the patentees.   The acquiescence of the Lord Chamberlains, from the time the Licensing Act was
passed to the reign of Lord Dartmouth, in the
wishes of the patentees, was proof to the latter
that the Lord Chamberlainship existed for the
sake of the patent houses, and that the Licensing Act simply legalized that relationship.   Lord
Dartmouth's appreciation of his functions as Lord
Chamberlain revealed the possibilities of conflicting authority which had lurked in the theatrical
monopoly ever since its creation, and especially
since 1737.

In support of the Lord Chamberlain's absolute authority in theatrical matters, precedent
was not wanting.   The patents themselves depended on that official for enforcement, even
when the patent houses alone were concerned.
When, in King William's reign, the clause was
violated, prohibiting one of the theatres receiving an actor from the other theatre without the
consent of the latter, the authority of the Lord
Chamberlain was sought to correct the abuse.
We have seen also, in the case of Betterton's revolt, that it was through the mediation of the
Lord Chamberlain that a license was secured from
the King for the revolters; and in the later re-

volts, already considered, the Lord Chamberlain's authority was not doubted, except in a single instance, and even then Steele was forced to submit to the silencing order of that official. This authority went so far as to restrain and chastise the conduct of actors when not employed at the theatres, for the Lord Chamberlain was the mouthpiece of the Crown in all theatrical affairs. Finally, the Licensing Act itself confirmed the absolutism of the Lord Chamberlain's power, and especially relegated to him the authority of licensing theatres. Viewed in this light, it mattered little to Lord Dartmouth that a contradiction of authority was contained in the Act of 1737. The attempt to exercise both authorities at the same time would prove which was the real one. If the conduct of actors, the licensing of theatres, the contentions of managers, and the differences between actors and managers fell within the jurisdiction of the Lord Chamberlain, there were grave reasons for believing in the final authority of that official. Relative to the last point, the disagreements of actors and managers, Lord Dartmouth had his deputy (T. B. Mash) make an investigation of the historical precedents on the subject. This led to the discovery of a document [1] in which the Lord Chamberlain's ultimate authority is established in all

[1] Unfortunately, this document is now, probably, lost, but

cases of controversy between actors and managers. Sir R. Steele's case is the only exception
noted of a denial of the Chamberlain's absolute
authority over theatrical matters.

The presentation of the patentees' case throws
light, also, on the Opera Arrangement of 1792.
It now (1807) transpires that the underlying
motive of the settlement was to reinforce the
"legal monopoly," and to make possible the rebuilding of Drury Lane Theatre. This appears
in the explanation of the purchase of the "dormant patent," and in the threat to use that patent if the "new projects" (the minor theatres)
were not abandoned forthwith, notwithstanding
the "guaranteed faith" of the *opera* arrangement. That the Outline was a blind to hide the
schemes of the patentees, especially of Sheridan,
is evident in the confession that the securing of
Italian opera to the King's Theatre was a mere
sop to be repudiated whenever the interests of
the patentees were endangered.

Another question of interest in the protest of
the patentees against the Lord Chamberlain is
connected with the "dormant patent." Did Sheridan think when he purchased it in 1792 to
strengthen his monopoly? If so, why did he not

the results of the investigation are extant in a letter from
T. B. Mash to Lord Dartmouth (dated Aug. 17, 1809). *Historical MSS. Commission*, Report XIII[4], p. 505.

make use of it instead of the 21-year license?
Or, rather, did he hold it in reserve, as indicated
by the above statement, as a safeguard against
any attempt to establish a rival theatre? And
did the patentees have any genuine confidence
in the efficacy of the "dormant patent" for any
purpose? The exact status of the old Killigrew
patent had not been determined in 1807, but
the time was not far distant when it, and the
whole question of patent rights in theatres, was
to be reviewed in a manner to test the sincerity
of the patentees' pretenses regarding it. Meantime, the fact was significant that Sheridan had
permitted the "dormant patent" to remain
asleep after its supposed purchase from Harris
in 1792, and the bluster about reviving it did not
seem to scare Lord Dartmouth. The resistance
of the patent houses to the authority of the
Lord Chamberlain in granting licenses to the
minor concerns was as useless as that of the
Haymarket had been against the encroachments
of the winter houses. A still greater danger,
which shook the old concerns to their very foun-
dations, was in store for the defenders of monopoly rights. But never in the history of the patent
houses did the zeal and courage of the patentees
appear to such advantage as when beset by the
direst events. The first catastrophe — the burning of both the "great houses," Covent Garden

in 1808, and Drury Lane in 1809 — was in itself sufficient to daunt the proprietors; while the attempt, following immediately on these disasters, to establish a third theatre in London, was even more discouraging. A consideration of this attempt, the most important single episode in the history of the struggle to break the shackles of the theatrical monopoly, will form the basis of the next chapter.

CHAPTER VIII

EARLY on the morning of September 20, 1808, Covent Garden Theatre was discovered to be on fire ; in a few hours it was entirely consumed. With unexampled energy, a new structure was begun before the close of the year, and almost precisely one year from the date of the conflagration, the new theatre, larger and more magnificent than ever, was thrown open for theatrical exhibitions. The immense expense to which the proprietors had been subjected in erecting the new building (the estimated cost was £300,000) led them to increase the price of admission to the performances. This action precipitated the notorious " O. P." (*i. e.* " Old Price") riots which lasted from the opening night, September 18, to December 17, 1809, when a compromise was reached between the managers and the public. The London theatre-goer of the seventeenth and eighteenth centuries had been used to fracases in the pit and boxes, and even to riots of brief duration and respectable limits. But the " O. P." riots touched the high-water mark, especially in the matter of time and the zeal with which they were conducted. Pandemonium reigned almost continuously for the sixty-seven nights on which the Covent Garden Theatre was open, during the period of three months following the opening night. Matching the persistence of the rioters — that is the audiences — were the obstinacy and haughty demeanor of the proprietors [1] in refusing to be dictated to at all by the rabble.

I have given above what is generally supposed to have been the cause of the " O. P." riots, namely, the advance in the admission prices to the theatre; and certainly this was one of the chief origins of the tumults. But there were other factors of great importance entering into the dispute. The increased dimensions of the new edifice, it was claimed, had been made at the sacrifice of the drama, for though a large house would hold more people than a small one and, in one respect, be more for the public accommodation, yet a great loss was sustained thereby to the drama itself, as no actor could hope to give the finer tones to expression and, at the same time, be heard and seen by the audience in all parts of the house. As a result, pantomime and spec-

---

[1] In 1802 John Philip Kemble purchased of Harris a one-sixth share in Covent Garden. The next year (1803) Kemble became acting-manager of that theatre.

tacle were resorted to, to the detriment of the dramatic art and to the lowering of the public taste.

Another cause of complaint, tending to produce the riots of 1809, was the employment of foreign troupes in the new theatre, in preference to English companies. The average Englishman had always been extremely sensitive on this point, and unquestionably it was a most inopportune time for the Covent Garden managers to import their actors and actresses when England's relations with the Continent were anything but settled. The mere mention of a foreigner for the English stage, even in times of profound peace, was sufficient to cause an outcry against the practice. As a result of this antipathy, Mme. Catalini, who had been engaged by the Covent Garden management to open the season, was compelled to cancel her engagement before the disturbances could be quelled.

Of a more serious nature was the indictment brought against the new arrangement of private boxes at Covent Garden Theatre. This was a question touching public morals directly; for, it was declared, the new private boxes were " in open defiance of public decency." It was a notorious fact that this new adjunct had been made to the theatre to accommodate the lewd women of the town. That this was one of the leading causes of the riot may be seen from the fact

that, in September, 1810, when Covent Garden
opened for the season, the riots were renewed
because the proprietors had not fulfilled that
part of the compromise of the year before, calling for a removal of the private boxes.[1]

Out of the riots themselves developed circumstances which were used as serious charges
against the proprietors. During the progress
of the disturbances, the attitude of the audiences became frequently so threatening that
the managers of the theatre thought to defend
themselves and property by opposing force with
force, if need arose. As a result of this foolish
policy, "pugilists, jews, and the most ruffianly
inhabitants of the metropolis, appeared in the
pit, to support the cause of the proprietors."
It was generally supposed at the time that these
bruisers were admitted to the theatre free of
charge, " for the sole object of preserving public tranquility." This manœuvre was almost, if
not quite, as unpopular as the cause generally
adduced for the riots, and only operated to ag-
gravate the mischief it was intended to reduce.[2]

[1] *London Chronicle*, September 11–25, 1810. The compiler
of the *Covent Garden Journal* says (in his Preface, i, 22)
apropos of the riots, " The most important feature in the following discussion, undoubtedly, is that of the private boxes."
See also *Advertiser* for October 26, 1809.

[2] *Considerations on the Past and Present State of the Stage*,
etc., pamphlet, pp. 54+Appendix, London, 1809. See also
London Times, November 14, 1809.

As might be expected, the managers of Covent Garden Theatre were arraigned by the
public for bringing about these disgraceful
scenes, by an injudicious, if not tyrannical, exercise of power; and the discussion which followed on the disorders sought to inquire into
the nature of the privileges contained in the
patents. It was openly charged on the proprietors that they had dared to advance the price
of admission, knowing that they had no competition, and that the public would be forced, therefore, to submit to their demands.[1] In regard to
the question of admission, the patentees rejoined
that the original patent issued by Charles II ex-
plicitly gave to the holders the privilege of fixing
the price of admission; that the theatrical business in London was "their own monopoly," and
that, being a monopoly, any attempt on the part
of the public to dictate the terms of management
was a violation of property rights. To this it
was retorted that the patents contained, likewise, the clear intimation that theatrical amusements were for the benefit of the public; that
the grants of Charles II to Davenant and Killigrew were unlike monopolies in general (which
give exclusive privileges to their possessors), in

[1] *Covent Garden Journal*, ii, 616. It should be remarked
that Drury Lane Theatre burned on the 24th of February,
1809. See also pamphlet signed "Candidus."

that they were held in trust for the benefit of
the public ; that any advantage accruing to the
patentees from the monopoly was in no sense
absolute, but conditional on a return to the public of services in proportion to the favor experienced by the Crown protection to the monopolists; and that any violation or abuse of the
privileges contained in the monopoly was sufficient cause to nullify it.   At best, the patents
were very shadowy documents, and their use to
invade the rights of the public was never intended, nor would it be tolerated.   The law of
custom was as much to be observed as any grant
of so doubtful title as the theatrical patents,
and the arbitrary advance of price to the theatre
could not be legally, or justly, sustained on the
plea of a " legal monopoly." [1]

On the other hand, there were moderate critics of the theatrical situation who looked upon
any attempt to compel the managers of Covent
Garden to sell entertainment to the people at the
price dictated by the purchaser to be a palpable
violation of the rights of property.   Those tak-

[1] *Cobbett's*, December 16, 1809 ; *Covent Garden Journal*, ii,
616–624, *et passim*. " The only ground on which such a monopoly can be defended," says the editor, " is the means it
gives to its possessors of catering for the public amusement
at a cheaper rate than they could do if their trade were
open and unlimited." See also, in this connection, *Considerations on the Past and Present State of the Stage.*

ing this view thought that extenuating circumstances might make it necessary to increase the price of entertainments as well as any other commodity; almost everything had doubled in price since the close of the French Revolution, and why not the admission to the theatre? Furthermore, it was pointed out by cool-headed, unprejudiced observers, the slight advance of one shilling to the boxes and sixpence to the pit was a matter too trifling to quibble over, much less to create a riot.[1]

But on the other counts brought against the managers, public opinion was scarcely divided. The deleterious effects of the increased dimensions of the theatre on the drama and on acting have been mentioned. The old building had been too large for the effective representation of Shakespeare's plays, for which reason buffoonery, pantomime, and melodrama had been substituted, to the detriment of the stage and the degradation of the public taste. The new theatre emphasized these evils, and for the banishment of the legitimate drama from the English stage the management was held responsible. It was irony, not charity, that dictated such criticism

---

[1] *Cobbett's*, December 7, and 16, 1809; *Covent Garden Journal*, ii, 707–710; 763–765. Cobbett admits one evil caused by the advanced prices to the pit and boxes (for the price to the galleries remained the same), namely, that poor people must necessarily take the back, and less satisfactory, seats.

as this : " But this [the then existing state of
the stage] is not such a sign of perverted taste
as it is of a prudent toleration of Blue Beards,
Kettledrums, or the distant view of the big-bel-
lied Virgins of the sun ; for if the manager did
not provide these, he could give the audience
nothing." A contrast between the theatre in the
days of Garrick and the new Covent Garden
Theatre was a subject for lament among those
who could remember the time when everything
connected with the dramatic and histrionic arts
was made to subserve the arts themselves. From
a tract, written by Frederick Howard, Earl of
Carlisle, at the time of the " O. P." riots, I quote
the following extract, pertinent to the discussion
in hand :

" A modern audience would be surprised to
hear how the public were accommodated forty
years ago [*i. e., circa* 1770]. The side boxes
were few in number, and very incommodious,
especially when the frequenters of those boxes
ever appeared in them in full dresses, the
women in hoops of various dimensions, and
the men with swords and habiliments all calculated to deny convenient space to their neighbours. Frocks were admitted into the front boxes,
but they were not usually worn by gentlemen in
the evening ; women of the town quietly took
their stations in the upper boxes, called the

green boxes; and men whom it did not suit
either to be at the expense of dress, or who had
not time to equip themselves, as before described,
resorted to the pit. This of course comprehended
a large description of persons, such as belonged
to the inns of court, men of liberal pursuits and
professions; and who, by an uniform attendance
at the playhouse, became no incompetent judges
of the drama.

"Their situation in the pit enabled them to
hear and to observe. Their habits of life led
them to an acquaintance with the authors and
the actors of the day; the latter were not ignorant they were continually before a tribunal
that makes itself respected, and whose sentence
conferred fame or censure; and they were convinced that negligence, ebriety, and buffoonery
would not be suffered to pass unnoticed or un-
punished. Garrick's voice, with that of many
others in his troop, reached without effort the
deepest part of the front boxes, nor was lost
even in the farthest rows of the galleries. The
general custom of wearing swords was certainly
productive of spilling blood before resentment
found time to cool; but as far as the theatre was
concerned it was instrumental to decorum; the
scene was hardly ever disconcerted by noisy
quarrels, blows, or such indecencies as we now
witness; the weapon was at hand, and the

appeal to it was rather more serious than to the fist, and enabled the weakest to contend with the most athletic. Women of the town were never permitted in the boxes below stairs with the single exception of the beautiful Kitty Fisher, whose appearance occasioned great dismay among all the frequenters, male and female, of the hitherto unpolluted front boxes. . . . The stage formerly seemed to have commanded more universal interest than at present. . . . These circumstances, with many others, incline me to believe that the beauties of the author, and the merits of the player, were much more constantly, than in these days, the topics of conversation and observation ; the natural consequence of hearing accurately, and of being able not only to compare one actor with another, but with himself ; a perpetual stimulant to the latter to exertion, and not to trifle with the audience. . . .

"The audience formerly, and in the times I am alluding to, were contented to attend favourite performances and performers under much inconvenience, and what would now be called disfigurement of the scene ; but still they saw and heard, and, even with the following enumerated abatements of the illusory charm, crowded the house. At a benefit of the principal actor or actress, a large division of the pit was added to the front boxes, leaving few rows of the former ;

besides this, many seats were placed on the stage,
so as to afford the actors a very contracted space,
not more perhaps than twenty feet square ; this
of course excluded for the night almost all the
accustomed decorations and change of scenery ;
but these inconveniences were thought lightly of,
partly because long habit had inured the spectators to suffer them, partly because the two
great faculties of the ear and eye were still retained ; while now we are made to accept as
compensation for the surrender of these, an
expensive and tinsel pantomime, the noisy music
of which may be heard where the human voice
could never reach, and the glittering robe of
a Blue Beard be discovered, where no eye could
observe upon any change or expression of the
actor's countenance." [1]

The matter of personal safety also entered
into the question of the size of the theatres. In
case of fire during a performance, it was pointed
out, in such large structures the casualty list
must necessarily be great, for a large audience
would be liable to stampede and trample many
to death.[2] A small theatre was freer from this

---

[1] *Thoughts upon the Present Condition of the Stage, and upon
the Construction of a New Theatre.* By Frederick Howard, Earl
of Carlisle, pp. 47 + Appendix, London, 1809.

[2] The Sadler's Wells horror (October 15, 1807) was fresh in
the minds of people. Owing to a false alarm of fire, a panic
ensued, in which more than twenty persons were crushed to
death.

danger. As to the plea of the patentees, that the
increased population of the metropolis required
larger theatres to accommodate the audiences,
the answer was sought in the simple question,
Why are there not more licensed theatres ? Some
went even so far as to suggest that the increased
dimensions of the new Covent Garden Theatre,
with the consequent bad effect on the public
good, was sufficient to work a revocation of the
patent. "Now," argues one, "though the exact
dimensions of the theatre cannot be supposed to
be dictated by the patent, yet the erection of the
building, adequate to the rational purposes of
the drama, must have been one of the virtual
stipulations on which it was granted; and if so
it may deserve consideration, how far the erecting the present structure (beautiful and appropriate to other objects, as I admit it to be) does
not, in strictness, work a forfeiture of the proprietors' monopoly." [1]

Of a far more serious nature was the indictment brought against the Covent Garden management for the arrangement of the private
boxes in the new theatre, "in open defiance of

[1] *Considerations on the Past and Present State of the Stage.*
The patent theatres, before their enlargement in 1790–94
would each hold about a £300 audience ; after the rebuilding
of the theatres after the fires of 1808–09, the two theatres
together would accommodate £1500 audiences, Drury Lane
alone, on occasion, holding over £800.

public decency." The excuse given by the proprietors for this innovation was, that some persons "feel it necessary, or convenient, to segregate
themselves and their families, more especially
the younger females, from some of those inconveniences inseparable from a public theatre." It
was evident to every one that the " inconveniences " had but one meaning, namely, the
women of the town who were a nuisance to the
real auditory and a disgrace to the management of
both the patent theatres. It was pertinently asked,
whether the private boxes were merely the retreat of decency alone, or rather were they not
constructed to serve the very opposite purpose?
" If," says Sir Frederick Howard in his " Thoughts
upon the Present Condition of the Stage," " the
internal part of the theatre had attractions to
keep those who pay at the door, in their places,
the lobbies would not be filled with profligates
of every description, familiarizing the yet uncor-
rupted and modest to scenes of such meretricious
impudence, hardly exaggerated by Hogarth in
the supper in his Rake's Progress. What parent
could conduct his wife and daughters through
this sty without trembling with the fear, that
though those sights are to them shocking and
horrible, they may not be so to-morrow? An
audience who went to the play to hear and see,
would quickly interfere with these orgies."

Worst of all, the managers were fearlessly accused of fostering immorality for the immense profits which accrued to them from the rental of the private boxes, and this was declared to be a perversion of the terms of the patents which were intended to sanction public theatres, not private bagnios.[1] "The royal patent can be no more construed to sanction improper practices in its holders than could the licence which was formerly given to public stews indemnify the owners of them from a like responsibility. . . . We take it upon ourselves fearlessly to affirm that there is not a night on which this [Covent Garden] or any of our theatres are open, when the managers are not liable to an indictment for keeping a disorderly house, under its most usual acceptation, viz., a brothel; and that of the most loathsome, mischievous, corrupt, and disgusting description."[2]

Admitting the triviality of some of the charges brought against the patentees, such as the engagement of a foreign singer, "the pensioned hireling of Buonaparte" (an allusion to Catalini), the alleged abuse of monopoly privileges

[1] *Sunday Advertiser*, October 29, 1809; quoted in *Covent Garden Journal*.

[2] Cobbett, in a strained effort to be liberal, denied that the private boxes increased immorality, evidently overlooking the main point, the effect on the decent part of the audience. *Covent Garden Journal*, ii, 707; Preface, 24, 25.

of a more serious nature demanded a thorough
examination of the whole question of theatrical
patents. Lord Dartmouth was appealed to in an
open letter to exercise his power, as Lord Chamberlain, to put a stop to the shameful conduct of
the theatre.[1] But his lordship was too wise to
meddle with a quarrel which was bound to take
its course anyhow. Threats of petitioning Parliament for leave to erect a new theatre in the
metropolis were advertised in the " Times," November 2, 1809. Plans for a new third theatre
were submitted to the public, containing various
schemes for obviating the evils inherent in the
patent houses.

"Service to the public," became the shibbo-
leth of the opposers to the patentees. The new
theatre, when built, should hold by the legitimate drama. Therefore, the structure must be
small, with the idea of private gain wholly
secondary. To avoid all difficulties growing out
of monopoly in perpetuity, the patent for the
new national theatre should be issued for not
longer than seven years, and be revocable for
cause. To lessen the danger from conflagrations
the theatre should be built of stone. The air
was suddenly filled with schemes for a third
theatre. Elaborate plans for a subscription the-

---

[1] *Times*, November 7, 1809; *Sunday Advertiser*, October 29,
1809; quoted in *Covent Garden Journal*, ii, 608, 657.

atre were published broadcast; others conceived
the idea of a joint-stock company; while others
still, apprehending the difficulty which was sure
to arise respecting the patents, proposed that
"the government make a liberal purchase of the
patents originally granted for the accommodation
of a population small comparatively with the
present." [1]

But there was a prior claim to all these to the
conception of a third London theatre. While
the rabble was howling itself hoarse in the " O.
P." riots, while the public and the managers
of Covent Garden were hurling invectives and
recrimination at each other, and the papers were
filled with accounts of the uproar and the in-
scriptions on the placards at Covent Garden,
a company of London gentlemen were quietly
formulating a plan for the erection of a third
winter theatre. Even before the opening of the
Covent Garden Theatre, and the " O. P." riots,
they had seen that the time had come for an attempt to oppose the monopoly with another stage
for the regular drama. By the middle of September, 1809, these gentlemen had already had
two meetings on the subject, and it had been
given out that they intended to erect a theatre

[1] For these various proposals, see *The Times*, Oct. 30, Nov.
2, 1809; Frederick Howard, *Thoughts upon the Present Condition
of the Stage*, Appendix; *Morning Chronicle*, Oct. 7, Nov. 8, 1809;
Considerations on the Past and Present State of the Stage.

in the East End of the city. It was also reported
that they were drawing up a petition to the
Crown to grant them a license for the purpose;
and that they had pledged themselves to the
amount of £250,000 towards carrying the undertaking into effect.

It was understood that the petitioners would
base their prayer on the plea that all monopolies
are injurious and prevent that fair competition
by which the public are benefited. The evils
arising from the theatrical monopoly were aggravated by the fact that London had increased
three fourths in extent and population since the
creation of the monopoly by Charles II, so that
many were deprived of the pleasure of the acted
drama, on account of the distance to the established winter theatres. The proposed new theatre was intended to relieve this emergency.
One rumor had the site of the new building in
Fleet Street, and it was to be a model of beauty
and convenience. It was also noised about that
the petition would contain an offer to fix a price
for admission the same as that at the Haymarket, box, 4s., pit, 2s. 6d., gallery, 1s. 6d., which
should not be altered under penalty of forfeit-
ing the license. It was proposed to call the new
playhouse The London Theatre Royal.[1]

Some of the rumors relating to the plans of

[1] *Sunday Examiner*, September 17, 1809.

the London gentlemen referred to were, doubtless, unfounded, or wholly false. But the essential part of the report was true, namely, that a petition for a third theatre was in preparation. This petition was signed by fifteen gentlemen, including the Lord Mayor of London (Thomas Smith), five members of Parliament, and Richard Cumberland, the dramatist. It was addressed to the King, and prayed for a charter-grant to establish a theatre for representing the regular drama. It averred that the petitioners had agreed to subscribe £200,000 for that purpose. The reason they gave for such a project was that the increased population of London and Westminster made another theatre desirable and expedient.[1]

The subject of the theatrical monopoly, which had its origin in the Crown, had run its cycle and was once more back to the Crown. But that which had been created by the Merrie Monarch without a moment's hesitation was too weighty a problem for His Majesty, in 1810, to solve off-

---

[1] *Proceedings before the Privy Council,* 1810, Appendix A. The Historical MSS. Commission make note of the petition of the Lord Mayor of London, and other gentlemen, for a Third Theatre, and have marked it, " n. d.," evidently knowing nothing of the Proceedings before the Privy Council for the consideration of the aforesaid petition, or of the time when the petition was made. See *Historical MSS. Com.,* Report XIII [4], p. 503, 1892.

hand. The King in Council, therefore, referred the petition to his Attorney and Solicitor-General for legal opinion in the matter, who advised against the grant, on the grounds, first, that such an incorporated charter as that prayed for would give to the corporation so constituted an advantage over all other theatres in the metropolis; and secondly, that "future creditors of such a theatre would be abridged of their legal remedies for the recovery of debts."

At the time of petitioning the King, a similar memorial was sent to the House of Commons, asking leave to bring in a bill for the purpose of erecting a third theatre in London, should His Majesty give his consent. After the Attorney and Solicitor-General rendered an adverse opinion to the scheme, the memorialists at once prayed for a hearing before the Privy Council. The date appointed for the Council proceedings was the 16th of March, 1810, and, until after this important event, it was useless to prepare a bill to be brought before Parliament. On the 19th, therefore, the House of Commons was petitioned by the promoters of the third theatre plan, for an extension of time for bringing in private bills.[1]

Sheridan strongly opposed granting the ex-

[1] For these petitions see *Proceedings before Privy Council*, 1810, Appendix B, C, P.

tension of time (three weeks) asked for by the
petitioners. He thought the application most
extraordinary. A committee " above stairs " had
been appointed to hear the memorialists for a
third theatre, yet the latter, declared the adroit
Drury Lane manager, "had not dared to come
before that committee since the 8th of February."
At the last hour they had come in praying for
time. The whole business seemed to Sheridan
" a tissue of finesse and insincerity." The appeal
to the Privy Council, after the Attorney and
Solicitor-General had rendered an opinion adverse to a third theatre scheme, and, at the same
time, the application to the House for an extension of time, proved that the petitioners wanted
two strings to their bow. In the petition to the
Privy Council the " Lord Mayor of London " appeared ; in that to the House of Commons it was
plain " Thomas Smith." Sheridan denounced
this as artifice. He then appealed to the House
to keep in mind the sacredness of vested property rights and the inviolableness of patents ;
but no attempt was made by the patentee at this
time to defend the principle of monopoly. The
temper of the House, however, was on this occasion at variance with the Drury Lane representative ; for, after a brief debate, the application of
the third theatre promoters was granted for an
extension of time to bring in their bill.

Meantime the Privy Council had had its first sitting on the petition of the Lord Mayor and others interested in the third theatre movement, praying to be heard against the Attorney and Solicitor-General's objection to the incorporation plan, and asking leave to suggest means by which creditors would always be safe from loss incurred by the theatre's indebtedness. These were the specific points for consideration before the Privy Council. But it was clear to every one concerned that the hearing was to be in reality an examination of the whole question of the patents granted by Charles II, and the claim of the patentees to a "legal monopoly." This was to be the battle royal for a free stage, and the most careful preparation was made by both sides; on the one hand, for an attack on all the weak points of patent rights, on the other, for a defense of individual, vested, property rights, based on a faith in the inviolableness of patent privileges.

For the purpose of hearing the champions of these diverse causes, the Lords of the Council met on the 16th of March, 1810. This august body consisted of the Lord President (Earl Camden), Earl of Aylesford, Earl Harrowby, Lord John Thynne, the Master of the Rolls (Sir William Grant), Sir William Scott, Mr. John Trevor, and the invincible Sheridan. The petition of the Lord Mayor and others was read. At the same time numerous counter-petitions were presented, praying that the first petition be rejected. The proprietors and shareholders in Drury Lane and Covent Garden manifested the greatest alarm at the petition for a third theatre, and memorialized the King in Council, showing how destructive to their interests a third winter theatre would prove. Their legal arguments against a rival were founded on the grants of Charles II, which, they claimed, gave to Killigrew and Davenant the exclusive right to erect two theatres, and on the suppression and silencing of all other theatres in London at the time the patents were issued; for this was construed by the patentees as creating a perpetual monopoly to the " heirs, executors, and assigns" of the original grantees. As counsel for the third theatre advocates, Mr. Warren appeared to answer these claims, as well as the other counter-petitions and the Attorney and Solicitor-General.[1]

Counsel for the petitioners gathered his arguments about two main topics, viz., the nature of crown prerogative, and the desirability of a third

[1] A full account of the Privy Council proceedings on the Petition for a Third Theatre (March 16, 19, 26, 1810) was published in pamphlet form at the time, together with copies of all the counter-petitions. This Report is the source of my account in this chapter. See, also, *London Chronicle*, March 17, 20, 1810.

winter theatre in London. On the first of these
heads it was contended that, if it were the prerogative of the Crown which made the theatrical
patents valid, then the prerogative must have
belonged to Charles II as King, and not as an
individual. If the latter alternative were true,
the flimsiness of the monopoly claim appears at
once ; and if the former interpretation be the
correct one, the power of succeeding kings
to grant patents must be conceded. In other
words the prerogative of a King is temporary,
that of the Crown perpetual, or until altered by
act of Parliament. The true meaning intended
by the clause in the patents giving " full power
and authority " to certain individuals, their heirs,
etc., and for the suppression of all other persons
acting plays without authority, is simply that
none shall act without authority, and it does not
establish a monopoly. That this was the construction placed by succeeding monarchs on the
clause in the patents referred to, attention was
called to Steele's patent (January 19, 1714),
to the one granted to Foote, and to the Opera,
and Lyceum.[1] So, also, did the Crown issue a
license to Wilks, Cibber, and Booth (July 3,

[1] S. J. Arnold was granted a license in 1809 for English
opera at the Lyceum. A consideration of this theatre will be
taken up in a succeeding chapter. The Opera, mentioned in
Warren's speech, refers to Vanbrugh's house in the Haymarket.

1732), another to Lacy and Garrick (June 24, 1747), which was renewed (October 26, 1762), and to Sheridan, Linley, and Ford, all for the like period of twenty-one years.

From these numerous instances, the conclusion was deduced that there was no restriction on succeeding kings arising from anything contained in the original patents. As a further evidence in support of this position, citation was made of that provision in the Licensing Act (art. v), wherein "no person or persons shall be authorized by virtue of any Letters Patent from His Majesty, . . . or by the licence of the Lord Chamberlain," to act anywhere in Great Britain, except in London and Westminster, as clearly implying the power of the Lord Chamberlain to issue licenses, and of the Crown to issue patents.[1] Otherwise the clause itself would be nugatory. But the reference to this clause in the Licensing Act required a consideration of the differences between a patent and a license. Warren held that there was no difference, so far as the monopoly was concerned; for both were infringements on the exclusive privileges claimed for the patents by the patentees. That the monopoly might be broken, and that for such an object a license was as effectual as a patent, the Little Theatre in the Haymarket, the Opera House in the Haymarket, and the Lyceum,

[1] Cf. *Statutes at Large*, 10 George II, cap. xxviii, art. v.

were instanced. For, since the two original patents specified no particular time of the year for acting, their privileges extended to all seasons, and the existence (by virtue of license or patent) of any other theatre for summer, spring, or winter was incontrovertible evidence that the grants of Charles II to Killigrew and Davenant did not create a monopoly in perpetuity, and that a license was as effectual as a patent.

Having, as he was convinced, answered the argument that the original theatrical patents created a perpetual monopoly, the leading counsel for the third theatre petitioners attempted to show cause why a third establishment for the regular drama was desirable. The counter-petitions from Drury Lane and Covent Garden had given as reasons why such a concern should not be chartered, the inviolable security of the patents themselves; the expense incurred in building and ornamenting the new Covent Garden Theatre ; and the jeopardy in which a third theatre would place the creditors of the patent theatre. As to the objection current that the new Covent Garden Theatre was too large, the patentees answered that the theatre had been so constructed to meet the accommodation of an increasing population.[1] This was a weak point

[1] The population of London in 1810 was about one million, or about double that of the time of Charles II.

in the armor of the patentees which had been frequently sought by the public. Carried to its logical conclusion, it meant that whatever the increase in the population, the capacity of the patent theatres could be enlarged in proportion. The contention was manifestly absurd. " They do not advert to this circumstance," retorted Warren, " that they may enlarge them to such a degree that many of the persons present can neither see nor hear." The Drury Lane petitioners had said that " the average nightly receipts of the Theatre of Drury Lane, and they believe also of Covent Garden, for a series of years, fully prove that the persons resorting thereto, have not amounted to more than one-half of the number those Theatres were capable of containing, . . ." From which assertion it was intended to prove that a third theatre was not expedient. The reply to this was, that the patent theatres were too large, the public stayed away because they could not be commodiously seated. " How does it happen that Covent Garden is not full, now that Drury Lane is not in existence ? " The answer, it was maintained with confidence, was the strongest plea for a third theatre. The large theatres were empty because of their size, and it was to correct this lack of theatrical accommodation for the public that the petitioners were before the Privy Council.

The Covent Garden counter-petition had intimated that the project for a third theatre was a result of the recent calamity to Drury Lane, and that the promoters of the scheme were in hopes that, if their petition were granted, it would deter the proprietors of Drury Lane from rebuilding. To this insinuation Warren answered for his clients that it was their intention to petition for a third theatre, irrespective of the plans and prospects of Drury Lane. They had no other thought but that Drury Lane would be rebuilt. Coming to the objections of the Attorney and Solicitor-General, that a charter of incorporation for a theatre, such as that applied for by the petitioners, would secure to the latter an advantage over the other theatres, by removing personal responsibilities for the (possible) liabilities of the corporation, Warren answered, that to relieve all doubts on this point, the projectors of a third theatre were ready to place in the hands of trustees a stipulated sum, say £40,000 or £50,000, over which they were willing to surrender all control, to meet the emergencies apprehended by the King's lawyer. It was contended by the advocate for the third theatre party that a corporation was far more stable than individual ownership in property ; certainly the patent houses could not be held up as a proof to the contrary. It was denied that advantage was sought over the other theatres by the charter prayed for ; the petitioners had the single desire of serving the public in the way of dramatic entertainment. "We are willing," said their counsel, " to take the Charter limited in any way that His Majesty's advisers may think proper. We shall consent to put ourselves under any restraint that will enable us to represent moral amusements to the Public."

Curwood assisted Warren in defending the cause of a third theatre. After repudiating Sheridan's insinuations that the petitioners for a new theatre had brought their case before the Privy Council in a surreptitious manner, hoping to get His Majesty's consent before the House of Commons could oppose the measure in Parliament, Curwood went straight to the essentials of the theatrical controversy. He flatly denied that entertainments could be controlled by crown prerogative. If they could, then such authority had existed from time beyond memory — which was contrary to historic fact.

But the core of the problem was probed when the legality of the theatrical monopoly was examined. It was admitted by Curwood that long after the time when monopolies were held to be void, a distinction was made between monopolies of trade and those of amusement. Attention was called to the case arising in the forty-fourth

year of Elizabeth's reign (reported by Sir E.
Coke, vol. 77), in which the monopoly of the
traffic in playing-cards (granted to Ralph Bowes
in 30 Elizabeth, and renewed in 42 Elizabeth)
was declared null, thus overruling the distinction previously made between exclusive privileges in trade and in amusements. The sequel
to this case may be traced to the *Statute of
Monopolies* in the reign of James I. From this
it was argued that the patents granted to Killigrew and Davenant were void *ab initio*.

This review of monopolistic legislation was
the more necessary as the counter-petition of
Sarah Richardson, owner of one fourth interest
in Drury Lane Theatre, expressly laid claim
to the exclusive privilege of Drury Lane and
Covent Garden to represent plays and other
theatrical performances. And here it is worthy of
note that the counter-petitions from Drury Lane
and Covent Garden assumed no right to a monopoly based on the patents, while the representatives of Covent Garden distinctly denied any
such pretension, emphasizing, however, the right
of "long-established custom" which the two theatres had enjoyed to act plays in the winter and
spring. On this point Curwood drew the distinction between a patent of favor and a patent
of right, adding that the counter-petitioners had
evidently mistaken the former for the latter;

but that in either case an abuse of the patent worked its forfeiture.

Adverting to the Attorney and Solicitor-General's fears thát a charter of incorporation would render the security of future creditors unstable, Curwood added a point to that made by his colleague. He explained that the corporation petitioned for was unlike commercial, insurance, and such-like corporations, in that, from the outset, the theatre corporation would have £200,000 *visible*, either in funds or in property, in addition to the accumulating fund which they proposed to set aside to secure their creditors. What better security had the patent houses to offer than this? it was asked. Sheridan had said in his petition that the renters (*i. e.*, stockholders) [1] of Dury Lane were liable for all security to creditors; but he had neglected to state that the renters were the chief creditors. Wherein lay the security to the smaller creditors?

Curwood also dwelt on the size of the patent

---

[1] Although stockholders, the " renters " of Drury Lane partook of no share in the profits of the concern. They had free admissions to the theatre, and received the legal rate of interest on their subscriptions; but were individually responsible to the extent of their private fortunes for the indebtedness of the theatre. On the other hand, the members of the proposed third theatre corporation would be liable only for their subscriptions. Herein lay the advantage pointed out by the Attorney and Solicitor-General.

houses: " The great size of the theatres entirely
defeats the object of the Drama, and looking
down from the height of the vast concave, the
Actors appear like the inhabitants of Lilliput
parading the great hall of the imperial palace of
Brobdingnag. Not a feature of the face can
be distinguished, far less the variations and flex-
ibility of muscles, the turn of the eye and grace-
ful action, which, in an accomplished Actor, gives
life and energy to the composition of an eloquent
Author." The saloons and lobbies, the dens of
immorality at the patent houses, were also condemned.

The arguments of Mr. Adam, the first of the
counsel representing the patentees to speak, were
made up largely of apologies, avowals, and denials,
and were hardly calculated to defend his clients'
cause. Some of the points, however, are worthy
of notice. As to the question of exclusive privileges enjoyed by the two patent houses, the
integrity of these, he said, should be respected,
because, for a vast period, the proprietors of
these theatres " had been acting upon the faith of
reasonable expectation, which forms as it were
the equitable principle of the equitable code of
any country." The history and the law involved
in the case fell outside of Mr. Adam's province;
he was content to base his claims on the statements of the counter-petitions. He denied that

the theatre-going public had increased in direct
proportion to the population, and to support
this denial the change in the business habits of
the town was alluded to. The new system
of carrying the mails had altered the business
hours of the merchants, and, as a result, fewer
people attended the theatres, in proportion to
the population, than formerly. Prior to 1810
much of the business of the metropolis was trans-
acted in the evening after an early dinner.
At the time of the third theatre project many
commercial men remained at their counting-
houses until seven o'clock to answer their letters
within post hours. By the time they could re-
gale themselves it was too late to go to the
theatre. "Thousands of other. . . manners and
customs of the people" also entered into the problem, declared Mr. Adam.

The "deplorable and unfortunate situation of
Drury Lane" and its effects upon "the widow and
fatherless" was presented to the Council's consideration. So, too, the interests of Mr. Harris,
and "a gentleman high in the public esteem as
an actor,"[1] were matters not to be lost sight of.
A joint-stock company was a terrible thing to
contemplate, said Mr. Adam, for it was sure to
grow into a monopoly (a privilege for which the

[1] Alluding to Kemble, who was a shareholder in, and manager of, Covent Garden.

patent houses were not contending), the greatest
danger of which would lie in the very safeguard
which the promoters proposed to establish to secure the creditors of the concern.   Because, as
the theatre grew in power, this fund would necessarily increase proportionately and get so large
at last as to endanger the creditors for whose
preservation it was created.

At the close of Adam's speech, which his coad-
jutor dignified with the epithet " impressive," the
Council proceedings adjourned until the following Monday, the nineteenth of March.   Immediately on convening the second sitting, the members were addressed by Mr. Randle Jackson,
counsel for the trustees of Drury Lane Theatre.
If the effort of Mr. Adam had been feeble, the
like may not be said of the arguments delivered
by Jackson.   For eloquence and persuasion, for
method and coherency, and, above all, for subtle
reasoning and a knowledge of legal authority,
his speech was among the most effective before
the Privy Council on this occasion.   A few times,
in the course of his address, Jackson pressed the
sympathies of the Council harder than was needful, as when he referred to Mrs. Richardson and
her " four amiable and interesting daughters " as
having no other protection than " Heaven and
your Lordships ; " and again, when speaking of
the actors and actresses of the burnt Drury Lane

Theatre as the "sons and daughters of Misfortune, these objects at once of admiration and sympathy, of merit and disaster." But these appeals never sank into the maudlin or ludicrous. And when ridicule was employed against the arguments of his opponents, the manner was always so genial and manly that it attracted rather than repelled.

For the most part, Jackson employed his time answering argument, and so masterfully was this done that, often, the weaknesses of his own side were turned to his advantage. The points made by the opposing counsel were answered in order. As to the opinion that the patents to Killigrew and Davenant were monopolies, and, hence, were void *ab initio*, Jackson denied the premise, supporting his position on, first, Blackstone's definition of a monopoly, viz., " a licence or privilege allowed by the King for the sole buying and selling, making, working, or using of anything whatsoever, whereby the subject in general is restrained from that liberty of manufacturing or trading *which he had before;*" and, secondly, the interpretation which should, as he saw it, be placed on the decision in the playing-card case, already referred to. The patent involved in that case, Jackson maintained, was for *trade* and *traffic*, and the decision against it had no reference to the *amusement* of card-playing; the crown prerogative, as regards amusements, remained unlimited by the findings in that case. Resorting to a doubtful quibble and relying on the definition of monopoly given above, Jackson impressed the point that the Drury Lane patent did not grant a *sole* privilege, and hence could not be adjudged a monopoly; for the creation of a rival patent at the same time put it beyond the power of Drury Lane to exercise an exclusive privilege. To the assertion that Charles II had no right to bind his successors, the case of Steele was raised in answer, in which it had been decided in favor of such right. " What is it then we contend for," concluded Jackson on this part of the subject, " but that . . . we still retain the exclusive right therein conveyed, of being one of two houses, and that we must retain that right, until it shall be shown by due course of law that public expediency calls for a third Theatre, or that we have so conducted ourselves as to deserve the suppression of our own ? "

Warren had put forward the argument that the two patents had ceased to be valid from the circumstance of other patents and licenses having existed subsequently. Jackson remarked that it was worthy of mention that so faithfully had the spirit of those patents been complied with that at no time during the whole period which had elapsed since they were granted had there been more than two regular theatres open at the same time; and that even when both patents had fallen into one hand, the rule was still observed as to the coexistence of two houses, no thought ever having occurred of consolidating the two into one house,[1] but rather to consider them as safeguards against the erection of a third theatre. It was shown that all licenses subsequent to the patents had been of a temporary and conditional nature, and not opposed to the patent houses. Warren was corrected as to his confusion of patent and license. The former, observed Jackson, was to be distinguished by its having "the sign manual" by its having passed through "all the solemnities of office;" while a license is the "mere act of indulgence of the Lord Chamberlain, and much more limited in its nature and extent." Charters had often been shown to be "sacred things," and on this long-established sanctity the patentees would rest the merits of their case.

The charge was reiterated that the petitioners for a third theatre had seized upon the critical moment when Drury Lane was in ashes, in the

---

[1] Whether this was a conscious or unconscious mistake I do not know. The history of the theatre was not very well known in 1810, Cibber and Malone being the chief authorities for those desiring to learn about the subject.

hopes of discouraging the subscription for the rebuilding of that theatre, and Jackson warned the
Council that if they granted the petitioners their
prayer there was no assurance that the Drury
Lane subscription would succeed. " The question
is not the building of a third theatre ; it is
whether the Lombard Street Petitioners or the
Patrons of Old Drury, shall build a second
Theatre? the town cannot maintain three in the
same neighborhood : if your Lordships exalt
them, we must become prostrate and extinct,
our fate will be sealed, and we shall sink to rise
no more." And their Lordships are assured by
the speaker that this is not addressed to their
"feelings merely."

All of the arguments presented by Adam were
strengthened by Jackson. The irresponsibility
of a joint-stock company was enforced by a
reference to the recent example of the Globe
Insurance Company,[1] application for a charter
for which had been denied on the very grounds
now (1810) raised against the third theatre
advocates. A further difficulty attaching to the
theatre corporation plan was discovered by Jackson. The penalty provided by the Licensing Act
for the offenses therein described is a stipulated
fine, in failure of which the *person* of the of-

[1] This was in 1806. See Hansard's *Parliamentary Debates*,
1st Series, for 1806, *passim*.

fender must answer. It was suggested that the *person* of a corporation would be hard to define.[1]

By the date of the second sitting of the Council, on the petition for a third theatre, a numerous and varied list of counter-petitions had been sent in. Some of these were read at the conclusion of Jackson's defense. One of them was from Henry Fulke Greville, Esquire, the opera enthusiast. His petition on this occasion laid claim to a priority of right in the matter of establishing a third theatre. Greville averred that he had, in 1809, prepared a plan for this purpose, but had been informed that he could represent only operas and farces, the Lord Chamberlain " not thinking it for the present just or right to break through the monopoly of the Patent Theatres." Upon this, he (Greville) had written to Mr. Perceval, " praying for the support of His Majesty's Government in favor of a bill he intended to bring into Parliament, for leave to act under a Patent, and to extend the nature of the Performances at the New Theatre he had already the authority of the Lord Chamberlain to set on foot." Perceval's answer to this request showed that gentleman's opinion on the subject

---

[1] Jackson must have been using this for effect, for he must have known that the actors in a chartered (corporate) theatre could not be prosecuted under the Licensing Act.

to be that he " does not immediately recollect
how far the King can or cannot, consistently
with existing Patents, grant one for a New
Theatre, but he conceives if the King cannot do
it Parliament could not, without infringing the
rights of the present Patentees, give its sanction to such an Establishment." It was then
too late for Greville to bring a private bill into
Parliament (Perceval's letter is dated April 15,
1809); and so he decided to exercise the authority already possessed for musical entertainments, as he felt persuaded, he said, that when
the necessity appeared to the Lord Chamberlain for permitting an unlimited range of the
drama, such privilege would be annexed to his
theatre.

But just at this stage of the Colonel's plans,
the wily Sheridan interposed his influence to put
a stop to Greville's operations. He made overtures to Greville for a coalition of theatrical
interests, and at the same time promised that
when the necessity for a third winter house should
appear, he would give not only the sanction of
his "dormant patent," but would also use his
" best endeavors to affix the third Patent at your
Petitioner's new projected Theatre." " In consequence of this arrangement," continues the petition, " a request was made to the Lord Chamberlain for a Licence to perform the Drama this

Season under your Petitioner's Licence, which has been done." [1]

S. J. Arnold, proprietor of the Lyceum Theatre, presented a companion petition to Colonel Greville's, in which he prayed for a joint grant to himself and Greville, in case a third theatre were deemed advisable, in view of their former petitions, and as a protection to investments already made by them. The friendly relations with Drury Lane were pointed out, for, since the burning of the great theatre, "your petitioner has been the means of keeping together the company of the late Theatre Royal Drury Lane at the Lyceum Theatre, under an arrangement with Mr. Sheridan and Mr. Greville." Relative to the transaction between Sheridan and Greville, referred to by the latter in his petition to the Privy Council, the following letter (dated August 17, 1809) from T. B. Mash, deputy-Chamberlain, to Lord Dartmouth, is significant

[1] The same year in which Drury Lane Theatre burned (1809), Greville secured a license for the English opera in the winter, and S. J. Arnold a similar license for the summer season. This was a source of alarm and jealousy to Sheridan, who determined to nip the matter in the bud. Looking about for quarters for his Drury Lane Company, he conceived the plan of flattering Arnold and Greville with a proposal of coalition, the three managers to join licenses and forces at the Lyceum. The ruse was successful, the Lyceum opening on the 25th of September, 1809, under the triumvirate. — See *London Chronicle*, Sept. 26, 1809.

as showing the motives and methods of Sheridan :

" It has been intimated to me that a very curious proposal has been made by Mr. Sheridan to Mr. Greville, viz., that he should relinquish such a paltry protection as that of the Lord Chamberlain's licence, which according to Mr. Sheridan's pretentions will avail him nothing when opposed by the Patentees, as they shall certainly crush all those places of entertainment acting under such authority, and that therefore for Mr. Greville's better security they should, with Taylor and his son Tom, jointly open the Opera House for four nights a week for English operas under the dormant patent. I have not seen Col. Greville since, but on the morning (last Thursday) he received the invitation from Mr. Sheridan to meet him at Kelly's the comedian, who keeps a music shop in Pall Mall, to dine with him there, he told me that if anything particular transpired he would call upon me the following morning, and not having seen him . . . looks I think a little as though Mr. Greville was nibbling at the bait Mr. Sheridan has thrown out. I am also further informed that Mr. Sheridan slept at Kelly's that night, as he said, for the purpose of being near Carlton House, to be ready the next morning to accompany the Prince of Wales in order that His Royal Highness might introduce him with his memorial to the King, and desired when he went to bed that he might be called at eight o'clock, but unfortunately having made too free with Kelly's wine, he could not rise till near two, and thereby lost a fine opportunity of carrying his threats into execution." [1]

On the facts stated in their petitions, counsel Adolphus founded the claims of Greville and Arnold. The desirability of a third theatre did not enter into the question with them, only if one were to be erected, they thought that justice demanded a recognition of their prior application. R. W. Elliston, the comedian, manager of the Royal Circus, in behalf of himself, suggested, in addition to the plea of justice, the economy and wisdom of conferring the privileges of a third theatre (if one were expedient) on some of the numerous proprietors who already had " devoted their property to such objects," and who had shown their capabilities of managing a theatrical concern.

Warren, in rebuttal, showed the worthlessness of the petitions just introduced, since, with all their pleas of priority, superior training for the business, and so forth, they had shown no material means of supporting their claims ; whereas the projectors of a third theatre had backed

[1] *Historical MSS. Commission*, Report XIII [4], p. 505.

their proposals with £200,000.[1] On the other
hand, the petitions of Greville and Arnold "assist us one-half of the way," since both recognized the necessity of a third theatre.

Warren showed the greatest acumen, probably, when meeting the argument made against
the corporation plan, and for his purpose he
found the most valuable witness in Sheridan
himself. The latter in his counter-petition had
ended it with the opinion that "the protection of
a Charter of Incorporation . . . was the only
practicable mode of re-building the [Drury Lane]
Theatre, and making a just and honourable arrangement with the numerous and respectable
persons interested in its prosperity." It was
hardly consistent to condemn the method of corporation proposed by the third theatre petitioners,
and, in the same breath, to declare that plan
the only business-like one on which to reëstab-
lish the patent house.

Another apparent weakness in the counter-
petitions, and in Jackson's arguments, was found
in the point continually dwelt on by the patentees and their representatives, that a third
theatre would add to the unfortunate condition
of "creditors, widows, and orphans." "They put
it as a private case," exclaimed Warren, "we

[1] This thrust caused Arnold and Greville to set a subscription on foot, and in two days they raised £70,000.

as a public one: . . . We are not to be told,
by way of argument, that private individuals
have laid out their money and their property in
theatrical concerns, have been unsuccessful, and
are ruined; that is no consideration for your
Lordships."

At the conclusion of Warren's reply, after he
had shown the flimsiness of the argument that
a corporation had no person on which the law
might seize (since the directors, or managers,
would stand in that relation), and corrected
the misconception respecting his arguments on
the invalidity of patent monopolies (denying
that he had said the patents were void as regards
monopolies, but as regards crown prerogative),
Sheridan sprung something of a surprise by rising in his place in the Council, and announcing
that on the following Monday (March 26) he
intended to show that the patents of the two
houses amounted to a monopoly. The Council
then adjourned its proceedings on the petition
for a third theatre until March 26.

In the interim the parties representing the
various theatrical interests in London girded
their loins for a final effort. Arnold and Greville secured the services of Brougham (who
had been on the Northern Circuit up to March
25), who gave dignity to their claims, and added
the very strong point in favor of the minors,

that though they had to depend on annual
licenses, nevertheless, since these had been
granted year after year without opposition, the
proprietors had made large investments on their
faith in the continuance of the licensed privileges. This was the identical ground on which
the patentees claimed protection under their
patents, and if the argument was effectual in
the one case it should also apply to the other.

Complications had arisen during the week
from March 19 to March 26. Sheridan, either
to defeat the petition of the applicants for a
charter of incorporation, or to take advantage of
the occasion to reorganize Drury Lane on a corporate plan, — or both, presented a petition at
the third sitting of the Council, " that if it be
fit to advise His Majesty to grant any Charter
of Incorporation for the purpose of erecting a
New Theatre, the same should in every principle of justice and equity," be granted to Drury
Lane, " in preference to the claim of any other
Applicant."

Sheridan was responsible for introducing still
other perplexities into the controversy. In his
first petition to the Council, he had referred to
the old Killigrew patent as follows : " If a third
regular established Theatre should indeed be
deemed necessary, and called for by the Public,
the Proprietors of Drury Lane Theatre have a

third reserved Patent, which has been purchased at a considerable price by the Trustees of the said Theatre, and which they are willing should be applied to the attainment of the above object, instead of allowing new speculators to interfere with their just rights." A brief sketch of the " dormant patent" has been given in a preceding chapter. It will be remembered that George White was to receive £5000 for his one-fourth share in the patent. It now turns out that no portion of that sum had ever been paid, and White, with other co-partners in the " dormant patent," rose up in righteous indignation at Sheridan's presumptions, and petitioned the King in Council to protect them in their rights ; " for to this hour no part of the said sum of £5000 or the interest thereof, hath been paid to your Petitioners, for the agreed purchase money, or price of their share and interest in the said Patent."

The contract alluded to was none other than the Outline for a General Opera Arrangement, which was hereupon produced and read, and was probably better understood than when it was drawn up (1792). White's prayer was to the effect that if a third theatre should be established on the authority of the " dormant patent," he ought to be admitted as a shareholder to the extent of £5000.

It was time for Sheridan to prove his monop-

oly. But if the curiosity of his hearers led them
to expect any novel arguments, they were disappointed. The assertion was made simply that
the patents granted to Killigrew and Davenant
formed a monopoly, or they were meaningless.
And persons were not wanting to accept the
alternative. The monopoly had been created,
whatever might be thought of the fact, and, argued Sheridan, ought not to be destroyed without first compensating those who had invested in
property in the faith that the exclusive privileges
contained therein were inviolable.

The Drury Lane patentee declined to discuss
the expediency of a third theatre, that was a
matter for others to decide; his main contention
was that the " dormant patent " should have first
consideration, in case a third theatre were desirable. The danger of raking up this old document
was quite apparent to Sheridan, and in his petition he had called it a " reserve Patent." Taylor
and White had brought the subject out still
more prominently, and too frequently for its own
good. Warren was not slow to pounce upon this
in his rejoinder. It was not clear to him, the
discrepancy between the "understanding " which
Sheridan and the other proprietors had at the
time of the Opera Arrangement, respecting the
" dormant patent," and the use to which Sheridan
now proposed to put it. Much pleasantry was

indulged in by Warren over the "Sleeping Beauty," to the evident discomfiture of the Drury Lane manager. Warren maintained that, once asleep, always asleep; and from the principle of *non-user*, he established the invalidity of that vexatious document.

A glimpse at the proceedings, before closing this part of the subject, will not be out of order. The following description was sent to Elliston (who was at that time in Bath) by a friend:

"Sheridan sat at the Council board, whose petition came on after yours. There was one also from the wife of Tom Sheridan [Thomas Sheridan was at this time in Spain, in a declining state of health]. All the petitions were in the hands of counsel, excepting Greville's, yours, Sheridan's, and that of Mrs. Thomas Sheridan. Sheridan was very declamatory, and certainly produced an effect; but, I think, yours was as persuasive as any. Lord Harrowby perused it with evident attention. The Attorney-General, who was officially present, gave strong indications of dislike and hostility to a third theatre, and shook his head wonderously like Lord Burleigh, or as you might have fancied the *Lord Mayor* in 'Richard the Third.'

"To your petition Sheridan listened with more gravity than he is accustomed to exhibit. Graham was present, and observed, 'you were a

pretty fellow to petition the King after violating
the laws of your *Circus ;* and that if you were
brought before him, he should deem the utmost
penalty under the Vagrant Act applicable to
your case.' The Justice was in a fury, much was
said about the illegality of your circus ' Macbeth,'
when Sheridan slily observed, the greatest violation was to the bard, in *your* attempting the
impersonation.   Adam attending on behalf of
Drury Lane Theatre — he was quite didactic and
pathetic." [1]

This closed the arguments of the famous proceedings in Council for a third theatre. Scarcely
a feature of the theatrical situation relative to
the patents had escaped the closest scrutiny.
All imaginable arguments, from the various
hostile attitudes of the Crown to the patentees,
from the grants of other licenses and patents,
from analogies in other monopolistic fields,
from the abstract question of crown prerogative,
down to the practical absurdity and injustice of
a theatrical (or any) monopoly in the nineteenth
century, were marshaled against the patentees.
But the Privy Council was like adamant. As
Sheridan had admitted, monopolies were generally looked upon as evils and probably were ;
nevertheless, the theatrical monopoly, by long-
established custom, had been made an exception,

[1] Raymond's *Life of Elliston*, pp. 169, 170.

and it was not for their Lordships to make the
first break into the "sacred rights" of the patents. Furthermore, they could evade the main
issue by holding their decision strictly to the matter of the corporation plan of the petitioners.

The result of the hearing before the Privy
Council was made public on the 14th of April
(1810).[1] The opinion of the Attorney and
Solicitor-General was sustained, and the question of the expediency of a third winter theatre
left unsettled. This finding was a foregone conclusion; but the arguments before His Majesty's
Council had served to bring out, as never before, all the questions connected with the theatrical patents. The proceedings developed the
fact also that there was a strong antagonism to
monopolies, even among the supporters of the
patentees,— Sheridan himself admitted his dislike for them in general. But the theatrical
monopoly still remained legally as firmly established as in the time of Charles II.

[1] *Gentleman's Magazine*, April, 1810.

CHAPTER IX

PETITION is the inalienable birthright of the
Briton. The defeat of the third theatre effort in the Privy Council was promptly followed
by a memorial to the King for a theatre patent.[1]
But what the petitioners could hope for in that
quarter is hard to conceive. Taking the cue
from these attempts, the performers at the late
theatre in Drury Lane petitioned His Majesty
(May 9, 1810), through the Lord Chamberlain, for a license to erect and conduct a new
theatre on the plan of the patent houses. Of
course the prayer was useless, but it contains
matter germane to the subject of a third theatre.
The performers set forth that, since the burning
of Drury Lane, they had been deprived of the
emoluments which were their due ; that, though
they had no desire to interfere with vested property rights, they had no confidence in the
proprietors' ability to rebuild the patent theatre ;
and that, if a third theatre were permitted to be

[1] *Gentleman's Magazine*, April, 1810.

built, the performers should have the preference.
Substantial reasons were given in support of
their petition. As to the means necessary for
such a venture they assured the King that, with
what had been proffered to them already, and
with what they could raise among themselves,
they would have ample means for the purpose
of erecting and conducting a theatre such as
Garrick acted in, "when seeing and hearing were principally and materially attended
to." [1] As argument in favor of theatrical management by experienced actors, the history of
the stage was cited. It was assumed as axiom-
atic that the representation of the drama would
be better conducted by artists than speculators.
It was promised that, in case their petition were
granted, they would establish a fund for the
benefit of the infirm and aged of their profession. Out of these suggestions were to appear,
later, benefits of practical worth to the actor;
though the present attempt to establish a third
theatre by professionals proved futile.

The proceedings in Council had been dragged
out to such length that the original petitioners
were prevented from getting a bill before Parliament before the close of the session. In the
mean time, Sheridan had taken time by the fore-
lock and petitioned the House of Commons for

[1] *London Chronicle*, May 15, 1810.

the privilege of transferring the Drury Lane
property to a large body of subscribers in order
that the claims of creditors to the establishment
might be satisfied, and for the purpose of rebuilding the theatre. It was especially implored
that the proposed subscribers should not be held
liable for more than their subscriptions.[1] This
was precisely the ground on which the third
theatre projectors had been denied ; but Sheridan was back of the scheme now, and that made
a difference.

But this move did not deter the agitators for
a third theatre. The next session of Parliament
found them in a stronger array than ever. No
serious attempt had been made to rebuild Drury
Lane Theatre, and this fact became a strong
argument for a new theatrical establishment,
although the promoters of a third theatre per-
sistently denied that Drury Lane, in reality or
in ashes, entered at all into their motives.
Nevertheless, the existence of but a single theatre, exercising a power more exclusive than
any since the days of Christopher Rich, giving
to the public a grade of entertainment, if not

[1] Cobbett's *Parliamentary Debates*, 1st Series, vol. xvi, col. 757.
It is noteworthy that when the Drury Lane Rebuilding Bill
was before the House of Lords, one (the Duke of Norfolk) who
was financially interested in Drury Lane Theatre expressed a
decided opinion that there ought to be a third theatre. Cobbett,
vol. xvii, col. 747. See also *London Chronicle*, March 3, 1812.

undeniably inferior in quality, at least highly unsatisfactory to the most enlightened taste, pleaded forcibly on the side of open competition.

A new champion now arose to assist in the struggle for a free stage. John Williams (1761–1818), satirist and critic, the "terror of actors and actresses, good and bad," entered the lists, and, as editor of the "Dramatic Censor for 1811," made the campaign against the patentees one of education. With less judgment than Aaron Hill, Williams was a more caustic critic than his worthy predecessor, and was willing to go to infinite pains to establish the charges made against the patentees. He went into a careful examination of the patents to determine, if possible, the source of an exclusive privilege which compelled the inhabitants of the city and suburbs of London "to make a weary and expensive pilgrimage of many miles, whenever they may want to suspend the operations of care, by a visit, with their families, to a colloquial theatre; and why their ears and eyes are offended, when they are there, by a pertinacious and insulting display of vulgar and ungrammatical pronunciation of language, and by debasing spectacles in action."[1] As Hill had maintained in 1735, so now it was pointed out, that it was the misuse of power in the hands of the patentees which lay at the bot-

[1] *Dramatic Censor,* col. 97, *et sq.*

tom of the complaints, and that a correction of
the evils would come the sooner, the greater the
abuse. Among the charges laid at the doors
of the winter theatres was the encouragement of
dullness, and the discountenance of genius. It
was declared that, "until the spell of monopoly
is dissolved and broken, neither the Public, nor
the Children of Genius, can have any alternative
but a desponding submission to the baneful
effects of an exclusive patent."

On the last day of January, 1811, the petition
for a third theatre in London was presented to
the House of Commons.[1] The plan proposed
for the new theatre differed from those thereto-
fore devised. The subscriptions were to be £1000
each, the subscribers to form a joint proprietor-
ship. The proprietors were to receive ten per
cent. on their subscriptions, if the profits
amounted to so much, otherwise there was to
be an equal and rateable division of the actual
profits of the concern. If more than ten per cent.
should be realized on the investment, the surplus,
up to five per cent., was to be distributed
amongst the public charities.

There were to be no " free admissions " of any
kind, or to any one.[2] A committee of four,

---

[1] *European Magazine*, vol. 59, p. 142; *Gentleman's Magazine*,
vol. 81, pt. 1, p. 164.

[2] This was one of the chief complaints against the patent

chosen for life as chief directors, together with
the Lord Chamberlain or his nominee, were to
constitute a Board of Superintendence, with
power to appoint annually a manager. The
manager was to have unlimited control over the
internal affairs of the theatre, with the proviso
that the engagement of performers and the
question of their salaries must be submitted to
the Board for approval. No actor, while a
public performer, could serve as manager.[1]
Prices of admission were fixed at 6s. to the
boxes, 3s. to the pit, 2s. to the lower gallery,
and 1s. to the upper gallery. The size of the
theatre was planned to be but little more than
that of Old Drury before 1791. No property
boxes were included in the plan, although the
stage boxes were to be at the disposal of the
performers for their friends; while the system
of " orders " found no place in the proposed
new theatre.

This plan had much to commend it. The evils
and abuses attendant on, and fostered by, the
patent houses were to be totally inhibited; the
accommodation of the public was kept constantly

houses. " Women of the town " would, at the opening of the
season, purchase, for a nominal sum, say £5, entrance to the
theatre for the entire year. This was called " free admission."

[1] This clause was aimed to cover the complaints against
Kemble at Covent Garden, apropos of the " O. P." riots.

in view ; and while a sufficiently liberal arrangement was offered to shareholders to induce them
to invest their capital in the concern, all tendencies towards running the theatre for private
gains were discouraged. It was confidently
hoped by the well-wishers of the plan that the
time was at last come to break the monopoly.
The more enthusiastic supporters of the idea
went so far as to announce an almost certain
victory. The patentees were told that they alone
had, "by their own misconduct, put an end to
that exclusion of competition, which it was their
interest to preserve." [1]

But zeal in a cause does not always insure
success. Once more the host had not been reck-
oned with. The spirit of Old Drury, like the
Killigrew patent, was only sleeping. Rousing
itself in the presence of danger, the committee,
appointed under the Rebuilding Act to examine
into and adjust the affairs of that theatre, met
(March 12, 1811) and resolved " to proceed
with *vigilance* and assiduity."

Taking timely alarm at the promulgation of
this report of the Drury Lane Rebuilding
Committee, the petitioners for a new theatre
(probably with a view to incite the members
of Parliament, friendly to their attempts, to be
present when the second reading of the bill

[1] *Dramatic Censor for 1811*, cols. 248–258.

came up) caused to be published a response to the action taken by the Drury Lane proprietors. The conduct of Sheridan in the Privy Council in 1810 was reviewed. They called attention to the impression which the astute manager left at that time, that there was a fair prospect of rebuilding the Drury Lane Theatre, for which ostensible purpose a subsequent bill of incorporation had been passed. When Sheridan had, by these tactics, succeeded in silencing his opponents, "his splendid abilities fell again into their wonted lethargy," and the announcement of the Drury Lane Committee that they had determined "to proceed with vigilance and assiduity," was the result of the "unwearied Petitioners renewing their application to Parliament." And again it was declared that the affairs of Drury Lane had no relation whatever to the third theatre project.

Other considerations of a cogent nature intervened to delay the decision of Parliament on the London Theatre Bill. On the 25th of March (1811), Mr. Mellish (member for Middlesex) moved the second reading. When the Speaker put the question, whether counsel were in attendance, the inevitable Sheridan arose and blandly stated that *he* had no intention of calling in the assistance of a lawyer, that a brief statement of the circumstances of the case would be sufficient to enable the House to determine the question before them. The representative of Drury Lane was of opinion that the originator of the motion had been influenced by the erroneous supposition that Drury Lane would not be rebuilt; but he (Sheridan) felt confident that when he assured them that this was a mistaken notion, and that there was the strongest possibility of its speedy reëstablishment, it would be deemed advisable to withdraw the bill. This story of the "orator, wit, classic, and statesman," that the rebuilding of Drury Lane Theatre was imminent, had been repeated often enough to form a standing joke. He had depended on it to defeat the projects of the petitioners for a new theatre in 1810, and now, two years after the theatre had been in ashes, he repeated the worn-out tale. Some there were, induced in good faith to contribute a small fortune towards rebuilding the patent house, who now looked upon the equivocating, procrastinating methods of the manager of that concern as the sheerest nonsense, used to cover up a wholesale swindling operation.[1]

Having mentioned the Rebuilding Act, Sher-

[1] See letter to *Dramatic Censor*, for April, 1811, cols. 219–221, from one who claimed to have subscribed £150,000 and who had been "to that hour unpaid, either principal or interest."

idan was under the necessity of explaining why
that legislation had not been taken advantage
of. His excuse was, that, after the bill had
passed, it had been intimated to him that the
Chamberlain (Lord Dartmouth) had intended
to question the legality of the " dormant patent,"
and that he had received from his Lordship a
letter (dated June 28, 1810), expressive of his
resolution to oppose the erection of any theatre
in Westminster. A compromise was reached,
however, by which it was agreed to leave the
" dormant patent " out of the question, and to
permit the running license to continue for twenty-
one years. These, said Sheridan, were the
causes of delay in rebuilding Drury Lane, and
time was what they now required. At any rate,
he maintained, it was not the custom for the
legislature to interfere with charter and patent
rights without adequate compensation. On the
other hand, it was pretty clear to many that
the notorious embarrassments of Drury Lane
had rendered the proprietors incapable of rebuilding it.[1] This fact had become apparent
to those most intimately concerned in the interests of the patent house. Sheridan's genius

[1] Cobbett's *Parliamentary Debates*, 1st series, vol. xix, cols.
496–500; *London Chronicle*, March 26, 1811; *Gentleman's
Magazine*, vol. 81, pt. 1, p. 373; *European Magazine*, vol. 59,
p. 300.

and finesse had succeeded for thirty years in baffling the foes of the monopoly, but, with the theatre in ashes and the finances of the institution hopelessly involved, it seemed beyond his power to extricate the affairs of Old Drury from the ruin which enveloped it. Furthermore, Sheridan's business methods were not of the sort to inspire confidence in his followers. He had exhausted his fund of tricks, which had once passed for magic, in raising enormous sums of money; and, without financial aid, Drury Lane Theatre could not be rebuilt. Meantime the arguments for a third theatre were growing more and more importunate.

In this crisis a recruit appeared on the side of theatrical monopoly to frustrate the hopes of the third theatre enthusiasts. More than this, by vigilance and zeal in behalf of Drury Lane, he succeeded in performing the seven-days wonder of rearing a phœnix out of the ashes of the burnt patent house. If one should turn the leaves of parliamentary history for the period under consideration, one would find a name recurring so frequently as to call for special attention. Scarcely a question of importance or public interest arose at this time in the metropolis without receiving the opinion of Samuel Whitbread, Esquire, the great London brewer, to whose judgment the greatest respect was accorded.

When the Rebuilding Act was passed (1810), incorporating the Drury Lane proprietors, Whitbread was named in the Committee to investigate the affairs of the theatre. He now appeared in the House of Commons and infused new spirit into the opposition to the London Theatre Bill. He sanctioned all that Sheridan had said; but he did more than merely supplement the orator and politician, — he became the new standard-bearer of theatrical patent rights. When Whitbread arose as sponsor for Drury Lane he received the attention due an oracle; and when he asserted that he confidently expected the restoration of Old Drury, cries of " Hear! Hear! " resounded from the House. He thought that, in view of the prospects of rebuilding the theatre, the third theatre advocates would be willing to postpone the second reading of the London Theatre Bill for six weeks, in which time he hoped to be able to speak decidedly as to the progress of the rebuilding committee. It was useless to reiterate to the House that the rebuilding of Drury Lane Theatre had nothing to do with the matter before them; since the decision of the Privy Council in 1810, the two questions had been indissolubly linked. All opposition to Whitbread's motion to postpone the second reading was futile, and the death-knell of a third theatre was struck.

But the battle was not over by any means.
During the six weeks' interval, the contestants
were busy. The "Dramatic Censor" continued
to put in earnest strokes against the monopoly.
Vigorous attempts were made to arouse a sentiment against the Rebuilding Act; the method
of carrying it "through both Houses of Parliament with a degree of silence unparalleled" was
stigmatized, and especially obnoxious was the
clause it contained providing for private boxes.

The injury to the histrionic profession by the
monopoly was greatly deprecated. The policy
that caused the dismissal of Holman and Pope
from Covent Garden was branded as "crooked."
The motive back of their ejectment was declared
"too palpable to be problematic." These artists,
it was asserted, were walking the streets unemployed, "with the broad arrow of managerial
interdiction" on their brows, the former "waiting for some friendly bark to transport him over
the trackless ocean;" the latter, "silent and sad,
in a state of proscription, idleness, and despair."
It was broadly insinuated that "the dog in the
manger" at Covent Garden was the cause of
the expatriation of some of England's best
actors.[1]

---

[1] One of the complaints brought against Kemble was that
he was jealous of good actors, and for that reason dismissed
all dangerous rivals, resorting to spectacle rather than risk

On the 9th of May Mellish again moved the second reading of the bill for a third theatre. Whitbread at once announced " the strongest probability that Drury Lane might be reconstructed," and recommended a further postponement of the motion before the House to the next session, at which time he would agree to pledge himself, as a member of Parliament, to take no active part against the application for a third theatre if Drury Lane Theatre was not, by that time, in the course of building. This was not satisfactory to the champions of the Theatre Bill. What Whitbread had stated was no more definite than what had been presented six weeks before, and even if it were, the essential question remained, — the expediency of a third theatre.[1] The debate on this occasion grew more general than usual. Both sides felt that the fight was to a finish. The chairman (Mr. Peter Moore) of the committee to inquire into the affairs of Drury Lane reported that the claims on the theatre were in a fair way of settlement, and that many of the creditors (including Sheridan) had released the proprietors from all obligations. He further stated that, if more time, say three

his professional reputation to the dangers of competition. Emigration of actors to America did not begin, however, to any extent, before about 1819.

[1] See speech of Mr. A. Browne, Cobbett's *Parliamentary Debates*, vol. 19, 1st Series, col. 1140.

months, were allowed them, they could assure
the rebuilding of " that noble structure."

General Tarleton grew sentimental when referring to Sheridan's generosity in contributing
the amount due him. As to a third theatre, the
General could not see the necessity of it when
Kemble had to introduce quadrupeds at Covent
Garden in lieu of actors. He intimated that, as
it was an age of speculation, the promoters of
the bill were " gentlemen speculating in theatres,
who never read the poets, and never entered
a play-house." Nothing could have been better
calculated to fire the enemies of the monopoly
than this speech. Mr. Marryatt was instantly
on his feet to disavow the charge of speculation.
He took occasion, in passing, to call attention
to the inconvenience to which the theatre-going
public of London were put, from the circumstance of having only one winter theatre. " If
a gentleman," he said, " applied for a box for
himself and family, he was informed he could
not get one for fourteen days; and thus taking
it on chance for that time, if they wanted to
laugh at a Comedy, they were perhaps seated
to cry at a Tragedy." It was quite clear to Mr.
Marryatt that the charge of speculation was
more applicable to the patent manager who
manipulated the monopoly for his own private
ends. The evil was still further aggravated, he

declared, by the fact that "some of the very best . . . performers in the country could not procure engagements, as they had been displaced by the quadrupeds which could be obtained at a cheaper rate, and could act on the largest theatre, as there was no necessity of watching the expressive turns of their countenances!" Kemble had but recently introduced elephants at Covent Garden.

This thrust was too much for Sheridan to remain quiet under. He replied warmly to the accusations against Kemble, and alleged that quadrupeds had been brought in to satisfy the depraved taste of the town. This, he was confident, was the true explanation ; for he recalled an instance when, against the judgment of his theatrical advisers, he had given a representation of Joanna Baillie's *De Monfort*, and though "this play was brought forward . . . with all the aid of Mr. Kemble and Mrs. Siddons, and the most superb scenery," nevertheless "through the perverted taste of the public it had failed."

Sheridan then reviewed the proceedings before the Privy Council in 1810, and expressed his confidence in Parliament that it would never contradict such high authority, nor usurp the prerogative of the Crown. The greatest effect was given to this dramatic speech when reference was made to Whitbread as surety for the

speaker's sincerity. The quickness with which
Sheridan had caught the current in favor of
the great brewer showed that he had lost none
of his former generalship. He sat down amidst
the " Hear! Hear! Hear!" of the auditors;
and although some further efforts were put forward by the supporters of the bill, its doom was
sealed. The vote for postponement of the second
reading stood 80 to 23 in the affirmative; and
postponement to the next session meant that
the bill was irrevocably lost. For the spirit
which Whitbread infused into the defense of
the monopoly, and the sturdy determination
manifested on the part of the third theatre projectors to push their bill through Parliament,
had given new life to the old concern. Proposals
were published for settlement with the creditors
of Drury Lane and for the rebuilding of the
theatre. And at two general meetings of the subscribers (one on the 14th, the other on the 31st,
of October, 1811), satisfactory arrangements
with all claimants were made. The rebuilding
of Drury Lane Theatre before the first of October, 1812, was assured, and in less than a year
from the first of those meetings, New Drury
Lane was opened (October 12, 1812) to the
public with " a flourish of trumpets and beating
of drums."[1]

[1] A full report of these proceedings was published in the

But the ghost of the third theatre would not down. Two weeks after the silencing of the bill, a motion was before the House, preliminary to the introduction of a similar measure at the next session of Parliament. Preparatory to this step the mover (Mr. Taylor) thought it advisable, during the recess, to ascertain the existing state of the stage as well as the privileges exercised by the monopoly over exclusive departments of the drama. The abstract principle upon which this motion and all similar applications for a third theatre were based, was the simple proposition that if the instructive amusement of the public was a good thing, then the public should have an unquestionable right to that good, and that no restrictions should be placed on the enjoyment of the right, except on the ground of political expediency, or absolute necessity. The contemplated motion to inquire into theatrical representations was the more necessary, because of the growing depravity of taste which had resulted from " the mummeries now exhibiting at some of the theatres." No aim to interfere with the interests of Drury Lane Theatre was intended by the motion " to inquire into

Dramatic Censor, for May, October, and November, 1811, cols. 257–259, 399–403, 416–420. See also Cobbett, *Parliamentary Debates*, vol. 19, 1st Series, 1140–1147; *Gentleman's Magazine*, June, 1811; *European Magazine*, vol. 60, p. 54.

and report upon the present state of the Dramatic and Scenic representation at the Theatres in this metropolis, together with the grounds and nature of the privileges and immunities claimed by the several Theatres, and the restraints imposed thereby on the amusements of the public." [1] The new Cerberus, Whitbread, immediately thrust himself into the breach thus made in the patent defenses, showing to the satisfaction of the House the evil intent as well as the certain bad consequences of the motion, should it pass. Any attempt to pry into "the abstract merits of any question touching the monopoly must tend to throw cold water upon the present public inclination " towards the rebuilding of Drury Lane Theatre. This had the desired effect, and the motion was withdrawn.

The importance of this abortive attempt to investigate the state of the drama and the nature of the privileges bestowed on the two patent theatres is not at once apparent. As a matter of fact, it was calculated to reach the root of the theatrical situation by the most direct method. It is the first genuine effort to go behind the scenes for the purpose of scrutinizing the claims of the monoply and the alleged abuse of privilege by the patentees. Those interested

[1] Cobbett's *Parliamentary Debates*, 1st Series, vol. xx, 288–290 ; *London Chronicle*, May 24, 1811.

in Drury Lane Theatre knew well enough the danger attending such an examination, and, naturally, preferred to keep the question in the background. So long as mere asseveration and conjecture were the only obstacles, the patentees could rest assured that political influence was a sufficient bulwark. But the motion to investigate the real conditions and facts about the great houses was not utterly lost. Twenty years later it reappeared, when it proved to be the beginning of the end.

Matters rested thus until the beginning of 1812, when, on the 7th of February, with a dogged persistence, the third theatre leaders were in Parliament again with a petition. This time the patentees were openly charged with degrading the drama by the introduction of horses, dogs, and an elephant on the stage. Kemble was also accused of professional jealousy which not only lowered the character of the representations at Covent Garden, but also threw the most gifted actors out of employment. The 20th of March was set for the second reading of the bill; and Sheridan being away from the House (owing to illness) on that date, Whitbread asked for a postponement of its consideration until Sheridan could be present. But delay had been the game for two years, and the petitioners were in no mood for such dilly-dallying methods. Forced on the defensive, Whitbread pleaded the cause of Drury Lane in the same old strain, and moved a postponement for six months. The grounds that had been traversed on both sides, *ad nauseam*, were again gone over. But it was evident that the third theatre party were clutching at the last straw, though, in the two years that had intervened since their first effort, they had filled out their ranks in Parliament until their minority was a respectable one at least. The motion to postpone was carried 58 to 34.[1] The Third Theatre Bill was dead. Lord Ossulton tried to revive it the next session, but the single opposition of Whitbread was sufficient to silence it forever, and on the 28th of April, 1813, it was withdrawn from the House of Commons.[2]

The immediate danger to the patents from the third theatre prosecutors was averted. An occasional echo of the contest was heard,[3] but the attempt to reach theatrical freedom by way of the Crown or Parliament was, for the time,

[1] *Parliamentary Debates*, 1st Series, vol. xxii, pp. 96–101; *London Chronicle*, March 23, 1812; *Gentleman's Magazine*, vol. 82, pt. 1, pp. 267, 467; *European Magazine*, vol. 61, p. 225.

[2] *European Magazine*, vol. 63, p. 523.

[3] See *The Pamphleteer*, no. iv, pp. 370–395, December, 1813, containing a plea for a third theatre, by Sir James Lawrence; also *Gentleman's Magazine*, March, 1811, proposal for "The Alfred Theatre."

given up, and the old contest between the winter and the summer theatres was resumed. The possibility of a struggle of an entirely different sort had also made its appearance, and, in time, was destined to accomplish what the bold defenders of the third theatre idea had failed to do. This was the guerrilla warfare between the minors and majors which had first manifested itself in 1807, as has been seen. Fostered by a Lord Chamberlain, who, on principle, was opposed to the theatrical monopoly, these lesser establishments became more and more the leading factors in the solution of the problem which had puzzled the heads of the promoters of a third theatre in 1810–12.

CHAPTER X

INTIMATELY associated with the struggle
for a free stage in London is the history of
the establishment of the English opera; for by
the beginning of the nineteenth century the patentees had grown envious of every species of
entertainment that in any way resembled a theatrical exhibition. Furthermore, although thus
far they had rarely exercised the privilege, their
patents secured to them a monopoly of the opera
if it secured exclusive privileges in anything;
and the necessity had at last arisen of guard-
ing even the unused rights claimed by them.
Italian opera had been surrendered by the two
patent houses, almost from the founding of Vanbrugh's Opera House in the Haymarket (1704),
and the terms of settlement provided by the
Opera Arrangement of 1792 gave a definite
sanction to the monopoly of foreign opera at the
King's Theatre.

In 1794, Dr. Arnold, the musical composer,
converted a portion of the building which until

the founding of the Royal Academy (1768) had been used for an art gallery, into a theatre, and intended to secure a license to open it, but was thwarted by the patentees. This was the Lyceum. A few years after this (1802) Colonel Greville started his " Pic-Nic Society " in Tottenham Street,[1] and two years later made proposals to the Lord Chamberlain for the establishment of a theatre for music, in which nothing but English talent should be employed. This fell through, as we have seen, but Greville still nourished his pet scheme for the native opera. Finally, in 1809, he secured from Lord Dartmouth a license for English opera *in music*, to which privilege, after a short time, dialogue was added, it being understood in the extension of the license that dialogue and music should be used only in so far as both of them should make out an operatic entertainment. Greville was on the point of putting his license into an elaborate execution, by purchasing and fitting up the Pantheon in Oxford Street, when Drury Lane Theatre burnt (February 24, 1809), at which time Arnold secured a license similar to his own.[2]

There is a curious story connected with George

---

[1] *London Chronicle*, February 20, 1802.

[2] See Brougham's speech before the Privy Council, March 26, 1810. *Account of Proceedings*, p. 86 *sq.*

III and the founding of the English Opera
House. The King was exceedingly fond of music and a devoted patron of the art. Dr. Arnold
was organist to His Majesty, and, in 1809, it
occurred to Samuel James Arnold, son of Dr.
Arnold, to take advantage of the circumstance
to obtain from the Crown permission to open a
new theatre for the especial purpose of fostering
the English opera. A prospectus was prepared,
setting forth the aims of the undertaking, a copy
of which had been previously submitted to the
Lord Chamberlain. The project pleased the
fancy of the King, the license was accordingly
issued, and the English opera prepared to launch
under the most favorable auspices. As the license was first issued, no limitation, as to season,
was contained therein. The zealous Greville at
once complained that he had prayed for a privilege similar to that in Arnold's license, and that
the Lord Chamberlain had promised him that if
any person besides the proprietors of Drury Lane
and Covent Garden should be invested with the
privilege of opening a winter theatre, that
person should be Colonel Greville. Thereupon
Lord Dartmouth hastily summoned Mr. Arnold
and explained that Greville's prior claim had
been overlooked in granting Arnold a license
for the entire year, at the same time acknowledging the privileges which Arnold's license gave

him of performing winter and summer. The Lord Chamberlain extricated himself from the dilemma by suggesting that Greville and Arnold divide the privileges of the two licenses between themselves. This advice was followed, Greville choosing the winter season for his operations, leaving the summer months to Arnold.[1]

But the burning of the Drury Lane Theatre materially altered these plans. Owing to this accident, Arnold and Greville deemed it advisable to join their licenses and open only one opera house, the Pantheon being chosen for the purpose. At this juncture the ready-witted Sheridan nipped the movement in the bud by proposing a union of all three interests. The advantages to all parties concerned were evident: Arnold and Greville would get all the privileges of the Drury Lane license added to their own, in addition to the insurance against persecution by the patentees; while Sheridan would, for the time, put an effectual stop to the English opera scheme, and also secure a house for his burnt-out company. The three licenses, accordingly, were merged into one, and the Lyceum was opened for the remainder of the winter season of 1809 under the three managers. In the agreement

---

[1] Solicitor-General's speech in behalf of Arnold in 1831, *London Chronicle*, January 12, 1831; see also Brougham's speech before the Privy Council, 1810.

arising out of these circumstances the licenses of
Arnold and Greville were distinctly recited, and
their right to keep open their theatres winter and
summer was not denied. Moreover, it should be
borne in mind that in the hearing before the
Privy Council in the following year (1810),
Arnold's rights, instead of being questioned, were
wholly admitted, whatever Sheridan's motive in
so doing.

The Drury Lane season — for such it was —
at the Lyceum closed on the 12th of June, 1809.
Arnold, on the 7th of the month, had made a
preliminary announcement that he would open
the theatre for a summer season of operas and
ballets. A few days later, the following advertisement appeared in the public prints :

" LYCEUM THEATRE

" The Public are respectfully informed, that
the period for which the Drury-lane Company
engaged the above Theatre, having expired — the
Theatre will, after This Evening be closed for
a few days, in order that the new decorations
which are prepared may be affixed throughout
the house, and in order to enable the Proprietors
to make the various alterations which have been
proposed to afford the utmost accommodation
to the Public within the Theatre, as well as by
improved facilities of ingress and egress. After

which the Theatre (by authority of the Lord
Chamberlain), *WILL OPEN* for the Summer
Season with an entirely new *COMIC OPERA*,
and a *GRAND BALLET*. Particulars of which
will be duly announced. A spacious new Lobby
will be opened to the Public; and the lower
circle of Boxes, enlarged and considerably improved, will be appropriated exclusively to Dress
Company."

The date for opening was fixed for June 19,
but on account of the " extensive alterations " in
the theatre, this was changed to June 22,[1] from
which it was again postponed to the 26th, when
the new venture actually started off with *Up All
Night*, followed by *Love in a Tub*. The advertisement ran, " The Doors to be open at Six
o'clock, and begin at Seven precisely. Boxes
5s. Pit 3s. Gallery 2s. Upper Gallery 1s." The
effort was favorably received by the public.
The convenient size of the theatre was especially
commended, the contrast, in this respect, with
the winter houses being remarked, and the effect-
iveness of the performance attributed to this.

The operas permitted to Arnold, at this time,
consisted of three acts only and might be performed as at the patent houses, except that the
dialogue might not be converted into recitative.

[1] See *Morning Chronicle* for June 7, 10, 12, 13, 15, 16, 17, 19,
24, 27, 1809; *London Chronicle*, June 27, 1809.

The after-piece was, at the period under consideration, confined to spectacles, ballets, or pieces consisting of songs and recitative. Something of the success attending the first night's performances at the Lyceum was due to the notoriety which the Drury Lane Company had given the place during the previous spring. And that circumstance contained another precedent, the consequence of which was unforeseen by Sheridan, namely, the acting of the regular drama. On the opening of Arnold's English Opera House, Sheridan intimated that the Lord Chamberlain had exceeded his authority in granting the license. The Covent Garden managers also expostulated against the grant, but the Earl of Dartmouth threatened that if they did not keep quiet on the subject he would extend Arnold's privileges.[1] As Arnold's license comprised the summer months only, it would seem that no competition could arise between the Lyceum and the patent houses, but rather with the Little Theatre in the Haymarket. Viewed in another light, there were now two summer theatres instead of one to resist the encroachments of the winter houses, and for the next few years the vicissitudes of the Haymarket and Lyceum, or English Opera House, run parallel and have a common interest.

[1] Oulton, *History of Theatres of London,* iii, 93, 94. Oulton's account is contemporaneous.

The summer season of 1810 opened at the Lyceum on June 4, when Arnold put on the musical farce *Hit or Miss*, borrowed from Drury Lane. It is well to note this introduction of the musical *farce*, as the victory for free competition in theatricals was ultimately won by the aggregate effect of such slight innovations as this. The same year, Colman petitioned the Prince Regent either to oblige the winter theatres to close earlier than usual, or to extend the time of performances at the Haymarket. The latter alternative was granted, and Colman obtained leave to continue to October 15. But the concession proved useless. The Haymarket closed at the time specified in the old license (September 15), the reason being that "so many obstacles now present themselves against the enjoyment of the grant." [1] The chief "obstacle" was that Covent Garden opened on the 10th of September, and the Haymarket performers were forced to leave Colman on that date in order to renew their articles at the patent house.[2]

Colman now determined to repeat the experiment of 1803, of opening his theatre with an independent company. Once more the provinces

[1] *London Chronicle*, September 17, 1810.

[2] *European Magazine*, vol. 58, p. 218. Arnold also applied for and got an extension of his season to October 15. In 1812 he ran up to October 9. — Oulton, iii, 142.

were invaded for recruits, and on the 15th of
May, 1811, the Little Theatre opened despite
the patent houses. Some of the actors had never
seen service on any stage, but that mattered
little in comparison with the main issue. " Yet
what can the manager of this Theatre do ? "
breaks out the incensed editor of the " Dramatic
Censor." " When Foote and the elder Colman
had it, they were enabled to open by the middle
of May, because that was the period when the
winter managers felt it expedient to repose from
their dramatic toil; and then an Edwin, a
Parsons, a Palmer, and a Bannister, were glad to
enlist under the banners of the minor chief, and
sweat and laugh during the summer solstice!
But *tempora mutantur*, Power hath become more
powerful, and the Winter Rats have usurped
the cheese of the Muses, and left the mere par-
ings to solace the mice in the dog days ! " [1]
Nevertheless, the Haymarket continued its performances until the 16th of October ; although
the last night was " by permission." Elliston, in
delivering the farewell address, spoke of the
season as " an experiment, . . . adopted to save
their interests from annihilation."

In the following year (1812), petition was
made, and granted, for an extension of the Hay-

[1] *Dramatic Censor*, May, 1811, col. 264, September and
October, cols. 369, 403.

market license to seven months. This license
was renewed until 1822, when it was reduced to
the original term of four months.[1] But the new
privileges were of little value to the proprietors
of the Haymarket Theatre. A series of disgraceful rows among the partners, a King's Bench
suit which deprived Colman of his personal liberty, together with the encroachments of the
winter houses, combined to ruin the prospects
of the theatre, which was not open for a single
night in the summer of 1813. The next season
it was opened for a short period only, and, in
1815, for two months, not commencing that year
until July 17, as Drury Lane continued up to
July 13, and Covent Garden to July 20.[2]

During these years of depression and gloom at
the Haymarket, the English Opera House had
been experiencing a harvest of successes. On
the closing night (September 15) of the summer
season of 1815, the annual address (delivered
by Raymond) referred to the seven successful
seasons of the theatre, and announced that the
proprietor was making arrangements to build
"an entirely new, airy, and commodious theatre,"

[1] I give this on the authority of a reported speech of Sir C.
Wetherell, made in the Chancellor's Court in 1831 in the case
of the Majors *vs.* the Minors. See *Morning Chronicle* for January 26, 1831. According to Oulton, iii, 242, the Haymarket
license was extended to eight months in 1812.

[2] *European Magazine*, July and September, 1815.

to be ready for the opening of the ensuing summer. Splendor was not promised, but comfort, safety, and convenience were. These promises were faithfully redeemed, if the published descriptions of the theatre by the architect (Beazley) is a criterion.[1] On the site of the old Lyceum in the Strand, the new English Opera House was erected. The work on it was pushed, as Arnold intended to put the already accepted interpretation on his license, to act any season of the year, and, if possible, to open his new theatre about Easter, 1816.[2] But the patentees were unable to brook any inroads of this nature. On the 12th of October (1815) the Drury Lane Committee was called together to hear the annual report. The bulk of this is taken up with the financial condition of the concern (which was in no wise flattering, the report showing a deficit of £19,387 for the year, with a gross shortage of £68,294). But a point of peculiar interest is contained in the clause calling the attention of the meeting to the announcement of " the proprietor of a *Summer Establishment*" to pursue his speculations to an indefinite extent. The committee reported

[1] Oulton, iii, 177–183; *London Examiner*, September 17, 1815.

[2] Colonel Greville, on the receipt of some real or imagined slight, had retired from the partnership in 1810, leaving Arnold in undivided possession of the English opera for winter and summer.

that the Covent Garden and Drury Lane proprietors had lost no time in petitioning the
Prince Regent (through the Lord Chamberlain)
against any invasion of their rights.[1]

In spite of this threatening forecast, Arnold
pursued his purpose to open in April. His license was originally issued in February, and,
being an *annual* license, he argued that it was
good from February to the next February. The
influence of the patentees against him was too
great, however, and effectually prevented the
operation of his unexpired license. Arnold,
therefore, was compelled to issue the following
announcement to the public ("Morning Chron-
cle," April 2, 1816):

"THEATRE ROYAL, ENGLISH OPERA HOUSE,
March 30th, 1816.

"Notice is hereby given to all parties interested, that it was the intention of the Proprietor to have opened the new Theatre on Monday the 15th of April next ensuing under the
powers of his unexpired License; but that in
consequence of a Petition presented to his Royal
Highness the Prince Regent, by the Patentees
of the Winter Theatres, he has received from
the Right Honorable Lord Chamberlain an intimation that the measure of opening the Theatre,

[1] *European Magazine*, October, 1815.

whilst the Petition was yet under consideration, would be opposed by his Lordship.

" The Proprietor of the English Opera License, with due respect to his Lordship's high authority, has therefore considered it proper to delay the opening of the Theatre until further notice."

After numerous delays, Arnold finally succeeded in gaining the Lord Chamberlain's grant for four months, and, thus restricted, the new Opera House in the Strand was announced to open on the 15th of June (1816). In the opening address (written by Arnold and delivered by Miss Kelly) pointed reference was made to the venom of the patentees, in these lines :

" Our Humble Edifice triumphant rose
In spite of threatening flames [1] and Patent foes !
The Foes who 'd stint your pleasure — but in vain,
To Covent Garden and to Drury Lane,
Who kindly wish to prove, as it appears,
Monopolizers of your smiles and tears !
Who love you all so dearly that they swear
You shall go nowhere — if you don't go there.
Pray, how d' ye like our House ? Is 't snug and easy ?
Upon our life we 've done our best to please ye !
You all can *hear* and *see*, I hope — Yes — all !
Those are rare virtues of a House that 's *small !*

[1] Alluding to a conflagration in Exeter Court, where Arnold sustained a severe loss to ornaments, interior trappings, etc., which were being made ready for his new theatre. It was in an uninhabited house, and the cause of the fire is unknown.

> For such, are *Actors* ever bound to pray,
> Where you can *see* the *Stage* and *hear* the *Play*.
> Where you with ease can mark our real faces,
> Without the aid of glasses or grimaces !
> And each inflection of the voice is heard,
> Your ears preserved, and our poor lungs are spared !"[1]

So bitter was the feeling on the part of the patentees against Arnold's past success and bright prospects at the Lyceum, that the performers at Drury Lane were threatened with a forfeiture of their engagements if they returned to the new Lyceum. It was for this reason that Raymond resigned his position as acting-manager at the English Opera House. Kinnaird of the Sub-Committee at Drury Lane was especially vindictive, and seems to have been chiefly responsible for the general quarrel which was precipitated through his endeavors to intimidate his performers into abandoning Arnold's theatre.[2] As a consequence of Kinnaird's menaces, most of the performers at the Lyceum were new; Dublin, Edinburgh, and Bath had been brought into requisition to make good the deficiencies caused by resignations. Three, however, of the old performers (Mr. Gattie, Mrs. Orger, and Miss Kelly) disregarded the prohibition of the

[1] *European Magazine*, June, 1816; *London Chronicle*, June 17, 1816.

[2] *European Magazine*, September, 1816.

patentees, and braved the consequences. The result was a public airing of the dissensions of the managers in a rather fierce, and decidedly ill-tempered, paper war, — the greatest since the early days of the Royalty.

The quarrel was brought to a head in the autumn, at the time of the opening of the winter houses. On the evening of September 9, 1816, previous to the commencement of the performance of *Rich and Poor* at the Lyceum, Bartley (successor to Raymond as acting-manager) came forward and read a rather unexpected address of some length from the proprietor, Mr. Arnold. All personal injuries sustained from the opposition of the patentees were passed by, and the grievances of the unoffending performers taken up. These, he declared, "are deprived of the means of obtaining a part of their subsistence, since they are even prohibited from appearing before you at this theatre on the *alternate* nights, when there are no representations at the others, and when they consequently receive *no salary.*

"At the opening of the New English Opera House, this season, the Proprietors of Covent Garden Theatre prohibited Mr. and Mrs. Liston (who had still a season of their engagement here unexpired) from acting in this place. To this unexampled act of rigour and restriction they were compelled to submit, in apprehension of the infliction of heavy penalties, or perhaps, dismissal from that Theatre, although their engagement to the Proprietors of the English Opera was made three years ago (and acted upon during two seasons) without the slightest hint of objection on the part of the Covent Garden Proprietors.

" Some accommodation in regard to Performers *was*, however, permitted by the Sub-Committee of Drury Lane, *because* the Proprietors of this Theatre had the power of offering them an equivalent. This equivalent consisted (by a priority of engagement) in the valuable services of a young Lady who never appears upon these or any other boards without receiving the warmest testimonials of public approbation and esteem."

The address then stated that the accommodation alluded to had been withdrawn, and that the Lyceum proprietor had been unable to elicit an answer from the Drury Lane Committee to a proposal to renew the arrangement. Arnold did not accuse the Drury Lane Sub-Committee collectively, but held a single individual responsible for the situation. From the person referred to (meaning Kinnaird), Arnold averred that he had received a verbal communication to the effect that none of the Drury Lane performers would be allowed to act at the Lyceum.

This long recital of complaints was justified by the apology offered to the audience for the non-appearance of Mrs. Orger and Mrs. Harlowe, whose names appeared on the play-bills for the evening, and who, it was alleged, had " received intimation that to perform here would be at their own peril, and would perhaps subject them to such severe penalties as they dare not encounter the risk of incurring." The following letter addressed to the manager was then produced and read to the audience : [1]

" My DEAR SIR: It is with extreme regret I am compelled to inform you, that Mr. Kinnaird has forbidden my performing any longer at the English Opera; intimating, that, if, neglectful of his injunction, I should appear there this evening, a heavy fine would be exacted.

                    " I am, etc., M. A. ORGER.
" Sept. 9, 1816."

The situation was further aggravated by the fact that Drury Lane was closed. While reading the communication from Arnold to the public, Bartley was frequently interrupted by applause, and cries of " Shame! shame!"   But

[1] An account of this singular performance, together with the text of Arnold's Address, appeared in the *Morning Chronicle*, September 10, 1816.   The succeeding numbers of that journal contain the rest of the correspondence.

the affair was not to end here. On the day following the publication of these proceedings at the Lyceum, Douglas Kinnaird appeared in one of the public prints in vindication of his action in forbidding performers to engage at the English Opera House. In this explanation a letter is quoted from H. Harris of the Covent Garden management, in which is cited precedent against permitting actors of the patent houses engaging at other theatres, even during the recess. Referring to the insinuations contained in Mrs. Orger's letter, Kinnaird called that lady's attention to the fact that the only conversation he had had with her on the subject of her performing at the Lyceum was on the Friday prior to the Monday of her appearance in the Lyceum bills. The occasion of that conversation was an application of Mrs. Orger to Kinnaird for permission to continue performing at the Lyceum on the nights when Drury Lane was closed. "This I told you was impossible for me to grant," continues Kinnaird, "as, if we permitted our performers to exert their talents against Covent garden theatre, when we were shut, they would do the like by us—and that then the benefits proposed, by our playing alternate nights, would be lost—and we might as well let our performers appear before the public at our theatre every night." Attention is also called to the articles

of agreement, " which you and all the performers
of the winter theatres signed. The salary given
is for the exclusive services of the performers at
this theatre. I recollect also explaining to you
that the Haymarket received the accommodation
till next *Saturday* [Sept. 14] *from old usage
alone.*" In the same issue of the "Morning
Chronicle" (September 11, 1816), "A Play-go-
ing Man" justifies the attitude of the patentees,
first, on the simple grounds of rivalry, and, secondly, because, when actors were engaged at two
theatres, at the same time, the "business" was
interfered with.

Arnold returned at once to the attack, de-
nouncing Kinnaird's conduct towards the actors
as tyrannical and oppressive, a course which had
not the sanction of the entire Sub-Committee
of Drury Lane, but was the individual action of
Kinnaird. It was denied that it had been the
custom to permit no regularly engaged performer
to play at any other theatre after the opening of
the winter season, — as Harris had asserted in his
letter to Kinnaird. "Formerly, indeed," pursues
Arnold, "no such permission was requisite. But
during the last eight years, since the winter
establishments have protracted their seasons of
performances, . . . the performers have . . .
been constantly allowed the privilege of acting
at the Haymarket Theatre *before* the closing, and

after the opening of the winter theatres." Arnold's position is sustained by the following interesting extract from Raymond's "Life of Elliston" (pp. 234, 235):

" In the old times, the Haymarket Theatre was open some ten days before the close of the winter houses. During these ten days there was but a skeleton company at the former, until the great patentees gave up their flesh and blood, by which it was clothed. Many, and frequently ridiculous, were the shifts to which this anatomized body was subject, in the short interval. One circumstance occurred, which, at the first blush (and verily it was of a character to raise one), would appear positively impracticable. It was that of Farley acting an important part in the play of Covent Garden, and also at the Haymarket, on the same night; the two *plays*, be it remembered, being the first pieces of the entertainments at both establishments.

" At Covent Garden the curtain rose at half past six o'clock, and in the Haymarket at seven; at the former, Farley was cast into one of Macbeth's witches, and at the latter, in the part of Sir Philip Modelove, in the comedy of *A Bold Stroke for a Wife*.

.   .   .   .

" The dove-tailing of this remarkable night's performance was . . . accomplished " by means of a hackney-coach, furnished with all the necessary habiliments of a dressing-room, and a servant, who assisted the actor to make the alterations for the part next to be represented, as the coach passed back and forth between the playhouses. During one of these trips, for the last scene at Covent Garden, the coach, in turning a corner, upset. " Half witch and half baronet — poor Farley was extricated from that door which fortune had thrown uppermost, and never actor surely made an appearance to more general applause."

The wordy warfare between the managers continued for a week, the public occasionally taking sides. On the whole, the facts adduced against the patentees on this occasion were anything but complimentary to their conduct. To admit that they were jealous of the English Opera House, by withdrawing the best performers from it, was to declare that there was no particular distinction attaching to the character of the performances at the patent houses ; and that, after all, it was the actor that drew the audience and gave fame to a theatre, whether it were Drury Lane or Saddler's Wells. Herein lay the secret of the encroachments of the winter houses, and the " lifting " of the best actors from the summer theatres. Herein, too, lay a suggestion to the managers of the minor concerns, namely, to make their best actors managers and proprietors, so that the patent houses could not buy them off. This largely accounts for the unmolested operations and successes of Foote; and, when the fact became practically apparent among the minors, it did more towards weakening the monopoly than all the correspondence wars, public addresses, and occasional prologues.

One other fact was slowly dawning on the minds of the enemies of the theatrical patents, and this contest between the patentees and Arnold served to emphasize its importance: if any sort of winning competition (or, rather, retaliation) was to be waged with the monopoly, the minors must adopt the tactics of the patentees and invade the provinces of the enemy. They must secure extended seasons; they must pay higher salaries for performers than the winter houses could afford; they must adapt their exhibitions to meet the demands of public taste, and at the same time fulfill the legal requirements. These outlines of attack and defense were still hazy, but they, or their equivalents, were sure to take form as soon as the right man should appear to give them effect.

Arnold was materially worsted by the crusade carried on against his new Opera House. It was a waste of time for him to urge that the " theatrical community has undergone a great revolution since the laws were established for the governance" of the patent houses. Everybody knew that. The fact of the monopoly remained, and it was useless to argue the point with the patentees on the abstract principle of benevolence and generosity. The Lyceum was compelled to close on the 5th of October, owing to the opening of the winter houses. Bartley spoke the final address, in the course of which he stated that "the unexpected limitation, which has been imposed on the licence to this Theatre, has rendered abortive the best exertions of the Proprietor, so far as relates to a fair and just view to his personal advantage, . . . He has had to contend with powerful enemies; and those enemies have hitherto so far triumphed, as to deprive him of a large portion of *talent* as well as a large part of the *means* of encourageing and rewarding it." [1]

Fortuitous circumstances at this time gave the summer theatres a temporary revenge. In April, 1817, owing, for whatever ultimate reason, to the lack of opportunity offered by the Covent Garden manager to his talent, Charles Mathews left the winter theatre and engaged at the Little Theatre in the Haymarket for the summer season.[2] The following year, adapting

[1] *European Magazine* and *London Review*, October, 1816.

[2] Mathews made his first appearance at Drury Lane in

one of Foote's eccentricities, he made his first
appearance "At Home" at the English Opera
House (April 2, 1818), and, for forty nights,
depending on his sole efforts, he gave to large
audiences a "series of entertainments, which
succeeded in exciting peals of laughter from the
beginning to the end." This series of monologues was of a far higher type of dramatic art,
and approached legitimate comedy more closely
than did the efforts at mimicry to which
the Covent Garden management had confined
Mathews. But the interpretation of the regular
drama, the exclusive privilege of the patent
houses, was invariably based on dialogue, whatever else entered into the definition. The patentees, therefore, had no power to interfere with
Mathews's successes. The first season of these
entertainments concluded on the 16th of June.
The strained relations between the patentees
and all others who dared venture on any species
of theatrical entertainment may be seen from
Mathews's farewell on the closing night:

"I beg to state distinctly," he said, "that

1804, with which company he remained until 1812, when,
failing to agree with the acting-manager (T. Sheridan), he
withdrew from Drury Lane, traveled for nine months, returned to London (October, 1812), and engaged for five years
at Covent Garden. Discontented with the narrow range of
characters given him, he broke the engagement as stated
above. *European Magazine*, vol. 73, pp. 283-287.

while I am advised that my performances are within the strict letter of the law, no fear shall deter me from proceeding, and that I will resist strenuously and firmly any measures that may be pursued to support an injurious monopoly to my injury ; and that I shall double all the energies of my resistance from the recollection that I am contending in the cause of the public, who have no right to be curtailed of their lawful amusements, or to be told by patentees, ' if you won't come to laugh with us, we shall take care that you shall not go to laugh elsewhere.' " [1]

And at the end of the regular summer season at the Opera House (October 5, 1818), the proprietor expressed the hope that, " without infringing on the supposed rights of patent monopolies, he may occasionally be enabled to invite you here with such performances and exhibitions *as the law allows*," [2] alluding, no doubt, to the " At Home " entertainments.

The encroachments of the winter houses not only continued but were extended. Drury Lane did not close until the 30th of June in 1818, while Covent Garden kept open until the middle of July.[3] At the close of the Haymarket's

---

[1] *European Magazine*, June, 1818.

[2] *Ibid.* vol. 74, p. 355.

[3] *London Chronicle*, July 16, 17, 1818.

season in 1817 it was announced that the Little Theatre would, the ensuing year, take advantage of the entire limit of its license (seven months); [1] but July 15 (1818) was the earliest date it could open. Each year the old complaint was poured into the public ear concerning "those mightier powers against whose strength our weakness must give way." [2] The contest was rapidly approaching a climax. The season of 1819 – 20 at Drury Lane did not end until July 8, and at Covent Garden until the 17th. The former reopened on the 15th of August. The vexation caused to Arnold, of the English Opera House, by this palpable invasion of his interests was too great to be contained. His feeling of indignation found vent in the following manifesto :

" THE WINTER THEATRES

" Since the Patentees of the Winter Theatres incessantly complain of the encroachments of other Theatres; and appeal by Petition against those that open under the Lord Chamberlain's

[1] The extended privileges had been in disuse so long that it is doubtful whether it would have been allowed to be exercised, even if the winter houses had not, by their encroachments, prevented it. This view is sustained by the fact that the seven months privilege was renewed in 1820.

[2] *London Chronicle*, September 14, 1819 ; *ibid.* September 16, 1817; *European Magazine*, vol. 72, p. 259 ; *ibid.* vol. 76, p. 264.

Licences and by Prosecutions against those that act under the Licences of the Magistrates,[1] it is time the attention of the Legislature, and of the Publick, should be called to the gradual encroachments made by these great establishments on their more limited and more defenceless neighbours.

"In Garrick's time, the Winter Theatres played never more than 150 or 160 nights in the year; till within the last ten years, they never exceeded an average of 200 nights; opening in the middle of September, and closing early in June. They have now gradually extended their performances from the *beginning* of September to towards the *end* of July, leaving only an interval of six or seven weeks, when the Town is comparatively empty (and in the dog-days), for the summer Theatres to reap their little scanty harvest.

" The Theatre Royal Drury Lane has now reopened in the *middle* of August, leaving the summer Theatres *twenty-one* Nights only free from an oppressive coveteousness, which it appears can only be bounded by the ruin of more humble rivals.

" The attention of the Publick is now respect-

[1] The allusion is to the petition of the patentees against the Olympic and Sans Pareil, 1818. This will be considered in the next chapter.

fully called to this brief statement; and their continued patronage earnestly solicited to the Theatre Royal English Opera House, in which the most animated exertions will continue to be made to merit their favour."

The only effect this had on the 'Great Lessee,' Elliston, who had taken charge of Drury Lane Theatre in 1819, was the following characteristic reply:

"The Patentees can not condescend to enter into a competition of scurrility, which is only fitted for *Minor* Theatres — what their powers really are, will be, without any public appeal, legally decided in November next, and any gasconade can only be supposed to be caused by cunning or poverty."[1]

Arnold retorted to this in the public prints and in "a new extempore, temporary sketch," entitled *Patent Seasons* (written by R. B. Peake). The audience showed its sympathy on the side of the summer house, for it "applauded most vociferously" the hits at the winter manager. The dramatic critic in the "London Review" (August, 1820) said of the performance and of the circumstances calling it forth: "As a temporary trifle, it well deserved its favourable reception, but we fear, that something even more

[1] *European Magazine*, July and August, 1820; *Lady's Magazine*, August, 1820.

than being so satirized or laughed at, must be adopted, to bring the *Patent Seasons* into a more reasonable compass."

The " Examiner " (August 27, 1820) treated the matter in a somewhat different way, but, though friendly to Elliston of Drury Lane, it was outspoken on the subject of free competition in theatrical entertainments. " We know not," says the dramatic editor of that weekly, commenting on the representation of the *Patent Seasons*, " we know not how the performers feel on such an occasion, but it must surely be a strong sense of the truth of what they are saying, which enables them so gravely to say it. It is certainly an awkward business on all sides. Actors, we are afraid, like other agreeable persons, get little with the town in general, by showing themselves in the light of sufferers, instead of merry makers. The chance is that want of success is attributed to them rather as a want of merit than anything else. The town, on the other hand, evidently feels less interested in the pathetic part of the representation than in the sarcasms on Mr. Elliston. It crowds to the pit in much the same taste as people crowd around a fight, for the sake of being entertained and excited at the expense of others. . . . But the right of complaint is undoubted on the part of the Lyceum, if not for the actual encroachment, for the manner of it. The truth is, that all the theatres, great and small, ought to be allowed to remain open all the year round, and the legislature should be applied to accordingly. We can hardly suppose that it would hold out long, against earnest and well-put representation."

There is a possible justification of Elliston's action in opening Drury Lane the middle of August, 1820. Edmund Kean was preparing to come to America for the season of 1820–21, and Elliston conceived the idea of getting him to give a series of " farewell " performances before sailing. Though ostensibly for the benefit of the public, this was a mere ruse used to cover up an " unprecedented and oppressive conduct towards the summer houses." When Kean closed this engagement (September 16), it was indignantly asserted by some that, " we cannot believe that such an experiment will ever be repeated," of keeping the patent theatre open during the summer.[1]

The patentees had not yet reached their limit in the matter of encroachments. But if there was ever a theatrical manager who knew, and dared to use, his capabilities in matters of an extreme nature, Robert William Elliston was that manager. The season of 1820–21 closed at

[1] *European Magazine,* vol. 78, p. 257.

Drury Lane on June 15. On the 27th of the same month it reopened for "a limited period," for the purpose of producing the masked festivals, the Victory of Waterloo, and the Coronation. "On the subject of interfering with the 'little hour' allotted to the career of the Summer Theatres, by this new arrangement," remarks the "European Magazine"[1] on this procedure, "we cannot but regret that Drury Lane should be thus reopened; and whatever interest may accrue from it to any party, as a species of monopoly, we most unhesitatingly condemn the principle. We leave all notice of the season's conclusion until we are sure that it is really finished; and positively and finally at an end."

The critic was saved the trouble of his "notice," for that season at Drury Lane did not "positively and finally end," but continued straight on through the year. In July, Kean returned to London after his unpleasant experience in America, and at once began to perform at Drury Lane (July 23). Not to be behind, Covent Garden entered the contest, and summer and winter houses struggled through the season. Though it was apparent that the motive of the patentees was completely to silence the summer theatres, nevertheless, by a resort to novelty,

[1] Vol. 79, p. 550; see also vol. 80, pp. 382, 383.

the latter succeeded in keeping their doors open. But the experience was too costly to hazard a repetition. It was time to determine, once for all, whether the English Opera House and the Little Theatre were to be exterminated or to exist independently and in spite of the patent houses; half-existence was no longer endurable. On the closing night at the Haymarket (October 14, 1820) the management announced that the next season would open in a new building. The old building, which had stood for just a century, was pulled down to make room for street improvements. The new Haymarket Theatre was erected on the adjoining lot. On the 4th of the following July, although the new theatre was not yet completed, it opened with an independent company and succeeded in keeping open for four months. At the close of the season (November 2), the manager boldly uttered his defiance at the patent houses, and announced his determination "to try his strength with the great Leviathans of the Drama." Now that the winter theatres had become summer ones, Morris, who was now the Haymarket proprietor, published his intention "to enter upon the open field of public competition, prepared to struggle and endure, ... willing to fight on until he may at last succeed in establishing a company, independent of the large theatres, . . . in a theatre honourably devoted to all the legitimate purposes of the British Drama."

This address contains some of the most radical advances made thus far in the struggle for supremacy between the patent houses and summer theatres. The threat to turn the tables on the patentees, to enter not only their season but also their exclusive monopoly of the legitimate drama, was a daring one, but not without its justification. On the accession of George IV (1820), an application was made (and granted) to extend the Haymarket license to seven months (April 15 to November 15), and the season of 1821 closed with a firm resolve on the part of the Little Theatre manager to take advantage of the privilege.[1]

This had the desired effect on the great houses. The following year (1822) a compromise was brought about, in the presence of the Lord Chamberlain (then the Duke of Montrose), concerning the respective seasons of the winter and summer theatres. The arrangement provided for a return to the original understanding — that the summer theatres should have the advantage of a four months season without interference from the winter houses. Elliston at once officially notified his performers of the agreement, in order that they might renew their connections

[1] *Examiner*, November 4, 1821.

with the summer theatres.[1] When the Duke of Devonshire succeeded the Duke of Montrose in the Lord Chamberlainship, an application was made for a renewal of the agreement of 1822, and was denied. This was followed (1832) by a petition for an extended license at the Haymarket, but as this circumstance is bound up with the general movement of the time, I shall reserve it for its proper place.

Thus ended the long war of encroachments, and the combatants turned their attention to another struggle which had of late years become of paramount importance in the contest for a free stage. This was the fierce competition which had grown up between the majors and minors, and which occupied the public attention from the period reached in our investigation to the close of the struggle.

[1] *London Chronicle*, April 3, 1822. As the English Opera House was still running on its four months license, it was not represented in this settlement, though, of course, reaping the benefits of it.

CHAPTER XI

MAJORS VS. MINORS

EARLY in the eighteenth century, in the days of Queen Anne, men of rank frequently assembled for amusement at a tavern at the rear of Oxford House in High Street, Marylebone Gardens. The place afterwards fell into disrepute, and is the scene of Macheath's debaucheries in the *Beggar's Opera*. About the year 1740 the Gardens were opened for public breakfasts and evening concerts. The entertainments resembled those at Vauxhall, including a varied range of pyrotechnic exhibitions. Among the musical novelties introduced at the Marylebone Gardens was a species which, later, "not only perplexed the sages of the Drama, but posed even the learned in the law," though at that time (when Dr. Arnold was connected with the Gardens) it gave little concern to the patent houses, or any one else.[1]

This was the "burletta," of Italian origin

---

[1] For accounts of places of amusement in London in the eighteenth century see Wroth, *London Pleasure Gardens of the Eighteenth Century*; Boulton, *Amusements of Old London*; Besant, *London in the Eighteenth Century*.

(diminutive of *burla*, mockery), afterwards performed at Covent Garden, and all the minors.
Among the various methods adopted by the
minor theatres, to evade the limitations placed
on their licenses, was to alter, by degrees, the
burletta, or musical farce, until it approximated
the legitimate drama in presentation, though
still retaining its original title. So imperceptible
were these changes that the monopoly had been
almost surrounded and undermined before
serious opposition was raised to the burletta;
and by then, precedent had so thoroughly associated that particular sort of entertainment
with the lesser establishments, distinguishing
them from the guardians of the legitimate drama,
that they could not be dispossessed of it after
the thing itself had become confused with the
regular drama. Furthermore, as we shall see,
the patentees, in an evil moment, sanctioned the
burletta after it had been metamorphosed into
the drama, by bringing on a regular piece under
the title of " burletta."

At the close of the eighteenth century a burletta was generally understood to be " a drama in
rhyme, which is entirely musical; a short comic
piece, consisting of recitative and singing, wholly
accompanied, more or less, by the orchestra." This
is the definition given by the younger Colman.[1]

[1] *Random Records*, i, 46–56.

The word itself seems to have been coined, and hence the dictionaries of the time are void as to its meaning, or so vague and general in defining it that little light was shed by them when the difficulty arose concerning that particular kind of entertainment. Astley got the burletta added to his amphitheatre license in 1787 ; and we have seen how a certain jealousy was manifested by the patentees towards Sadler's Wells when the latter (1788) tried to get a legal sanction for its usurped performances. By stealthy advances the burletta so evolved that, by the time a dozen or so of the minors were well under way, it became a most desirable addition to the annual license ; as by that time it had been made to cover every imaginable phase of the drama from the most trivial farce to *Macbeth* and *Hamlet*.

In 1809, two years after the immense impetus given to minor theatres by the licensing of a half-dozen or more, we may learn something of the meaning of a burletta from the following letter respecting one of the minors. The letter is dated August 29, 1809, and is from the Deputy-Chamberlain to Lord Dartmouth, Chamberlain. It is as follows :

" Mr. Scott, the proprietor of the small theatre [Sans Pareil] situate in Bullen Court in the Strand has just called to solicit a renewal of his licence, and humbly hopes that your Lordship will see no objection to the introduction of the word ' Burlettas,' which are strict musical pieces without dialogue, and which have hitherto been performed under his present licence for music, dancing, song recitative, recitation, and pantomime with optical and mechanical exhibition, but which is not, like Mr. Astley, sufficient to authorize him to continue such representation, and is therefore only desirous that the word 'Burletta' should be inserted, merely for the sake of security, without the smallest intention of extending his performance in the least."[1]

The repeated assurance that Mr. Scott had no intention of gaining any more privileges, but nevertheless wanted the word put into his license, is significant. The attention of the Lord Chamberlain had to be called by the patentees to the abuse practiced by the managers of the minor theatres in their interpretation of "burletta," but that official, feeling his inability to define the species, brought the matter for canvass before the Privy Council. The lawyers, called in to decide the meaning and state the law regulating the burletta, were equally incompetent and timorous.

As if such a decision — or lack of decision — were not victory enough for the minors (since they were thus left practically to de-

[1] *Historical MSS. Commission*, Report XIII⁴, p. 505.

fine for themselves the meaning of their annual
licenses), Covent Garden gave them another
loose to their string by announcing for its own
boards Fielding's *Tom Thumb*, containing dialogue *without* music, giving it the title of "burletta," thus affording the minors a precedent for
interpreting the term in future. The Lord
Chamberlain extricated himself from the difficulty as best he could ; he simply continued to
license the performances known as burlettas on
the grounds that they had been licensed, and he
had been unable to obtain proof or professional
opinion that the performances so licensed were
not burlettas. The Duke of Montrose modified
this decision somewhat (1827), but left the conditions practically unchanged ; he granted licenses to the minors for the performance "call'd
by the manager a Burletta, . . . provided it be,
in legal acceptance, a Burletta." The Chamberlain thus relieved himself of further responsibility in the matter ; the minor manager was still
left to define his own powers, and if the patentees were dissatisfied with the competition that
arose, their attention was called to a recourse in
the Courts of Justice.

By 1833 the mystery attaching to the burletta was dispelled, it had become indistinguish-
able from the drama. " The question of what is
or is not a burletta," writes the editor of the

"Morning Chronicle" (November 29, 1833), "has now, in practice at least, been settled ; it means a drama, with amusing plot, sprightly dialogue, and light sketchy characters, without any music." And it is safe to say that this was a fair definition, taken, as it was, from an examination of a new burletta (by Charles Dance), brought out at the Olympic on the 25th of November, 1833. An amusing illustration will demonstrate the scope assumed by the burletta at this time. In the course of an action in the Queen's Bench, in which Yates of the Adelphi was defendant in a breach of contract suit brought against him by Levy of the Victoria, the question was asked, " What is a burletta ? " Edward Stirling was in the witness chair, and answered, that it was " of French origin, containing necessary singing and music." " Pray," continued the counsel for Levy, " is Mrs. Fitzwilliams an actress or singer ? " " Both," was the answer. " Perhaps you can inform us if it is essential that Ophelia should sing in *Hamlet ?* " pursued the lawyer. " Pardon me," replied Stirling, " I think Shakespeare settled that question before we were born." [1]

I have given this hasty survey of the progress of the musical farce under the *alias* of " burletta," in order that the difficulties, as they arise

[1] *Old Drury Lane*, i, 172.

between the patent theatres and the lesser establishments, may be the better appreciated. Other
evasions and perversions were practiced by the
minors, such as, for example, the uses which
the melodrama were made to serve, as also the
opera, operetta, and so forth; but as these terms
need no explanation, I pass them by. The burletta was the main loop-hole through which the
minors sought escape, though not always successfully, when pursued by the majors. A series
of instances will illustrate.

In 1771 Charles Hughes built and opened an
amphitheatre in Blackfriars-Road to compete with
Philip Astley's circus, which started the previous
year. Charles Dibdin became a partner with
Hughes in 1782, when the name of the place
was changed to the Royal Circus. Here Dibdin
originated the "equestrian drama." The management was in all sorts of difficulties from the
first, and Dibdin made frequent visits to the
King's Bench. In 1805 the Royal Circus burned
down, but was rebuilt and opened the following
year. At first children were the only (human)
actors. Thus far little had occurred to distinguish the Royal Circus from the species signified
by its name. But it was to become one of the
prominent minors by means of an alchemy that
was soon to alter the whole theatrical situation
in London.

On the 23d of February, 1809, — the day
before the burning of Drury Lane Theatre,
— Robert William Elliston became lessee, for
seven years, of the Royal Circus. This transaction marks the real beginning of the revolution
that was to destroy the theatrical monopoly ;
for although the movement was in the air, until
Elliston brought his genius to bear on the situation, no practical line of action had as yet been
laid out. Elliston is a typical example of "the
times and the man." A month after the transaction referred to above, the new manager announced that the house would open on the
ensuing Easter Monday. Pursuant to this advertisement, the newly fitted-up theatre opened
with a new prelude, a melodramatic spectacle,
entitled *The Invisible Avengers*. Although Elliston's engagement at the Lyceum (where the
burnt-out Drury Lane Company was then performing) prevented his appearance at his own
theatre before the middle of June, nevertheless
the opening of the Royal Circus (renamed the
Surrey) was auspicious. The inventive genius of
Elliston in arranging novel performances assured
success from the outset. Among the great number of skillful methods employed by him attention may be called to his alteration of the *Beaux
Stratagem* into a burletta. "The success of this
dramatic transmutation induced a second of a

similar nature ; and some weeks subsequently the
Bold Stroke for a Wife was adroitly invigor-
ated with a decoction of music and mesdames,
the joint patentees of the *nostrum*." The climax,
however, of Elliston's audacity was reached when,
in September, 1809, he actually transformed
Macbeth into a ballet of action, with music, and
represented it at his new Surrey Theatre! [1] It
was in allusion to this circumstance that Sheridan, when in the Privy Council, 1810, cynically
remarked that Elliston had done greater violence
to Shakespeare than to the law.

But so long as Elliston was successful in the
popular eye, he took little account of the means
employed. The first season at the Surrey proved
so successful, that the intrepid manager was induced to attempt an enlargement of his privileges. It has already been remarked that the
licenses hitherto issued to the proprietors of
minor theatres did not permit dialogue, except
with an accompaniment of music. It was the
violation of this provision which caused some
of the actors at Palmer's Royalty Theatre to be
prosecuted by the patentees. On the 5th of

[1] For the chief facts connected with Elliston's managership
of the Surrey (Royal Circus), I have followed Raymond's
Life and Enterprises of Robert William Elliston, Comedian,
pp. 156-171. As Raymond knew Elliston well, and had access
to his private papers and correspondence, I take it that his
book is authoritative.

March, 1810, Sir Thomas Turton presented a petition to the House of Commons to enable Elliston to exhibit and perform at the Surrey Theatre all such entertainments of music as are commonly called pantomimes and ballets, together with operatic or musical pieces, accompanied with dialogue. An alteration in the petition was suggested to Turton, to exempt the proprietor of the Royal Circus from certain penalties under the law regulating dramatic exhibitions. It seems altogether probable that this was a scheme to defeat the petition, for the change called for an exemption of Elliston from penalties that might be incurred for breach of existing laws. Turton consented to the alteration, and the petition was, of course, defeated. The following year Sir T. Turton was one of the chief defenders of patent rights, and it seems strange that he should have been selected to pilot Elliston's petition through Parliament.

Soon after the defeat of his petition Elliston addressed the minister (Perceval) on the subject of an extension of privileges at the Royal Circus, and received as answer the opinion that such a request could not be granted, " except upon a ground which would go to alter the whole principle upon which theatrical entertainments are at present regulated within the metropolis and twenty miles round it." The Surrey, therefore,

continued after the order of its first year's performances, which usually went off "with the
greatest applause" from audiences "of a very
respectable description." [1]

Meantime the Sans Pareil had been added to
the list of minors with the burletta clause in its
license. Astley's and Sadler's Wells were the
other chief competitors of the Surrey at this
time. The Tottenham Concert Rooms, which had
been the home of Colonel Greville's "Pic-Nic
Society," was converted into a circus in 1808,
and in 1810 purchased by a pawnbroker by the
name of Paul, altered for theatrical purposes,
and opened for the first time on the 23d of
April of that year, with burletta attractions.
This latter venture, however, was a failure, and
need not be considered among the minors of
importance.

One other minor of this early period deserves
separate notice. This was the Olympic Pavilion,
erected by Astley, the circus king and horse-
tamer, on a spot in Wych Street where the old
Craven House once stood. This latter building
— which has its own history — had been constructed by Lord Craven early in the seventeenth
century. It was pulled down in 1805, and the
ground leased to Philip Astley. The Amphitheatre at the foot of Westminster Bridge had

[1] *London Chronicle*, April 24, 1810.

but recently burned down (1803), and the manager looked about for a substitute while it was rebuilding, with the result that he secured the Olympic Pavilion. For some time the theatre was quite successful, but this did not long continue and Astley put the place up for sale.

Now, whenever a theatre in England was for sale during the first quarter of the nineteenth century, there was at least one ready purchaser. This was Robert William Elliston, comedian and theatrical manager, who, at that very time, was negotiating for theatres in Dublin, Birmingham, and Edinburgh. On the eighteenth of March, 1813, the managership of the Olympic Pavilion was transferred to Elliston, and on Easter Monday (April nineteenth) of the same year, — the usual time for opening the minors, — the new proprietor opened the place under the name of " Little Drury Lane Theatre, " because of its proximity to Old Drury Lane Theatre. The circumstance of this venture soon brought the patent houses down on Elliston. When the latter secured the Olympic from Astley, he received a guarantee for the continuance of the license, which, as originally granted, extended through the whole year. It was with this understanding that the theatre was now opened for burlettas and musical pieces. Elliston's ambition for theatrical managership was sufficient to arouse the jealousy

of the patentees, while the appropriation of a circus license for theatrical uses incensed them beyond endurance. They at once memorialized the
Lord Chamberlain to the effect that Astley's license permitted him to act at the Pavilion only
when the Amphitheatre was closed, that he had
promised, at the time his license for the Pavilion
was issuing, that he would not violate the arrangement therein contained, and, further, that his
license was for equestrian exhibitions only. The
Lord Chamberlain (Lord Dartmouth) pretended
to have overlooked these details in permitting
Elliston to open the Olympic. Pressed by the proprietors of Covent Garden and Drury Lane, he
felt under the necessity of recalling the permission granted to Elliston to act at " Little Drury. "
Accordingly, Elliston's operations were brought to
a sudden standstill, and the establishment in Wych
Street was closed until the following December,
when the name " Little Drury Lane Theatre "
disappeared, and the " Olympic " was again
adopted, — for it would seem that the former
title, quite as much as the license granted to
Elliston, had aroused the anger of the patentees.[1]

The relative situation of the majors and
minors, sketched in the foregoing paragraphs,
remained unchanged until about 1818 or 1820.
The minors had a comfortable, though by no

[1] Raymond's *Life of Elliston*, p. 216; *Belgravia*, viii, 402.

means exalted, existence on their light fare of musical farces, or burlettas, singing, dancing, rope-walking, and the like. However, the Surrey and Olympic easily led the others in the character of their performances. Drury Lane Theatre had been saved by the providential appearance and engagement of Edmund Kean, "the little man in the cloaks," while Covent Garden was flourishing on exhibitions, little or nothing above those at the minor establishments. Thus far these smaller concerns can hardly be said to have menaced the patent houses, yet the jealousy of the latter was very apparent at every privilege gained by the former.

It was at this period in the history of the London theatres that the minors pushed rapidly to the front, and, for the first time, became really inimical to the welfare of the "great houses." The causes may be traced to numerous sources, — to be dealt with in another place. At present it is sufficient to enumerate the most important of these causes. The gradual development of the burletta has already been noticed, and to Elliston, more than any one else, was this innovation due, though T. Dibdin of the Surrey also deserves a front rank among minor managers. As the exhibitions of the minors approached the regular drama, the tendency was assisted by the decline of the per-

formances at the patent theatres, and especially
at Covent Garden, where spectacles, melodramas, and animal shows banished the legitimate drama from their boards. This, of course,
brought the majors and minors towards a common ground for competition, while the process
emphasized the importance of the smaller concerns. The appearance of Sir Walter's novels,
and, later, those of Cooper and others, gave an
impetus to the movement already begun, as the
melodramatic incidents of these works of fiction
were immediately dramatized for the stage, and
brought out at the patent houses and the minors
indiscriminately. It was a time of melodramatic
tastes, and the success of the smaller theatres
— from which melodrama was not excluded,
because it did not belong to the legitimate cate-
gory — in bringing these out, drove the "great
houses" into the competition for popular favor.

Add to this, the main fact to keep sight of,
another, namely, that it cost the patent houses
more to "dress" a piece for the stage, and we
may well understand the disadvantage to which
they were put in the competition. Furthermore,
the copyright law was no defense, either to
dramatic authors or to the patentees ; the
minors were free to appropriate any piece they
desired, which they did as soon as it had been
tried at one of the large houses.

Still other causes magnified the situation, among which may be mentioned the mismanagement which characterized the patent houses at this time; the appearance of trans-Atlantic steamships, by which, towards the close of the struggle, actors could seek an asylum on the American side when dissatisfied with the patentees, thus depriving the latter of their chief attractions and support; the accession of a new king (1820), an event usually followed by a clamor for privileges of all sorts; and, finally, a general stirring of the reform movement, in no sense congenial to the theatrical monopoly. From this on (*circa* 1818), the newspaper and magazine assume an interest in the theatrical contest, such as had not previously appeared.

At this time another minor was added to the already considerable list of " irregular " theatres. The foundation stone of this new theatre was laid (by proxy), in the fall of 1816, by Prince Leopold of Coburg, husband to the Princess Charlotte, chief patron of the undertaking. In honor of the Prince the new theatre was called the " Coburg." In 1833 (on the occasion of a visit from the Princess) the name was changed to " Victoria." The place was first opened on Saturday evening, May 9, 1818, with a private rehearsal, and, on the following Monday evening, it presented to the public *The*

Trial by Battle, which ran a number of times and was well received.[1] This little theatre was a troublesome competitor from the start, not only of the patent houses, but also of the other minors.

The main contest, however, at this time, was waged by the Surrey and the Olympic, with T. Dibdin at the head of the former, and Elliston at the latter. On the 23d of January, 1818, " a new grand melo-drama, founded on Mr. Coleridge's favourite dramatic Poem, called Zapolya, or The War Wolf," was announced (in the " Morning Chronicle ") by the Surrey manager as the attraction for Monday, the 2d of February. A week later (January 30) the advertisement was changed, *Zapolya* was pushed forward to the 9th of February, and *House Warming*, with *The Italian Wife*, placed for the 2d of February. No reason is given for this alteration in the bills, and the announcement of these plays is printed in ordinary type. Moreover, it was customary at the Surrey to announce coming attractions at least a week in advance of their representation. In the case of *Fazio*, or *The Italian Wife*, the advertisement appeared in the daily prints only two days before the performance.

[1] *London Chronicle*, May 12, 1818 ; *Morning Chronicle*, May 21, 1818 ; *European Magazine*, May, 1818.

These proceedings are accounted for by the popularity *Fazio* was making for itself at the Bath Theatre, where it was first produced on the 6th of January (1818).[1] Dibdin, learning of its success, saw the opportunity for increasing the rank of his already favored theatre, and, altering his plans on short notice, represented *Fazio* as an *acting* play on the 2d of February.[2] The piece did not disappoint the expectations of the Surrey manager; but it aroused the ire of the patentees, for, as given by Dibdin, it belonged really to the regular drama. Besides, the Covent Garden manager contemplated bringing it out himself, and to be thus forestalled in the undertaking was the source of much offense to him. On the 4th of February, however, Covent Garden gave out in capitals the "new tragedy of FAZIO," for "tomorrow evening." Three days later, Dibdin again dared to offer to the public " (for this night only) the very favourite serious Melo-drama, as originally produced at this Theatre, taken from Mr. Millman's Tragedy of Fazio, called The ITALIAN WIFE." After this, the piece ap-

[1] Genest, viii, 669.

[2] The previous season (1817) the Surrey did not close until the 28th of October. It opened again on the 28th of December, "for a short winter season," closing on the 2d of March (1818). *European Magazine*, vol. 72, pp. 458–550.

peared at Covent Garden twelve times [1] before
the middle of April, and then gave place to
more popular attractions.

This piece of audacity on the part of Dibdin
had scarcely been equaled at any of the other
minors. The competition between the minor and
major on this occasion was unquestionable, and
the fact was irritating to the patentees. Elliston,
over at the Olympic, was not far behind Dibdin
at the Surrey, and, the same year in which the
above circumstance occurred, succeeded in bringing the large houses down on him with a petition
to the Lord Chamberlain. The patentees complain that they find "their long established patent
rights destroyed, upon the faith of which a million of money have been embarked in their two
theatres," and that they must suffer " certain
ruin " if the Olympic and Sans Pareil were allowed to continue. The Sans Pareil was probably
included in the complaint as a mere blind to
cover the enmity of the patentees for the Olympic.
Elliston came out with an answer to this memorial, in a manner so characteristic as to bear
quoting in part. He denied that the minors had
commenced the system of encroachments, — these

---

[1] Viz., Feb. 9, 16, 19, 23, 28, March 2, 5, 9, 27, April 3,
10, 15. See *Morning Chronicle* for dates. *Fazio* was revived
at Covent Garden on the 12th of February, 1831. *Morning
Chronicle*, February 13, 1831.

tactics had originated with the patentees. "The Patent Theatres have become theatres for the display of the *irregular* drama," said Elliston in his reply. "The encroachment was, in truth, commenced by the Patent Theatres on the Minor Theatres, and not by the Minor Theatres on the Patent Theatres; and it was in the rage of en-grossing the whole store of stage exhibition, from the deep pathos of tragedy to the highest flights of tight-rope dancing—from the amblings of the poet to the amblings of the riding-horse — from the splendid illusions of the scene-painter to the sloppings of the stage with 'real water' — from the Attic playfulness of 'Congreve' to the more congenial playfulness of 'Puss in Boots.'. . .

"Posture-masters must be found (for the Minor Theatres), who should writhe themselves into more contortions than Mr. Pack was employed to do on the stage of the Theatre Royal, Drury Lane: dogs must be found who should bark more eloquently than the 'Dog of Montarges' was engaged to do on the stage of the Theatre Royal, Covent Garden: Children[1] must be found to support the dignity of the Minor Stage,

[1] The craze for child actors began when Master Betty made his appearance in 1804, and continued to revive, on occasion, as late as 1830, when Master Burke represented Shylock at one of the patent houses. The climax of this folly may be found in an advertisement in June, 1807, when Miss Biddy (four years old) was announced as Caliban!

as effectually as ' the dignity ' of ' the great
national concern ' of Drury Lane was supported,
lately, by the little girl who personated ' Richard
the Third : ' horses must be found to prance, if
possible, more classically than those that sustained the ' regular ' and ' national drama ' of
' Timour the Tartar.' Poor Mr. Astley ! (the
original proprietor of the Olympic) used to exclaim pathetically, ' Why do they take my horses?
I never tried to engage Mrs. Siddons.' " [1]

Notwithstanding the burlesque running
through this defense, it is, in the main, true
to actual conditions, and so forcibly did Elliston
impress this fact on the Lord Chamberlain's
understanding that he was persuaded to sustain
the Olympic manager in his course. The public,
too, felt that the action of the patentees was particularly ill-advised at that time. One of their
pleas had been that the two minors (Olympic
and Sans Pareil) customarily took in £150 nightly at their doors, thus depriving the two winter
houses of " their chance of profit and the means
of supporting the dignity of the national drama."
This was a weak admission, in view of the fact
that the success of the minors was due to their
acting plays similar to those at the patent houses,[2]

[1] *New Monthly Magazine*, 1829, pt. i, p. 176; *Life of Elliston*, p. 251.

[2] See letter of "T. B." in *Literary Journal*, August 29, 1818. It

and it was on this evidence that Elliston maintained his position.

Towards the close of the following year (1819) the patentees again broke out in opposition to the minors, intending utterly to exterminate them. Threats were made of restricting the lesser theatres to the old mummery of dumb show, a taste for which the public had long since outgrown, and which would have been tolerated only in a Bartholomew Fair. The Coburg manager (Glossop) retorted to these menaces, and "Dramaticus" defended the minors in a letter to the "Literary Chronicle" (January 22, 1820). The monopoly was fiercely attacked, and the growing jealousy of the patentees was accounted for by the respectability of the minors. It was hoped that, if conviction followed the prosecution of the minors, legislation would result, making future outrages of the kind impossible.

But the time had passed for annihilating the minors. Neither the strength of the patent houses nor the inclination of public opinion would justify such extreme measures. The patentees might pester the small theatres with persecutions, but the minors were now too numerous and too

is amusing to observe the change of front Elliston assumed within a year from this time. We have already seen the *hauteur* which, as lessee of Drury Lane, he displayed towards the minors.

vigorous to be driven from the field. In 1819 the Surrey and the Coburg closed their doors only two weeks, and then only to be refurbished for the Easter performances, opening again on the 12th of April. At the Surrey " the House was well filled, and the curtain fell amidst peals of applause." At the Coburg "the house was crowded to excess, and augured a successful season." Even the amphitheatre "notwithstanding the wetness of the night was well filled." Such is the flattering testimony of one of the leading papers of the day.[1] The other minors, too, were in the line of progress, commanding the attention of the theatre-going public, and of the critics. "The houses usually designated *Minor*," comments one of the editors of the dramatic column of the " Literary Chronicle " (December 4, 1819), " continue to display an activity which we should like to see imitated by less humble establishments. . . . New pieces have been produced at the *Adelphi*,[2] the Coburg, the East London, and *Astley's* theatres, all of which have been successful and continue to attract crowded houses." In one issue of the " London Magazine " (March, 1820) fifteen columns are devoted to a review of the

[1] *London Chronicle*, April 13, 1819.

[2] In 1819 Jones and Rodwell leased the Sans Pareil, opening it on October 18, under the name of Adelphi. The East London Theatre was the same as the Royalty.

minors; and though some severe criticism is passed (on the low order of the audiences at the Coburg, for example), a spirit of praise dominates the article. Alluding to the East London Theatre the critic laconically disposes of it in this significant passage: " It is sufficient to observe that Mr. Rae is the principal tragic actor there, and Mr. Peter Moore the chief manager. After this, is it to be wondered at that Covent Garden is almost deserted, and that Mr. Elliston cannot yet afford to give up the practice of puffing at the bottom of his play-bills ! " At the Coburg, T. P. Cooke was giving vigor and success to the new establishment by his acting.

Even Sadler's Wells caught the spirit of the time, erected a respectable new building, banished buffoonery, made an approach to the regular drama, and so improved the character of its *dramatis personae* that the old complaint of vitiated taste and bad morals attaching to the establishment was dispelled.[1] But the Olympic probably led the minors in competition, taking rank with Covent Garden. " Too much praise," says one of the periodicals of the time, " cannot be given to the taste and liberality of the new proprietors,[2] who . . . have at once put their

[1] *Literary Chronicle*, September 23, 1820.

[2] When Elliston took Drury Lane Theatre (1819) he leased the Olympic to Messrs. Barlow and Reeve for ten years.

theatre on an equal footing with their winter
rival. In no respect but in size does the Olympic
differ from the patent habitation of the Muses;
and how far this is a disadvantage still remains
a point of question. We must confess our own
prejudices are and have been strongly in favour
of Covent Garden, but the public feeling goes
evidently with the smaller houses: the Olympic
has been nightly crowded to excess, and people
have been regularly dismissed in crowds for
want of room." [1]

The Adelphi also deserves special mention
as early manifesting a respectability, making it
a dangerous rival to the " great houses." Under
the management of Jones and Rodwell, the
Adelphi was put into condition for attracting
public attention, though possibly with too much
of the tinsel about it to rank it with the Olympic
or the Little Theatre in the Haymarket. [2] It
was under the managership of Terry that the
Adelphi pulled away from the majority of the
minors, and took its place along with the Olympic as a formidable rival of the patent houses. [3]
Under Yates and Mathews, the Adelphi was
finally put in the first rank by public favor. " I
trust you do not put the Adelphi on a level with

[1] *Lady's Magazine*, October, 1820.

[2] See *Examiner* for October 28, 1821.

[3] *European Magazine*, February, 1826.

its restricted neighbours," complains a "Play-
goer" to the " Tatler " (November 17, 1830) for
not printing the complete play-bill of that theatre.
"Can Covent Garden produce a list of comedians
equal to Mathews, Yates, Reeve, Buckstone, and
Wilkinson?" And another enthusiast breaks
out, " We must observe, that the acting of Mrs.
Yates in a domestic tragedy (as it is termed)
called *Grace Huntley*, at the Adelphi, is just as
near perfection as anything on a stage can be.
She is a Garrick in petticoats. . . . " [1] For
the ten years following the beginnings of this
rapid rise of the minors into prominence, the
newspapers and magazines were filled with a
marked approval of the tendency, similar to
that shown in the few excerpts quoted.

The patent houses did not seem to decline in
proportion to the growing importance of the
minors. The Keans and the Kembles had kept
the old hulks from sinking ; but the successes
of the patent houses during this period were
merely temporary. Some good days were yet
before the "great houses," but this served only
to bring out the decadence which was upon the
old establishments. The harbinger of this decline may be traced from the beginning of the
century, but certainly nowhere more distinctly
than in the brilliant recklessness of Elliston's

[1] *New Monthly Magazine* for 1833, pt. iii, p. 351.

managership of Drury Lane Theatre, — covering the very years when the minors were getting into line for the final conflict. "These theatres," says "Tait's" (November, 1832), remarking on the minors, "from their number, and supported by the talent consequent on competition, have assumed a position formidable to the patent houses by rivalry in excellence, and important to the public in opening up new channels for the efflux of amusements, 'various yet the same,' and of far more attainable price. Within the last three or four years they have challenged an attention they seldom previously received, and rarely deserved; and by unceasing and well-directed efforts have at length fairly effected a more than equal division in the public patronage. . . . There is at this moment scarcely a minor theatre in London that does not possess one or more *stars*, persons of established celebrity either, or of rapidly rising reputation." Liston, Mrs. Orger, and Madame Vestris were at the Olympic; at the Surrey were Osbaldison and Mrs. West; Sadler's Wells boasted Mrs. Fitzwilliams; while the Strand (recently founded by Rayner) was " a practical refutation to the arguments of the monopolists, and a crying rebuke to illiberal licensers."

This fairly won position was not reached, however, without many a tilt with the patentees, who, the nearer they approached their doom, grew the fiercer towards the minors. In 1826 the old contest between the winter and summer houses (among which latter were numbered various of the minors) broke out again.[1] Led on by the Adelphi and Surrey, where tragedy, comedy, opera, farce, and melodrama were produced in giddy succession, the lesser establishments bade defiance to the patentees, and courted the penalties of the law regulating theatricals.[2] Some of the minor managers became so fearless in the game against the patent houses that they had a special clause inserted in the articles of the actors, guaranteeing the latter against arrest while the " business " of the stage was in progress. In other words, arrangements were secured with the officers of the law whereby a writ might wait the pleasure of the actor before being served.[3] Various other schemes were adopted for evading the law, while in some instances, as already mentioned, no attempt was made by the managers to screen themselves from the wrath

[1] In the *Wasp* for October 21, 1826, there is a sharp burlesque on the patentees for their action on this occasion.

[2] *New Monthly Magazine*, December, 1828, pt. iii, p. 528. Elliston was once more back at the Surrey, whither he went after failing at Drury Lane in 1826.

[3] This was related of the Victoria (*i. e.* Coburg) especially. See *New Monthly Magazine*, 1836, pt. iii, p. 171.

of the patentees. Occasionally, however, they went too far in their bold defiance (feeling safe in the protection of public opinion), and made the opportunity too strong an invitation for the patentees to pounce upon them in revenge.

In 1830 such an opportunity was afforded the patent houses, and they were not long in availing themselves of it. The persecutions begun at this time developed into a crusade against the minors, which scarcely ceased for the next five or six years, and was influential in hastening the downfall of the established theatres. The first object of attack singled out by the patentees was Chapman, manager of the Tottenham Street Theatre. Information was laid against him by the large theatres, charging him with giving stage entertainments without a license from the Lord Chamberlain. That the charge was true was notorious. An examination of the play-bills suffices to prove that something more than "dancing, singing, and dumb shows" were represented at the theatre in Tottenham Street. However, as the result of a technical slip, the patentees were unable to prove what everybody knew to be a fact, and the information against Chapman was dismissed by the Bow Street magistrate. At once mending their case, the monopolists made another trial; but in the opinion of the Justice, they did not mend it aright; and the Tottenham company were free to practice the old offenses over again.[1]

As a matter of legal justice, there can be no doubt that the patentees were in the right ; but the sympathy of the public was almost wholly opposed to the law, and the police court simply echoed the sentiment of the public when it dismissed Chapman. The more sober-minded, however, who believed in enforcing law so long as it remained on the statute-books, thought that the patentees had not received fair treatment, either from the court or from the assembled auditors. The treatment of C. Kemble, of Covent Garden, and his counsel on this occasion was especially rude, the crowd breaking out into jeers and insults against them. But the managers of the great houses were not to be browbeaten after any such fashion. Stinging under defeat and the taint of obloquy, the patentees bided their time for revenge. Meantime the Tottenham Theatre pursued its course in boastful safety.

For nearly six months the affairs of Chapman continued in a prosperous condition. But on the 6th of December (1830) the following advertisement of his theatre appeared in the daily papers : " LAST NIGHT but FIVE of the present

[1] *New Monthly Magazine*, August, 1830 ; London correspondent in *Edinburgh Literary Journal*, July 8, December 4, 1830. See also case of *Patentees vs. Chapman*.

COMPANY'S PERFORMING. A full explanation of the causes which have led to this sudden result will be given to the Public in the Bills of Thursday next." On the same day announcement was made that the Tottenham Theatre had been leased for twenty-one years by George MacFarren, who, it was reported, had secured Winston as manager. On Saturday evening, December 11 (1830), the theatre closed.[1] After the performance, W. Vining, in behalf of the proprietors (Melrose and Chapman), explained to the audience the circumstance causing the theatre to be closed. This had been due to an information (the third) laid by the patentees against the managers for representing the regular drama in violation of the Licensing Act. This time the patentees had been cautious enough to carry their suit to Lord Tenterden of the King's Bench, a man noted for his scrupulous integrity in interpreting the law. There was but one course open to such a judge, the defendants were found guilty; and the Tottenham Theatre was closed.

This decision was the occasion of an outburst of indignation against the monopoly. The ultimate decision, it was declared, would be influenced mainly by public opinion — and that was strongly opposed to every species of monopoly. People would not permit their enjoyments to be

[1] *Morning Chronicle*, under dates.

restricted because of some antiquated act of Parliament, the operations of which were unequal. No one would dream of contending, continued the argument in favor of the minors, that some people have a right to the convenience of a theatre at their door, while others ought to be precluded from such privileges.[1] The feeling against the theatrical monopoly ran so high that a remonstrance meeting was finally called at the Albion Tavern, in the interests of the dramatists and minor managers. Serle, the dramatist, delivered an effective speech, and Webster, Rayner, Davidge, and others, interested in theatrical property outside the patent houses, vented their opinions on the occasion. The result of this discussion took form in a series of resolutions. These called attention to the respectability of the minors; the injustice of the prosecutions brought against them; the perverted uses to which the patents had been put, and the changed conditions in the metropolis demanding an abolition of the monopoly; ending with an appeal to the press to assist the cause of the minors, and a determination to petition King and Parliament for a repeal of the restrictive laws.[2]

[1] *Tatler*, December 22, 1831.

[2] *Tatler*, December 26, 1831; *Gentleman's Magazine*, vol. ci, pt. 2, Supplement, p. 643; *Ladies' Museum*, January, 1832.

Much was looked for from the contemplated petition of the minors, not only for the theatres themselves, but for authors as well. For it seemed certain that the claims of the latter to protection must enter into any parliamentary discussion of the state of the drama. Relative to this meeting of the minor managers a writer in the " New Monthly Magazine " for February, 1832, says, " That the law must afford these establishments protection is evident ; and from the convenient dimensions of these theatres, . . . it is probable that a revival of the genuine English drama will take place ; by the equity of the legislature may the hope of the dramatist at length be realized." And the belief was expressed that the time was at last at hand to break down the monopoly of the "great theatres " that had degraded the drama and forced the actor to substitute trickery for talent. But more of this in another place. On leaving the Tottenham Street Theatre, Chapman took refuge in a building in Grub (Milton) Street that had been but the year before (1829) converted from a chapel into a theatre, called the City Theatre (later, the City Pantheon). But the patentees followed him up and compelled him to abandon the business of a manager.

A number of new minors sprang up about this time. The Pavilion, in the ghetto quarters, was opened in 1829 by Wyatt and Farrell. The following year the Garrick was opened in Leman Street, near the site of the Royalty Theatre and that of the Goodman's Fields, where Garrick had made his *début* to a London audience. Braham, the tenor, began his St. James Theatre in 1835, and the City of London Theatre (Norton Folgate) also started that same year. Two years later the Royal Standard was added to the list. But by far the most important of these recruits was Rayner's New Subscription Theatre in the Strand. This theatre had been used, prior to 1831, for panoramic exhibitions, but in that year Rayner, the impersonator, converted it into a theatre and opened it on the 25th of January, 1832, without the Lord Chamberlain's license. The proprietor attempted to evade the law by the stratagem of selling his tickets of admission at a neighboring chocolate-house, it being understood that the audience should be admitted gratis, after purchasing a ticket as aforesaid.

This bold ruse was more than the patentees could stand, and, as their blood was already up from the contest with Chapman, they caused informations to be laid against, and warrants to be issued for the arrest of Mrs. Waylett, and Messrs. Abbot and Keeley for acting at an unlicensed theatre. The change of tactics, from in-

forming against the manager of a minor theatre
to laying their charges against the actors, had
been suggested as a result of their numerous suits
against Chapman (and others) before getting a
decision in their favor. Furthermore, it occurred
to them that the penalty for violating the " for
hire, gain, or reward " clause applied as strin-
gently to *all* the actors as to the *one* manager.
Hence more damage would be caused the minors
by the course adopted on the present occasion.
But no sooner had the patentees taken this step
than they saw their blunder, for it was no easy
matter to prove that the actors were receiving
any benefits from the chocolate-house dodge, or
from any other source.

The announcement that the patentees had determined on prosecuting the Strand actors was
made at the annual meeting of the Drury Lane
Committee, July 7, 1832, but the few members
present showed little interest in the warlike
proclamation, which grew out of Captain Polhill's
plea of his inability to pay the entire amount
of the rental due on Drury Lane, owing to the
formidable rivalry of the minor theatres.[1] There
seems to have been a good deal of halting and
cross-purpose action on the part of the com-

[1] This account follows the reports given in the *Morning
Chronicle* for July 9, 16, 23, 1832. Captain Polhill was at this
time lessee of Drury Lane Theatre.

mittee against the Strand actors, for in a short
time after the report that a prosecution was in
hand it was suddenly given out that the counsel for the patentees had found themselves
wrong in their course, and that the threatened
prosecution• had been abandoned. To protect
themselves from ridicule, the Drury Lane Committee caused it to be noised about that their
menace was only intended for a joke. But everybody knew that the monopolists were in no jocose
mood, and it was asserted, by those who pretended to know, that the prosecution had been
stopped, not because the patentees were afraid
they could not convict the Strand actors, but
because the query would be forthcoming why
they had not resorted to this plain and simple
remedy years before, instead of complaining
that the law was not sufficient to protect their
property.

Whatever the cause, the Strand prosecution
was, for the moment, dropped. In the ensuing
autumn (1832), at their regular meeting for
licensing theatres, the Middlesex magistrates
refused to grant any privileges to the Strand
proprietor. Nothing daunted by this rebuff, the
manager continued to keep open his theatre after
the manner devised at the first,[1] until information was laid against Davenport (manager of a

[1] *Lady's Magazine*, November, 1832.

minor called The Westminster, then but recently
erected in York Street), followed by his conviction, when it closed. In the following year Miss
Kelly applied for a license to open the Strand,
but she also was refused, probably because the
committee in Parliament in charge of Bulwer's
Dramatic Performance Bill (to be considered in
the next chapter) had not included the Strand
in its recommended schedule of London theatres.
This action of the committee involved not only
the Strand Theatre, but also the two other theatres recently established (the City of London,
and the Garrick). This treatment was looked
upon as a great injustice ; for although the performances at the Strand were not of the highest
dramatic order, " surely," says the " Observer,"
" these are not times for drawing nice distinctions ; and everybody will acknowledge them to
be a vast deal more ' legitimate,' entertaining,
and useful, than half the performances at the
two *soi-disant* PATENT Theatres during the
whole of last season." [1] Unwilling to take chances
on the methods pursued by Rayner, Miss Kelly
began a series of mono-dramatic entertainments
for that summer.

The precarious tenure on which the Strand
was compelled to operate, if at all, caused it to
change hands frequently. On the 30th of Sep-

[1] Quoted in *Morning Chronicle*, July 1, 1833.

tember, 1833, it opened under the management of Messrs. Wrench and Russell. The performance on this occasion began with an address intended to burlesque the struggle between the majors and minors. The competition of the theatres was described in the language of a sailing match. The inequality of opportunity given the " vessels" was emphasized, and the hits at the patent houses were frequent and pointed.[1] The operations of the new managers came to a sudden standstill, however, within a few weeks after the opening. The official attention of the Lord Chamberlain (Duke of Devonshire) was called to the fact that, notwithstanding the recent conviction of Davenport in the Court of Common Pleas, the Strand was again open with dramatic entertainments. To avoid prosecution the managers were compelled to close their theatre. The "Observer" hastened to explain that "it will be perceived at once that the circumstances connected with the Strand Theatre are peculiar, and such as do not belong to any other place of amusement, whether licensed or unlicensed, in the Kingdom. It does not by any means follow that the Duke of Devonshire is to embroil himself with other Minor Theatres in the metropolis, when the law has pointed out a short and clear remedy should parties interested in licensed

[1] *Morning Chronicle*, October 1, 1833.

houses think it worth while to proceed against them." [1]

Fifty persons were thrown out of employment by the closing of the Strand Theatre. The personal character of Russell, the celerity with which he obeyed the suggestion of the Lord Chamberlain to discontinue his performances, together with the spirited and honest endeavor he put forth to give employment to his company of actors, merited, and received, the sympathy of the public. Notwithstanding the open lawlessness which had attended the managership of the Strand thus far, the circumstance of the numerous prosecutions of the actors and managers was an ultimate victory for the minors.

But the ill-starred Strand was destined to further persecutions by the patentees.[2] Early in 1835 we find this diatribe against the powers that were : ." The Chamberlain, the Mashes, and their myrmidons, *common informers*, to wit, are arrayed in battle against this neat and well-conducted little theatre. The Duke of Devonshire evinced some degree of delicacy in his official capacity, for though he suffered the theatre to be prosecuted, he would neither suffer his name to

---

[1] Quoted in *Morning Chronicle*, October 21, 1833.

[2] After the closing of the theatre in 1833 Russell began to give some dramatic monologues, modeled on Mathew's "Annual." *Morning Chronicle*, November 26, 1833.

appear in it or allow the solicitor for the office to conduct the case. . . . Williams and Forrester are summoned to Bow Street on Tuesday next, and we trust their defence will be such as to show clearly to the world the rottenness of the cause against them, and cover their prosecutors with shame. If the actors are convicted, there is not a minor theatre in London that will remain unattacked."

After needless delays, the two actors were tried,[1] and, following the precedent of the previous Strand cases, there was but one verdict open to the Justices. If Rayner, Davenport, and Russell had been guilty of violating the Licensing Act, so had Williams and Forrester.

It would seem that such a record of misfortune from the outset would deter theatrical aspirants from undertaking the management of the Strand. However, such was not the case. At the beginning of 1836 MacFarren, the actor, gave out that he would open the theatre on the 11th of January. This date was postponed to the 16th, when the Strand was opened on the plan of an Italian theatre. But it was no sooner open than an order came from the Lord Chamberlain's office commanding that its doors be shut.[2] The story of the struggle grows

---

[1] *Examiner*, February 15, 22, 1835.

[2] *Spectator*, January 9, 16, 23, 1836.

monotonous. The opening and closing of the
Strand Theatre for the first four years of its
existence followed each other in kaleidoscopic
succession. Within two weeks after MacFarren was driven out, Rayner was once more at
the old stand to try his fortune, but succeeded
only in adding another victory to the majors.[1]
Finally, on the accession of the Marquis of Conyngham to the office of Chamberlain, a license
was granted to Rayner for the Strand Theatre,
placing it on equal terms with the most favored
of the minors, the Adelphi and Olympic.[2] Soon
after this the management of the Strand passed
into the hands of Douglas Jerrold and his son-
in-law Hammond,[3] future lessee of Drury Lane
Theatre, under whom it was opened on Monday,
April 25, 1836. Jerrold made his first appearance as an actor on the initial evening.

Once more before the downfall of the monopoly was the Strand to suffer the persecution of
the patentees. In the summer of 1840 a portion of Hammond's company opened the theatre,
but it was suddenly closed in consequence of an
information against three of the actors for playing for hire without the Lord Chamberlain's
license. The charge was not proved, the Bow-

---

[1] Fraser's *Literary Chronicle*, February 6, 1836.

[2] *Examiner*, March 20, 1836.

[3] *Spectator*, April 30, 1836.

Street magistrate dismissed the defendants, and the informers were compelled to settle the costs. The company, however, did not recommence their performances at the Strand, the heavy penalties seeming to them too hazardous.[1] Meantime other theatrical events were occurring and combining to draw the long struggle for a free stage to a close.

[1] *Spectator*, August 22, 1840.

CHAPTER XII

THE new school of dramatists now took up the fight in earnest against the theatrical monopoly, primarily in their own interests, but unavoidably involving the fortunes of the minor theatres. Since the "great houses" claimed the exclusive privilege of acting the national drama, the increasing dramatic output was limited to a narrow field of available demand. Furthermore, under the monopoly, which might (and often did) reject good plays, — knowing that they had the whole range to choose from, — the dramatists had no recourse, with their unaccepted plays, to other managers. Carelessness and ignorance too frequently resulted in the examination of dramas under the patent system, with injustice to the talents of aspiring dramatists. Add to these complaints the lack of copyright protection, and the case of the dramatic writers will appear deserving of attention.

The dramatists and the minors, having a common cause for dissatisfaction, now joined forces against the majors. The remonstrance meeting held towards the close of 1831, as a result of the Tottenham Theatre persecutions, was led by Serle, and the resolutions passed at that time were drawn up by him. Out of this preliminary meeting sprang another, held on the 24th of February, 1832, at the City of London Tavern, for the purpose of memorializing Parliament "against the system of oppression which has so long fettered and discouraged dramatic authors." This time, Mr. Edward Bulwer presided, and, as at the former meeting, the charges against the monopoly were numerous and vigorous. "Surely," writes the London correspondent to the "Edinburgh Spectator" (March 3, 1832), "it is but just to require that the court of competition be open to all; that a fair reading be given before competent judges, and the play, if approved, be submitted to a prompt stage trial;" and the effort of the dramatists "to emancipate dramatic genius from the monopoly under which it now writhes" is highly commended. Moncrieff gave an illustration of the methods employed by the patentees in their treatment of the dramatists. He had submitted a play to Covent Garden. After waiting an unusual time for a reply, he finally demanded a return of the piece. After much trouble expended in searching for it, he received it from the hands of the fireman at the theatre, who had, presumably, been appointed to read and pass judgment on it. It was from the indignity and injustice such as this that the dramatists now determined to free themselves.

On the 22d of May, 1832, in the House of Commons, Bulwer presented a petition signed by " noblemen, gentlemen, merchants, traders, and others, of London," praying for a repeal of all legislative enactments tending to restrict the performance of the drama in the metropolis. Mr. Bulwer announced his intention of moving a Select Committee to examine into the state of dramatic literature, with a view to founding a bill upon the report. The member (Mr. Hunt) seconding the motion went straight to the point, saying that it was high time the monopoly was abolished.

The proprietors of Drury Lane and Covent Garden Theatres followed this action with a petition (May 30) praying for a protection of their rights. On the last day of the month Bulwer brought forward his motion to appoint a Select Committee for the purpose stated above. It was thought, at the time, that this was a result of the decision against the minors by the Lord Chancellor, the previous year; but that formed but a single factor in the case, and the demand for investigating the dramatic situation would have come anyhow. Bulwer prefaced his motion by a long and forcible speech, in which he demonstrated that not only had the conditions producing the monopoly ceased long since, but also that the monopoly had not executed the function intrusted to its care, — the support and dignity of the national drama. In the Restoration period Davenant had been guilty of resorting to scenic display and spectacular exhibitions ; but especially during the period immediately preceding 1832 the patent houses had been prolific of amusements of a cheap order. Now, therefore, argued Mr. Bulwer, since the legislature had protected the patent theatres in their vast and exclusive privileges, for the sole purpose of maintaining the national drama, it was the duty of that body to say to the monopoly, " Where are the plays to produce and encourage which we gave you the exclusive privilege ? Where are the immortal tragedies, where are the chaste and brilliant comedies ? You were to preserve the dignity of the drama from being corrupted by mountebank actors and absurd performances ; you have, therefore, we trust, driven jugglers and harlequins from the national stage ; you have admitted no wild beasts ; you have introduced no fire-eaters and sword-swallowers ; you have preserved the dignity of the national drama inviolate ; you have left it such as it was when you took it from the hands of Ben Jonson or

Shakespeare ; for if you have not done this, then you have not fulfilled that object for which we took from your brethren those privileges we have intrusted to you." [1]

It was confidently denied that the objects of the monopoly had been realized ; and to enforce a law to support such a monopoly was a " monstrous injustice . . . inflicted on the public." Moreover it was absurd to ask the theatre-goers of London to tramp from every quarter of the metropolis to Drury Lane and Covent Garden, and when there, to see, not a tragedy or comedy, but " a very fine scene in a very bad melo-drama — or, perhaps, if they were in eminent luck, a couple of lions and a diorama by way of keeping up the national drama." The size of the patent theatres had been largely responsible, it was admitted, for this state of affairs. If, as the patentees had so frequently declared, the theatres had been enlarged to accommodate the increased population of the metropolis, that fact, as well as the resulting degraded drama, led to one conclusion : more theatres were needed, and they should be free from the precarious conditions then existing. If it were retorted to this, that the minor theatres were allowed to exist in spite

[1] *Hansard's Debates*, 3d Series, vol. xiii, 239–259 ; *Mirror of Parliament*, 10th Parliament, 2d Sess., pp. 2154, 2344, 2357.

of their illegality, then the rejoinder was at
hand, that the law still existed on the statute-
books, making the tenure of the minor manager
too uncertain. That law, if enforced, was denounced as unjust; if a dead letter, it was a
mockery. The law must be defined, demanded
Bulwer. The public should know which theatres
should exist; the actors, which plays might be
performed. As the law then stood, it was "an
iniquitous uncertainty, which, while it rendered
the property of the minor theatres so precarious
and illegal, frittered away by contraband far
more than it would by open rivalry, the property
of the great theatres." Endless prosecutions and
constant litigations were the products of the
laws as they then stood.

The office of examiner of plays was also attacked as a useless and objectionable feature of the
dramatic system. Bulwer insisted that "the only
true censor of the age was the spirit of the age."
The public and the press were thought to be
better censors by far than any "ignorant and
bungling official" appointed for that purpose.
And as to the number of theatres, of that too
the public should be the judges. They were not
likely to build more than they could support,
and they should be permitted to have all they
needed. So also no restrictions should be placed
on the legitimate drama; it was absurd to sanc-

tion what is frivolous, and forbid what is great.
Bulwer would have the stage free as it was in
the days of "Massinger, and Beaumont and
Fletcher, Jonson and Shakespeare, when seventeen theatres were constantly open to a metropolis a tenth part of the size of London at present,
and a population a hundred degrees less wealthy
and intelligent."

The objections raised to Bulwer's motion were
various: "The object of the motion was directly
opposed to the Lord Chancellor's opinion (1831);
it would also interfere with the crown prerogative; a multiplication of theatres would not
produce greater performances or greater authors,
nor would morals be improved thereby; the
question was too large for the Commons to cope
with, it should have originated in the Lords,
where the crown officers had seats; the degeneracy of dramatic exhibitions was due to the
illicit rivalry of the minors; the patent theatres
had rights to be defended; though a proper
footing for the minors was loudly called for,
the drama should never be taken from the authority of the Crown."

Sir William Brougham agreed with the main
arguments of Bulwer, relative to the necessity
of amending the statutes regulating theatricals.
As the law then stood, he said, every minor
theatre within twenty miles of the metropolis

violated its license when it represented any
pieces except burlettas, and every actor in such
theatre was liable to a penalty of fifty pounds
for each performance. It was notorious that this
law was violated with impunity every night. This
fact was a sufficient reason for legalizing all
those theatres required by public necessity. He
(Brougham) had gone carefully into the law on
the subject, and was positive that every minor
theatre performing the drama, with or without
the Chamberlain's license, was liable to an information. A question had arisen over the definition
of a burletta ; Brougham was certain that regular tragedies and comedies were performed at
the minor theatres. He had been informed that
Othello had been performed as a burletta, which
was accomplished by having a low piano-forte
accompaniment, the musician striking a chord
once in five minutes — but always so as to be
totally inaudible. This was the extent of the
musical element distinguishing *Othello* from
the dialogue of the regular drama.

Another member (Mr. John Campbell) went
farther than this, saying that the minors had
ceased to resort even to the subterfuge just mentioned ; and, he added, " where the laws and the
habits of a people are at variance, there is something vicious in the system." Either the law
should be made to conform to the habits of a

people, or the habits of a people to the law, for
the sake of a rational basis. For his part, the
speaker thought that free trade was desirable in
the matter of public amusements, and that the
Government should never interfere except to
enforce the observance of decorum, or to protect
private character and public morals. As to the
patent houses, Campbell declared that they were
worse than the minors, and were a reproach to
the country. Others took the same view. They
suggested that while Parliament was in the
business of doing away with monopolies, " they
should also put an end to that very injurious and
most indefensible one — a theatrical monopoly."

The general tendency of the House of Commons was decidedly in favor of the proposed investigation. The motion passed and a committee
was appointed with Bulwer as its chairman. The
work of the Committee was laborious and searching. Its sittings extended over several weeks, and
the full text of its examination filled scores
of pages. Authors, actors, prompters, managers,
were called before it for the purpose of giving
evidence. The methods and practices of the
patent theatres as regards performances, plays,
the prices of admission, the relations of authors
and managers, — and every topic relating to the
theatrical monopoly, as well as the minors, were
all examined with the eye of scrutiny.

All parties agreed that the laws governing the theatres ought to be revised and placed on an intelligible footing. The patentees held up the inviolableness of their property rights against all infringements, even of Chamberlain and King; and Morton, the dramatist, instead of " bearing witness " before the committee, advocated the cause of the patent houses outright. Macready thought that all plays hitherto produced should be given to the large theatres, allowing to the minors only those to be produced thereafter. Davidge of the Coburg advocated the abrogation of all law respecting the theatres, and, facetiously comments the " Morning Chronicle " (July 2, 1832), he " seems to act on this opinion." Mr. Place, of Charing-Cross, also was opposed to any legal regulation of the stage; but this was an extreme position, ill calculated to aid the cause of the minors. Kenney, the dramatist, deposed that he had been tricked out of his *Masaniello*, for which he had never received a penny from Drury Lane, although the piece had been played there for nearly two hundred nights. For his *Irish Ambassador* seventy pounds were still due from the manager of Covent Garden. The monopoly, he was sure, was the cause of this hardship.

One of the numerous sensations of the proceedings of the Committee was produced when

Sir Richard Birnie and Mr. Hall were examined (July 10, 1832). The latter asserted that, notwithstanding the fact that he had once been overruled in judging in favor of a minor theatre in the case of an information brought before him for hearing, in a similar case he would decide again as he had done. Birnie and Hall were the Bow Street magistrates who had refused to convict the Tottenham Theatre performers, on the ground that sufficient evidence had not been produced by the informants to show that the minor theatre had not been licensed.

Bulwer, of course, and his brother, were for no restraints. Duncombe was for a middle course; while Sheil, though opposed to the monopoly, doubted the feasibility of legislative remedy. Earl Belfast placed himself on the side of the Lord Chamberlain's authority. Mr. Alderman Waithman expressed himself for the minors. Rayner thought it a good plan to demand of the monopolists their patents, and to see if those documents did not contain a clause to the effect that they were granted " for the advancement of our morals — the refinement of taste — and the improvement of dramatic literature," and if they did contain such an express purpose, then the managers of the large theatres ought to be questioned whether the production of *The Dog of Montarges*, *Jack the Giant-Killer*, *The*

Lions of Mysore, " and five hundred other pieces
of a similar description " had fostered the high
ideals of the patent grants. If the answer were
in the negative, then the patents should be declared null and void. At any rate, they ought to
be restricted by law, never in future to represent melodrama, burlesque, or pantomime.[1]

On August 2, 1832, the Committee had completed its investigation, and were ready to report
to the House. The report comprehended eight
main divisions, as arranged by Bulwer. The
first of these consisted of the plain statement that
the Committee had found " a considerable decline, both in the literature of the stage, and the
Taste of the public for theatrical performances."
The enumerated causes of this state of affairs
were, the prevailing fashion of late dining, the
want of royal encouragement, and the supposed
indisposition of some religious sects towards theatres. These all lay outside of legislative control.
But there were additional causes which Government might consider, such as the uncertain
administration of the laws, lack of proper encouragement to dramatic authorship, and the want of
regulation as regards the number and distribu-
tion of theatres.

The second section of the report struck at the

---

[1] For comments on the Select Committee's investigations,
see *Morning Chronicle*, July 2, 16, 23, 25, 1832.

root of the evil respecting the licensing of theatres, — the cause of most of the grievances of
the minor theatres, and the years of contention
between them and the patentees. It was recom-
ménded that the sole power of licensing theatres
be confined to the Lord Chamberlain; that the
jurisdiction of that official be extended to
a distance of twenty miles about London (that
being the point at which, by the Act of 28 George
III, the authority of the magistrates to license
theatres for the regular drama began); and that,
for the sake of a fair competition, the Lord
Chamberlain should continue to license all the
theatres then holding licenses from whichever
source — magistrates or Lord Chamberlain. The
difficulty of defining the " legitimate drama " was
admitted, and, to obviate this, the very liberal
proposal was made of allowing proprietors and
managers of theatres to exhibit " at their option
the legitimate drama and all such plays as have
received or shall receive the sanction of the censor." This second clause of the report is deserving of attention, as out of it, a decade later,
developed the law ending the long struggle.

In the next place the Committee thought that,
since theatres are for the amusement of the public, the public should have a voice in determining
the number. It was, therefore, strongly recommended to the House, that whenever a requisi-

tion, signed by a majority of the inhabitants of
any large and populous parish or district, praying for a new theatre, should be presented to the
Lord Chamberlain, that official should be compelled to comply with the public wish. In case
of any outrageous abuse of privilege, it was
suggested that the Chamberlain have recourse
to the Home Department for power to suppress
the license. Should a manager attempt to act
without a license, it was to be deemed *prima
facie* evidence that the community was opposed
to the theatre. In such emergencies the Lord
Chamberlain was to have the silencing power.

As to the question of licensing plays, it was
advised that the office of the censor should exist
at the sole discretion of the Lord Chamberlain.
This would not only give dignity to, but would
also fix responsibility of, the office of examiner
of plays. The old system of fees, whereby no
distinction was made between the fee for licensing a slight song and a complete drama, was
recommended to be abolished, and a graduated
scale substituted.[1]

The Committee did not apprehend that the
changes proposed by them would, if adopted,

[1] As the fee system stood in 1832, for a comedy altered to
a burletta there would be charged at least six distinct and
equal fees by the examiner, — one for the comedy, and one
for each of the (required) five songs. This fee system was
graduated in 1836.

have a depressing effect on the patent theatres; for, admitting that enormous investments had been made in those establishments on the faith of the continuance of the monopoly, it did not appear that the exclusive privileges had preserved either the dignity of the drama, or the financial prosperity of the patentees.

Coming to the question of the ill usage of dramatists as a result of the monopoly, a plea was entered for the better protection of dramatic authors, by legally establishing their rights, as in the case of authors of productions other than dramatic. It was hoped by the Committee that the adoption of this, and the other suggestions of the report, in some legal form, would extend a benefit to actors, who would then have a wider field for their abilities; to authors, who would have not only a greater demand, but also a greater protection for the products of their genius; and lastly, to the public, who would become the final recipient of all the promised benefits.

It was conceded that the report of the Dramatic Committee could not affect the status of the drama as represented at either of the great or small houses; because the craze for melodramas and burlettas made that species far more lucrative to the managers than the legitimate drama.[1]

---

[1] See *Morning Chronicle*, August 6, 1832; *Gentleman's Magazine* for August, 1832.

At the same time, this very fact was damaging
to the monopoly, as it stood particularly for the
regular drama. Whatever Parliament saw fit to
do with the report, it was certainly very dis-
tasteful to the patentees; for their weaknesses
had all been laid bare in the course of the investigation.

Some looked upon the work of the Committee
as little short of an audacious imposition. Tait's
"Edinburgh Magazine" (August, 1832) thus
cynically remarks on the subject:

"The unhappy Drama (almost ashamed to
know herself), a miserable pauper, who has been
passed from parish to parish, pressed during
the war, and turned adrift in her rags in time of
peace; pelted with mud by the editors of the fifteen daily and thirteen weekly journals of London,—now sentenced to the workhouse, and now
to the penitentiary,— is at length condemned
to the *peine forte et dure* of a Parliamentary
Committee! Not a farce-writing dunce, not a
ninny, not a candle-snuffer, but has been called
to speak to *her* character, and prate away his
own! . . . Certain senators, having premised
that there are no dramatic authors extant, insist
on bringing in a bill for their protection."

But the authors had a cause to support, and
no amount of adverse criticism was able to
dampen their zeal. The same day (August 2)

on which Bulwer read the report of the Dramatic Committee, one of the House members (Mr. Shiel) presented a petition from James Sheridan Knowles, praying for protection to dramatic productions. At the same time Bulwer gave notice that, if reëlected to Parliament, he would, the next session, move leave to bring in a bill for regulating the claims of dramatic authors.[1]

Pursuant to this announcement, on the 12th of March, 1833, permission was given to the member from St. Ives to introduce a bill " for licencing theatres, and for the better regulation of dramatic performances in the cities of London and Westminster, and within twenty miles thereof." This was known as the Dramatic Performances Bill, and was an outgrowth of that clause in the report of the Committee on Dramatic Literature, in which it was advised that the sole power of licensing plays be lodged in the Lord Chamberlain. The object of the measure was threefold: to throw open the regular drama to all the then licensed theatres, to defend the inhabitants of any district from the annoyances of mere theatrical speculations, and to centralize in the Lord Chamberlain authority over the theatres.

[1] *Mirror of Parliament*, 2d Session, 10th Parliament, vol. iv, p. 3519.

With these objects in view the bill proposed to enact, in the first instance, that any person desirous of obtaining a license for the exhibition of dramatic performances, at any place within the limits of the act, must, at least three months before the annual licensing day at which the application for license was intended to be made, post a notice to that effect on the outer door of the theatre where such performances were proposed to be exhibited. Copies of the said notice must be served also on the church-wardens and overseers of the parish, and insertions of the same made once a week for the three months in two daily morning papers. Should a majority of the persons interested in the property contiguous to the theatre petition the Lord Chamberlain two months in advance of the licensing day, against the license thus applied for, the said license should be denied. If no such petition were presented, then the Lord Chamberlain should be under the necessity of issuing the license prayed for.[1] However, provision was made for refusal to grant a license, could the act in any way be construed to conflict with the common law. Persons applying for a license should be required to

---

[1] Hansard's *Parliamentary Debates*, 3d Series, vol. 16, 561–567; see also *Mirror of Parliament*, 1st Session, 11th Parliament, pp. 711–713; and *Gentleman's Magazine*, vol. 103, pt. 1, p. 261.

present a certificate, signed by three architects, or surveyors, vouching for the stability and safety of the building intended for theatrical purposes.[1] It was proposed to give the Lord Chamberlain summary power in cases where unlicensed performances were exhibited, or where proprietors of theatres in any way exceeded the privileges of their licenses. But the Chamberlain was to have no discretionary powers over proprietors complying with the provisions of the act, nor, in case a memorial had not been presented within the time specified, against the granting of the license.

In presenting the bill Bulwer stated that, although the Dramatic Committee had thought the office of examiner of plays a needless one, they had retained it in the proposed bill, fearing that any attempt to abolish that office might militate against the bill itself. However, provisions were made for a graduated scale of fees. In the debate which followed Mr. Bulwer's speech, the necessity for some such measure as that proposed was very evident ; although some doubts were expressed as to the advisability of attempting the control of public taste by legis-

[1] This precaution may have been suggested by the then recent disaster at the Brunswick (*i. e.* Royalty) Theatre, which collapsed (February 28, 1828), three days after opening, killing a number of persons.

lative action. As in 1737, the summary power proposed to be vested in the Lord Chamberlain caused some apprehensions. And, too, the attack on the censorship was thought too radical. On the other hand, some would go beyond Bulwer in the movement towards reform; the censor and chamberlain, it was declared, " had trammelled the drama until it became as it now was; fees were demanded here and fees there. . . . There should be a free trade in the drama as well as anything else." One member (Warburton), who held a £500 renter's share in Covent Garden Theatre, thought that the monopoly system was calculated to afford irrational amusement at the dearest rate, and that the object of the bill was to reverse this state of affairs. If, continued the same speaker, the existing monopoly claimed the right to be protected in its vested interests, he wished to tell the House that there remained no such interests to be protected; for those supposed to exist were mortgaged to treble their value, and, of course, were worthless. For his part, he was willing to sacrifice his £500 share in Covent Garden in order to enable the minor theatres to perform the regular drama.

Opposition to the Dramatic Performances Bill was not wanting, either in or out of the House of Commons. The patentees had the memorial, which they had formerly presented to the Lord Chamberlain against the extension of the licenses of the Haymarket and Lyceum, printed and circulated broadcast, in the hope that it might effect the defeat of Bulwer's bill.[1] Alfred Bunn, the new lessee of both patent theatres, had two or three interviews with Bulwer for the purpose of prevailing on the latter to amend the bill to the advantage of the established houses, but the " young reformer " could not be dissuaded from his course.[2] The patentee then addressed the Crown, and also prepared a memorial to the House of Lords, in the hopes of obstructing the passage of the bill there, should it get through the lower House.

The press was by no means unanimously friendly to the bill, as presented. It contained certain defects which augured its defeat, and these were early pointed out by the " Observer." For example, one clause in the proposed measure, as first prepared, made it imperative on the Lord Chamberlain to grant a license to an applicant if a dissenting petition were not filed by persons living in the neighborhood; while another portion of the bill required that a consenting memorial should be lodged with the Lord Chamberlain from persons living near the theatre.[3] The " Ob-

[1] *Morning Chronicle,* Mar. 18, 1833.   [2] Bunn, *The Stage,* i, 111.
[3] *Morning Chronicle,* March 25, 1833.

server," from the start, predicted the failure of
the bill, on other grounds. Dissensions arose in
the Committee in charge of the measure, one or
two of the members threatening to withdraw, for
the reason that the schedule of theatres proposed
by the bill would make the monopoly stricter
than it had been. It was the impression of the
advocates of the minors that the schedule was
intended to include all the then existing London
theatres, whereas it provided only for those that
had been licensed. Such an arrangement would
debar the Strand, City, and Garrick theatres
from legal protection; and for this reason the
bill was violently opposed by some of the Committee. To meet the objections raised to the
schedule of theatres proposed by the bill, one
of the metropolitan members offered a compromise, whereby the Lord Chamberlain should, by
the aid of a jury, be enabled to decide whether a
theatre was or was not desired by the inhabitants of any particular district. But this cumber-
some and expensive method was immediately
attacked by the papers, and the whole matter
was left as originally proposed.

Relative to licensing the Victoria (Coburg)
and the other theatres outside the Chamberlain's
jurisdiction, the leading theatrical paper of the
day [1] remarks: " What mere folly it seems not

[1] *Morning Chronicle*, July 1, 1833, quoting *Observer*. **Miss**

to give the Lord Chamberlain at once jurisdiction there, by which care could be taken that unobjectionable pieces only should be represented. Here is a short and easy remedy, at least for part of the existing evils, without useless and endless discussion about a Bill which never will be passed."

The bill, which had passed its second reading and been committed on the 30th of May, was reported on the 8th of July. On the 19th of July, Alderman Wood, of the metropolis, succeeded in getting an amendment added, exempting the city of London from the act, on the ground that the mayor and aldermen had previously exercised the power of granting and refusing licenses within their jurisdiction.[1] On the 24th of July Bulwer moved the third reading. One of the members (Mr. Rotch) of the House, in objecting to the bill, used such severe language against the profession of actors as to create a sensation, and brought upon himself a well-deserved opprobrium. A theatre, he declared, served the purpose only of bringing together a set of unfortunate outcasts who had no means of existence, and it was beneath the dignity of

Kelly, who was at this time planning to open the Strand, at once petitioned Parliament for protection.

[1] *Mirror of Parliament*, 1st Session, 11th Parliament, pp. 2006, 2813, 3188, 3309, 3312, 3463, 3490.

Parliament to legislate for such a class.[1] This fierce invective did not prevent the bill from passing the House of Commons, which it did by a vote of 38 to 7. The following day (July 25) Bulwer carried the bill to the House of Lords.

The minors were elated over the success of their measure in the Commons, and prophesied certain victory in the upper House.[2] The Marquis of Clanricarde undertook to conduct the bill through the House of Lords, and secured its first reading on the day of its receipt. Notice was given for the second reading to come up in one week. By the appointed day both sides had gathered their strength for the fray. Lord Wynford presented a petition signed by one hundred and sixty persons, "proprietors, managers, performers, musicians," and others, interested in the Victoria Theatre. The petition stated that over three hundred persons were employed in and about that theatre, and that none but the works of the best dramatic authors were performed there. They set forth their precarious situation, due to the then existing law laying each of them liable to a fine of fifty pounds for every night they performed. They, therefore, prayed that the bill then before the Lords might pass. In

---

[1] Hansard's *Parliamentary Debates*, 3d Series, vol. xix, p. 1220.

[2] *Morning Chronicle*, July 29, 1833.

presenting this memorial, Lord Wynford did not deny the truthfulness of the petitioners' complaint, but entertained some doubts as to whether the £50 penalty could be enforced.

A petition, similar to the foregoing one, bearing the signatures of thirteen hundred inhabitants of London and Westminster, was read by the Duke of Somerset. Both of these memorials were tabled. Other petitions, favoring the bill, were presented from the minors of the metropolis, from actors and authors interested therein, from merchants, traders, and others of London, and from the inhabitants of St. Mary, Lambeth, and the other sections adjacent to the metropolis.[1] Covent Garden and Drury Lane, of course, petitioned against the bill.

Something of the ardor which stirred the public in general to promote the Dramatic Performances Bill may be appreciated from a single instance. On August 1, the day before the time set for the second reading of the bill in the House of Lords, a public mass meeting was called at the Crown and Anchor to consider the propriety of memorializing Parliament in favor of the measure. A number of notable persons were present at this conference, representing authors, actors, members of Parliament, and the public in general. Among these were Messrs. Serle, Warde,

[1] *Mirror of Parliament*, 1st Sess. 11th Parl., pp. 1384, 3490.

Wrench, Abbott, Egerton, Elton, Farrell, Jerrold, Osbaldiston, Davidge, Keeley, Mitchell, Vining, Bulwer, and many others. The Duke of Somerset, who was in the chair, opened the meeting with a brief address. Serle made, perhaps, the leading speech of the occasion. He stated that the appeal they were then making to the public was in behalf of three thousand persons whose livelihood was concerned in the issue between the two large theatres and the minors. They were asking for no exclusive privileges, he said, but merely the liberty to exercise their art. The history of the prosecutions of the minor theatres was then entered upon. It was averred that if the large theatres had not persecuted the minors with such vindictiveness, but had allowed them a degree of liberty, they would have been content with a less measure of justice than they now demanded. Nothing but the utter abolition of the monopoly would now relieve the situation and satisfy those most seriously affected.

The oft-repeated assertion, that a multiplicity of theatres would lead to a deterioration of the drama, was denied, and doubts were expressed whether it could possibly be in a worse state. It was a well-known fact that Sheridan Knowles's play, *The Wife*, and the regular English company of actors had been driven from Covent Garden to make room for foreigners;[1] while at the minors Shakesperean and other great plays had been acted repeatedly with success. At the Olympic Pavilion *Hamlet* had drawn large audiences over and over again. Experience of other countries had proven competition to be the cause of improvement of the drama, and so would it in England, if permitted. Serle then alluded to the treatment which Knowles, Dowton, and Kenney had received at the hands of the patentees, when seeking an opportunity for presenting their productions.

The charge was denied that the minors were to blame for the embarrassments which had overtaken the patent houses. Drury Lane Theatre, as everybody knew, had been built during " war prices," and values had declined with the return of normal financial conditions.[2] Drury Lane was not the only concern that had suffered from the same cause. As to " vested rights," it was maintained that a monopoly, existing solely for the benefit of a few, which kept the bread

[1] This occurred in 1832 under the management of Laporte.

[2] " Scarcely any description of property has been more seriously affected by the general distress than the Public Theatres: even in the Capital they have been severely visited ; but in the Provincial circuits they have been, almost without exception, entirely shut up, or their rents reduced one-third ; some to half their former produce, and others allowed to be used for the payment of taxes and repairs." *Gentleman's Magazine*, March, 1817, p. 270.

out of the mouths of thousands, and prevented
the public from enjoying rational amusements,
had no right to be permitted. Serle closed his
speech by reiterating that the drama could live
and prosper only when free; that the exertions
then being made were aimed to rescue it from the
thralldom of the existing monopoly; and that
if the House of Lords should think fit to reject
the bill then before them, nevertheless its promoters would in no wise feel that their cause was
weakened, but, on the contrary, they would make
more extensively known the justice of their demands, and " they would knock again and again
at the doors of the Parliament till justice was
admitted." [1]

The sentiments of the meeting were written
down in the form of a petition, which was at
once forwarded to the House of Lords. On the
following day (August 2), as announced, the
Marquis of Clanricarde, the original mover of
the bill in the Lords, opened the debate for the
second reading. The anomalous condition of the
laws regulating the theatres was, he said, contrary to the wishes of the people, injurious to the
public morals, and derogatory to the profession
of acting. The anomaly consisted in the conflict
of the law on the subject and the fact as backed
by public opinion. East of Temple Bar, across

[1] *Morning Chronicle*, August 2, 1833.

in Surrey outside of Westminster, theatres,
"some of them very good, and others less so,"
were acting without the license of the Lord
Chamberlain, and had no means of obtaining one.
The development of this inconsistent state of
affairs was significant; so long as the minor
theatres had devoted themselves to a low and
vulgar order of amusements — "whilst they were
no better than haunts of vice and idleness"—
the patent theatres raised not one point of objection ; but the moment the minor concerns became
respectable, and made an attempt to give a class
of performances " to which the intelligent might
resort with advantage," the great patent houses
put the arm of law into motion to crush them.
That the public had been aroused against this
injustice to the minor theatres, to say nothing of
the violence to morality, was witnessed by the
petitions, favoring the bill, presented to both
houses of Parliament, and by the report of the
Committee on Dramatic Literature.

A free competition of the theatres, with protective guards against licentiousness, was needed
to alleviate the situation ; and the Dramatic
Performances Bill was believed to contain the
remedy sought. As the law then stood, there
was no power to restrain managers from exhibiting performances wholly at variance with decency and morality ; for the Chamberlain's power

in such matters was only permissive, not prevent-
ive. As to an indefinite number of theatres
being fostered by the bill, should it pass, the
very opposite was expected from it by its friends,
for some of the places then exhibiting would, it
was predicted, be suppressed by the operations of
the act. Indeed, as to the matter of respectability,
it was pointed out, the two patent houses themselves were national disgraces, often guilty of
giving exhibitions both " indelicate and disgusting." Moreover, it had been a complaint for
years that those theatres derived considerable
sums every year from certain classes of persons
who went there confessedly for purposes immoral and vicious.

If it were held by some that the bill ought
not to pass because it would be an infringement
on the monopoly, the Marquis of Clanricarde
desired to tell the Lords that such a position
was both " absurd in principle and untenable in
law." Did the Lords not know that there were
no monopolies, that by the Act of 21 James I, all
monopolies were expressly prohibited, and that
any attempt on the part of the patentees to exercise a monopoly rendered them liable to the penalties of a *praemunire?* Furthermore, was it not
a patent fact that Drury Lane was then, and had
been for years, running on the authority of a limited license, and was this not sufficient evidence

that the monopoly, as well as the "vested property rights," was a mere fiction? It seemed absurd to the Marquis to speak of infringing property rights, the value of which was measurable only in terms of debts and mortgages.

The Earl of Glengall, who was directly interested in the patent theatres, represented the cause of the patentees and repeated arguments with which we have been made acquainted in the course of these pages. But the most unique turn to the debate on the bill in the House of Lords was given by the Bishop of London, who, in a spirited manner, pronounced a lengthy anathema against the immorality of the stage, not sparing the patent houses. A lamentable picture was drawn by the bishop, in respect of the Garrick Theatre, where "the value of property had deteriorated, houses could not be let, offences multiplied, and the district alarmed by riots by night." The good prelate was chagrined that a bill should be introduced to increase these places of evil. By some sort of mathematical jugglery he calculated the possibility of two hundred and fifty theatres within a radius of two miles from the General Post Office, in case the bill passed; nor could the spiritual Lord consent to the second reading of a bill that promised to multiply dens of iniquity at such a rate.[1]

[1] In 1835 Farrell, proprietor of the Royal Pavilion Theatre

On the merits of and necessity for the Dramatic Performances Bill, the House of Lords were almost equally divided, with the deciding majority opposed to it. On the motion for a second reading, the bill was lost, lacking five votes only.[1] Notwithstanding the prediction of certain wiseacres that Bulwer's bill would fail to work its way through Parliament, its rejection by the House of Lords was a great surprise, even to the enemies of the measure. So confident were some that it would become a law that a canvass had been made to ascertain whether a third theatre project would meet with any great opposition, and several thousand pounds had been subscribed for such a purpose. But the defeat of the bill in nowise daunted its promoters. Though the session of Parliament was almost at its close, many were anxious to renew the effort before the prorogation should take place. A number of plans were discussed, only one of which stood any chance of passing without

in Whitechapel Road, was called before the magistrates at the instigation of the Bishop of London, who complained that two pieces founded on scriptural subjects had been enacted at the Pavilion and Garrick theatres. After investigation the justice dismissed the case.

[1] For the best account of the debates in the House of Lords on the Dramatic Performances Bill I have followed the *Mirror of Parliament*, 1st Session, 11th Parliament, pp. 3384, 3490–3494. See also *Gentleman's Magazine*, vol. 103, pt. 2, p. 167.

strenuous opposition.[1] This one was proposed
by Mr. Otley, who wished to introduce a short
bill empowering magistrates with discretionary
authority in mitigating the fifty pound penalty
for acting in an unlicensed theatre. As the law
stood, magistrates were powerless to graduate
the fine provided by the Licensing Act. However, on the whole, the extreme severity of this
provision operated favorably to the actors in
the minor theatres, for in 1833, and long before,
there was little disposition in any quarter to
carry the old act into effect.

The minors were greatly opposed to Otley's
compromising measure, and nothing came of it.
The old order of things continued. But the
monopoly had received such a shock from
Knowles's attempt to establish a third theatre,
from the extension of the privileges of the leading minors, and from the vigorous combined
attacks of minors and authors, that it was never
to recover from it. It was nearly ten years before the dramatists were to concert again in
defense of their rights, but in that period the
internal decay of the patent houses, and the
external attacks of their foes, made the closing
ceremony of pronouncing the doom of the " great
theatres " a mere perfunctory legislative act.

[1] *Morning Chronicle*, August 5, 12, 1833.

CHAPTER XIII

TO the long list of theatrical conflagrations
was added that of the New English Opera
House on February 10, 1830.[1] Arnold was still
the proprietor of that theatre, and, before rebuilding, he conceived it to be to his interests to
obtain an extension of privileges to his license.
It will be remembered that the license issued to
him in 1809 was claimed by Arnold to be for
the year, and that it was afterwards abridged to
four months, from June to October. Accordingly, in September, 1830, Arnold petitioned
the King for a renewal of the original license
for English opera. This action caused a tem-
pest of agitation among the patentees, who, as
was their wont on such occasions, immediately
presented counter-petitions praying for protection to their " inviolable patents " and " vested
property rights." The storm which these pre-
liminaries threatened to brew was directed by
the Crown towards the Lord Chancellor's Court;

[1] For the season of 1830 the Lyceum Company went to
the Adelphi, in the Strand; in 1832 to the Olympic.

for it seemed certain that the struggle of 1810 would be repeated.

The hearing of Arnold's petition and the counter-claims of the patentees was set for the 11th of January, 1831, at seven o'clock in the evening. The interest taken in the case by the public may be inferred from the opening scene at the court-room, as reported by the " Morning Chronicle " (January 12, 1831):

" Upon this occasion there were associated with the Lord Chancellor the Chief Justice of the Common Pleas, the Vice-Chancellor, and Mr. Justice James Parke. As early as six o'clock the doors were beset by an impatient multitude eager for access. . . . A favourite few obtained admission through the private door. Within a quarter of seven the public entrance was thrown open, when the rush fully equalled any scene of confusion ever witnessed in the pit of a theatre, . . . on the first night of a new tragedy."

A number of noted theatrical persons were present, and the general interest manifested in the case promised to be even greater than that taken in the famous proceedings of 1810 ; for by 1831 the feeling against the monopoly had become part and parcel of the reform movement. Arnold was represented by the Solicitor-General (Mr. Horne), Sir Edward Sugden, and other

counsel of note. They based the claims of their
client on the original license of 1809, and its
recognition by Sheridan and the Privy Council;
and especially on the fact that the recent im-
portation of foreign opera in competition with
native talent rendered it doubly necessary that
the season of the English Opera House be
extended to coincide with that of the winter
theatres, if anything like a fair competition
could be hoped for by Mr. Arnold. It was denied that the present application contained in it
any intent to break the monopoly then existing,
at least "no further than it had already been
done."

The whole question of crown prerogative was
again entered into, but, as the arguments were
the same as those given in 1810, they need not
be reviewed here. One point, however, emphasized by the Solicitor-General to the confusion
of the patentees, was the invalidity of *both* the
patents from the moment of the union in 1682.
The argument adduced from this union was
that the two patents were at that time incorporated, not only by the permission and suggestion
of the Crown, but by Charles II, the grantor of
the original patents; and that this very fact of
incorporation obliterated the separate distinction
of the patents, — a point in law not to be con-
troverted. The incorporation *per se* of the

two patents worked their forfeiture completely. The subsequent action of King William in granting Betterton a license in order to carry out the original intention (of two theatres) supported this view. Moreover, any use of the patents not intended by the original grant worked their forfeiture; and in this light it was unnecessary to inquire whether succeeding princes could violate the patent grants of Charles II, but simply whether any one could. If it were claimed by the patentees that there had been a revival of the merged patents (in 1792), then which patent had done the reviving, and which one was operative in Betterton's time?[1]

Of all the numerous instances of violating the patents, reviewed by Arnold's counsel in 1831, one other is worthy of mention. When Rich was ejected from Drury Lane Theatre in 1709, Queen Anne signified her willingness to grant a license to any one who would surrender his claims to the patents granted by Charles II. Collier, a shareholder in the Drury Lane patent, complied with this request, submitted to Her Majesty, and received a license to open Drury Lane Theatre. The opponents to the patentees

[1] It is a curious fact that during the union, though it was Killigrew's patent that became dormant, the united company was known as the King's Company, operating under Davenant's patent at Drury Lane. Later, Rich opened Covent Garden with the same patent.

now claimed that this circumstance was founded
on the surrender of the patents to the Crown,
at which time the prerogative over theatrical
affairs was resumed. It was also pointed out
that, if the patents gave a monopoly, Italian
opera was also included. In granting O'Reilly
a license for Italian opera at the Pantheon
(1790), Chancellor Thurlow decided that the
King's prerogative in such matters was unlimited.

Such an array of precedents against the
theory that the theatrical patents were inviolable had never before been marshaled. Against
these, counsel for the patentees recited all the
acts of Parliament, from the " Rogue, Vagabond, and Sturdy Beggar " act of Queen Elizabeth, through the Licensing Act of 1737, to the
" Arrangement " of 1792, sanctioned by the King
and others high in authority. As to the lapsing
of patents on the ground of non-user, Mr. Arnold's attention was called to the fact that his
own Lyceum license was invalid, as having remained unused from 1812 to 1815.[1] Finally,
the patentees did not rest their claims on the

[1] Arnold made answer to this that, as he was director of
the Drury Lane Company for those three years, it had been
hardly the proper thing for him to establish a rival theatre on
his license. The allusion is to the period when Sheridan joined
his burnt-out Drury Lane Company to that of Arnold at the
Lyceum, pending the rebuilding of Drury Lane Theatre.

patents granted by Charles II, but rather on the historic recognition of the rights of the patent owners, and on the justice inherent in the inviolability of property investments. And the touching on this phase of the question entailed a recapitulation of the financial calamities of the two patent houses for the previous half-century. It does not seem to have occurred to the patentees that these very disasters — at least those due to mismanagement — would, sooner or later, be looked at with a different effect from the one aimed at on the present occasion. Alluding to the objections made against monopolies, counsel for the patentees apprehended that, under free competition, the most tyrannous of monopolies would result, for, ultimately, one theatre must succeed in driving all others from the field. Aaron Hill would have added, " or raise them to a higher plane," which was the aim of the opponents to the monopoly.

A complication at this juncture arose in the proceedings of the Lord Chancellor's Court.[1] On the 25th of January, Morris, proprietor of the Little Theatre in the Haymarket, memorialized the King to take his theatre into considera-

---

[1] The importance of the case required the court to sit a number of times from January 11 to 31. For the proceedings see *Morning Chronicle*, January 12, 14, 19, 25, 26, February 1, 1831.

tion when deciding on Arnold's petition, which
was looked upon by the Haymarket manager as
nothing more nor less than an attempt to establish a third winter theatre. On the basis of justice and policy Morris thought that his theatre
should have precedence over the English Opera
House in the matter of a third establishment,
inasmuch as the Haymarket had been a truer
representative of the legitimate drama. The con-
version of the regular drama into an " operatized
form " at the English Opera House was characterized as "spurious," the representation of which
was in violation of the spirit of Arnold's license.

Arnold's rejoinder, that the pieces put on at
the Lyceum were sanctioned by the Lord Chamberlain, was unanswerable; and as to non-user
working the forfeiture of a license, that was
a two-edged sword on the present occasion. So
too might the plea of financial disaster be worked
on both sides. But financial success or failure
was denied to have anything to do with the controversy. The essential point was the question
of public benefit. Referring to the attitude of
the Haymarket, an attitude presumably taken
in support of the monopoly, Arnold's counsel
(Sir C. Wetherell) uttered a note of warning to
the Little Theatre : " With respect to the common cause which the little theatres had made
with the great Moguls, who fought with ele-

phants, he could only say that the little poten-
tate of the Haymarket and others would soon find
that if Mr. Arnold were defeated they would be
likewise swallowed up." The persecution of the
Tottenham and Strand proprietors followed on
the heels of this prediction.

After due deliberation, the Lord Chancellor
advised the King that the crown prerogative cannot be so affected by previous patent grants as
to preclude the granting of similar patents; but
that, under the circumstances of the case then
under consideration, he gave it as his opinion
that the new English Opera House should be
limited to six months every year, commencing
with May and ending with October. To this
decision the King added a second, calculated to
relieve a much vexed question, relating to the
licensing of minor theatres. It was laid down
that, thereafter, all minor theatres should receive their licenses from the Lord Chamberlain's
office, and not from the magistrates.[1] This was
a step towards reducing the confusion connected
with the promiscuous licensing of theatres ; for
hitherto managers had generally been able to
find some magistrate who could, and would, exercise a liberal interpretation of a variety of
laws in the granting of licenses for theatrical
amusements. But the decision was far from satis-

[1] *New Monthly Magazine,* April, 1831.

factory in many ways; it added a new confusion to the Lord Chamberlain's power, for by the Licensing Act that officer's jurisdiction extended no farther than the liberties of Westminster. This conflict of jurisdiction, legalized by statute, had been the source of most of the theatrical rows since the days of John Palmer; and though the attempt to localize responsibility respecting the theatres was a worthy one, it was not calculated to remove the main difficulty, — the disparity of protection secured to the patent theatres and the minors. From an immediate outlook the decision in the case of Arnold's petition was unsatisfactory, because of the halfway course adopted in granting a license for six months. Neither party could claim a victory, yet on the whole the effect was disheartening to the minors.

A year and a half went by, and the new English Opera House was not yet completed. In the summer of 1832 both the Italian Opera House (King's Theatre in the Haymarket) and Covent Garden [1] were kept open with a French company, in competition with the two regular summer theatres. In this extremity Morris presented a memorial (July, 1832) to the Lord Chamberlain,

[1] Covent Garden Theatre and the Italian Opera House were at this time under the sole management of Laporte, who was making the wildest efforts to keep from sinking financially.

praying for an extension of his season. The Duke of Devonshire withheld an immediate reply, pending the investigation of the Dramatic Committee. However, many weeks passed after the report of that Committee had been made, and Morris had not yet been answered. Some time in September (1832) a rumor got afloat that the licenses of both Morris and Arnold had been extended. This was too uncertain to furnish much relief to the memorialist. When the Haymarket closed its season on the 8th of October it was evident, from the address of the manager to the public on that occasion, that Morris had received no official answer to his petition. Finally, about Christmas, it was given out on good authority that the prayer of the Little Theatre had been granted, and that Morris was preparing to open his theatre on the ensuing Easter (1833) for an eight months season.[1] The Lyceum was also included in this extension, the privileges to both theatres being granted at the special instance of King William IV. A scruple was at once raised whether this was not a breach of the arrangement made in 1822 with the winter houses, relative to the time of opening. This point was dismissed, however, by the summer managers on the ground that no

[1] For the history of these extensions I have followed the reports given by the *Morning Chronicle*, July 23, Sept. 3, Oct. 9, Dec. 24, 1832, Jan. 28, July 29, 1833.

such agreement subsisted between *them* and the patentees (Polhill of Drury Lane, and Laporte of Covent Garden).[1] The latter at once entered a protest with the Lord Chamberlain against the extension of the summer licenses, but to no purpose. For the first season (1833), however, Arnold relinquished his privilege of opening at Easter, because he was unable to collect an adequate company in so short a time.

The extension of the licenses of the Haymarket and Lyceum caused rejoicing among playwrights and actors alike, and a corresponding dolor among " certain other great people pertaining to certain great patented structures of name needless to tell." [2] It was a step in the abridgment of monopoly, and the herald of certain victory for the promoters of free competi-

[1] The frequent changes in the lesseeship of the patent theatres during this period in some sense suggests the financial condition of the tottering concerns. Elliston had Drury Lane from 1819 to 1826. It was then taken by Stephen Price, an American, who succeeded in holding it for four years before becoming bankrupt. Alexander Lee then risked his chance, remaining less than a year, and was succeeded by Captain Polhill in 1831. Two years later Alfred Bunn became the sole lessee of Drury Lane and Covent Garden, staying at the former until 1839. Covent Garden furnishes a similar story. Harris was succeeded in 1821 by C. Kemble ; the latter by Laporte in 1832, then Polhill the same year, Bunn in 1833 ; Fitzball for one day in 1835, then Osbaldiston, and Macready before 1840.

[2] Tait's *Edinburgh Magazine*, February, 1833.

tion in theatricals. It mattered little that the new privileges produced no immediately perceptible effect in the success of the two old summer houses ; the essential fact remained, that successful inroads had been made into the sacred domains of the patent theatres. The other minors at once sought similar favors from the Crown, and not without success. In 1835 Braham, the tenor singer, failing to make satisfactory terms with the Drury Lane patentee, applied for and secured a license for a theatre of his own. Purchasing a site in King's Street, in a remarkably short time he erected a new theatre which he styled the St. James. In March, 1837, the St. James, along with the Adelphi and Olympic, had, by royal command, their licenses extended two months beyond the usual term. They were now permitted to take advantage of the Eastertide, one of the best in the year for the theatrical business. This favor to the three minors was probably brought about by the indefatigable exertions of Madame Vestris, of the Olympic. Taking advantage of a day when her theatre was closed, she posted down to Brighton, where His Majesty " received her with much kindness and condescension." Within a few days from this interview the extension of the three licenses was granted.[1] Their season was now practically

---

[1] *Examiner*, March 5, 1837.

coextensive with that of the patent houses, and in the cases of the Adelphi and Olympic the performances were of a competitive nature to those at the " great houses."

A mere glance at some of the other minor theatres will serve to show the inroads that were constantly being made into the theatrical monopoly. Thursday, October 19, 1837, was licensing day in Middlesex, when the following list of "musical licenses" was issued, indicating how easy it had become to get around the decision of the King in 1831, that, thereafter, all dramatic licenses should be issued by the Lord Chamberlain. On the above date licenses were granted to E. Hughes, R. Dixon, and Charlotte Jones, of Sadler's Wells; John Perry, of the Queen's (*i. e.*, Haymarket) Opera; John Farrell, at the head of the Royal Pavilion; R. Gomersall and W. J. Bennett, owners of the Garrick; L. B. Rayner, manager of the New Strand; Chris. Cookerton, of the Norton Folgate; and John Braham, proprietor of the Colosseum. Thomas Hámlet was refused a license for his " Queen's Bazaar " in Oxford Street. John Gibson's application for the Royal Standard was at first denied, on the ground that it was too near the Norton Folgate; but the question being put, the license was granted by a vote of 13 to 12. " The decision was received with loud plaudits, notwithstanding the efforts of the court to suppress them." [1]

The licenses of the Olympic, Adelphi, and St. James were extended under the chamberlainship of Lord Conyngham, who succeeded to the office in 1836. One of his first acts had been, as we have seen, to license the Strand Theatre, something which even the magistrates had refused to do. As the first effective opposition to the monopoly in the early part of the century had originated in the Lord Chamberlain's office (Lord Dartmouth), so the finishing strokes were to be aided by the King's servant (Lord Conyngham). Whenever the Lord Chamberlain's power had been put to the test, in times past, it had always been with the result that the patentees were obedient to his mandates. In this connection an interesting question arose at this time, namely, as to the jurisdiction of the Lord Chamberlain over the theatres on the opposite side of the river, Astley's, Surrey, and Coburg. Opinions were variously stated on both sides of the question, showing the great confusion which still reigned as to just what was and what was not law respecting the theatres.[2] While as a

[1] *Examiner*, October 22, 1837.

[2] By the Act of 25 George II (1751) justices of the peace were enabled to license music, dancing, and public entertainments after five o'clock P. M. From the penalties of this act

matter of fact there was no doubting the authority of the Lord Chamberlain in all matters relating to the theatres, "it is not for him," said the "Morning Chronicle" (July 30, 1832), "'to run amuck' against the Minors, when the Majors remain perfectly passive, and allow their property, as they contend, to be injured, when they have the complete remedy in their own hands."

As if the natural tendencies of the times — the rise of the minors, altered customs and taste of the people, and the almost universal demand for reform — were not sufficient to insure the speedy dissolution of the old theatrical monopoly, the conduct of the patentees alone, in their management (or mismanagement) of the "great houses," was hastening the downfall of the patent theatres. Elliston's gilded reign over Drury Lane left him a bankrupt (1826).[1] Stephen Price was in the Committee's debt to the amount of £2000 when he quitted the old concern in 1830. Alexander Lee drew Captain Polhill and his fortune into the sinking ship, leaving him at the end of the

the patent houses, and the licenses issued by either the Crown or Lord Chamberlain, were exempted. This law had come to be interpreted in keeping with the public demands. See Chapter VI.

[1] After Elliston was forced to surrender Drury Lane, he returned to the Surrey, where he waged an incessant and defiant warfare on the patentees. It is significant that the latter made no effort to prosecute Elliston for "infringing patent rights."

first year to extricate himself from the ruin as best he might.

Covent Garden presents no brighter picture. As Drury Lane had once been bid for by a lottery agent (Bish, 1826), so Covent Garden now (1832) was "let" to an enterprising foreigner, Monsieur Laporte. To make matters worse the patent houses began the season of 1832–33 in open feud. Laporte commenced the campaign with a flourish of French plays and Paganini concerts, followed by the ballet of *Masaniello*, a popular pantomime, and the *Israelites in Egypt*, given as an oratorio in action, "assisted by the customary *accessoires* of a theatre," the first attempt of the kind in England. Drury Lane retaliated with Kean and Macready in *Othello*, a complete *corps de ballet* "imported from France," a German company, and Malibran. This competition was too fierce to last long, especially when the contestants were already weary from their strifes with external foes. In March (1833) Laporte succeeded in capturing Kean from Polhill; the latter threatened an injunction, and at the same time was compelled to close Drury Lane Theatre, since the main attraction, the erstwhile savior of the establishment, was gone.[1] But Laporte

---

[1] Bunn implies that Kean left Drury Lane because Captain Polhill denied him the loan of £500. *The Stage*, i, 103. Kean died in May (1833) succeeding these events.

gained only a temporary victory by the *coup*. Death had already marked Kean for his own, and during his first appearance at Covent Garden he was compelled to leave the stage before reaching the third act of *Othello*. Both theatres were thus practically stranded.[1]

Indeed, long before this stage had been reached, early in the season, after the fruits of his first victory, Laporte sounded a note of alarm by giving out that he intended to keep Covent Garden open for only four nights in the week. He was led to this decision by the poor box receipts, which often fell below £100.[2] This meant, of course, that the actors were to be put on half-pay, and take chances at that. Another source of anxiety and dissatisfaction to the performers was the disposition to supplant the English actors with foreign troupes. The introduction of foreign operas and ballets aroused, also, the advocates of the national drama. Serle had had one of his tragedies returned to him by the Drury Lane management (December, 1832), not because the piece was unworthy, but because Drury Lane was unable to bring it out; while Knowles and others received even worse treatment than this. In self-defense, the authors

---

[1] This rivalry between Covent Garden and Drury Lane is related by Bunn, i, 98–106.

[2] *Morning Chronicle*, October 22, 1832.

hatched a project, in case the patent houses should banish the English drama from the stage, to establish a theatre " in which the production of English authors might take refuge." Capitalists were found who actually subscribed a large sum for the erection of a third theatre in the vicinity of Drury Lane and Covent Garden. The plan included the engagement of a half-dozen English authors of reputation (such as Knowles, Kenney, Pool, Serle, Morton, etc.) to contribute regularly to the undertaking.[1] But the necessity for carrying these views into execution was cut suddenly short by the extension of the Haymarket license, as related in the first part of this chapter.

The ruinous rivalry between the old houses now caused a new report to be circulated, more alarming than any hitherto. It was conceived by certain managerial geniuses that the salvation of the patent theatres lay in their union. This was a return to the principle adopted in the time of Charles II (1682) to avoid the utter extermination of both houses. Alfred Bunn, Captain Polhill's manager of Drury Lane Theatre, a position which he held under Elliston also, was talked of as the proposed proprietor of the two theatres. Such a venture was at once violently opposed. The proposal was condemned as a total perver-

[1] *Morning Chronicle*, January 28, 1833, quoting *Observer*.

sion of the original idea of two rival theatres, the competition between which was intended to raise the standard of dramatic productions and stage performances. Viewed from Bunn's side, it was admitted that he showed wisdom in thinking of taking both houses under his sole control; but if, as it was reported, he contemplated running the two theatres with one company, his judgment in that was certainly short-sighted. "Select one house," he was advised by a cynical critic, "say Covent Garden, because we believe in the larger, jam into it all the dignity, sentiment, pathos, pantomime, comedy, farce, and interlude to be got; stuff it like a turkey at Christmas, and shut up Old Drury. As it is, neither house is ever full." [1]

The talked-of union of the patent houses revived the project for a third theatre. A movement was set on foot to secure and remodel the Pantheon in Oxford Street and, if possible, to obtain a license for the regular drama. This idea, however, was given up, and the plan of erecting an entirely new theatre was again much talked of, though the recent experience of the "great houses" caused some to doubt the feasibility of a third theatre speculation, — even if they were successful in securing a license. [2]

---

[1] *New Monthly Magazine*, for 1833, pt. iii, p. 350.

[2] *Observer*, April 21, 1833, quoted in *Morning Chronicle*, April 22, 1833.

The strained relations existing between authors and actors, on the one hand, and the
patentees, on the other, were aggravated and
brought to a hasty climax by the crooked conduct of Laporte. On the 16th of April (1833)
he suddenly closed Covent Garden Theatre,
without consent of, or formal notice to, his performers. It was announced that the theatre would
be closed for a fortnight; but the actors were
suspicious and became at once alert. Of course
their salaries ceased the moment the theatre
closed. Fearing lest they might be thrown entirely out of employment, they put Laporte's
intentions to the test by applying to the Lord
Chamberlain for permission to perform at the
Olympic during the two weeks interval of the
closing of Covent Garden. This request was
granted. But although Laporte had offered to
release all his performers from their articles at
the time he shut his theatre, he no sooner heard
of the contemplated opening of the Olympic by
his unemployed actors than he immediately resolved to recommence operations at Covent Garden.[1] This intention he carried out on the 24th,

[1] The cause of closing Covent Garden was well known to
be the low financial state of the concern. The Opera House,
Drury Lane, and the Strand closed the same night (April 16),
but in some of the cases this was due to an epidemic of influ-
enza among the actors. *Morning Chronicle*, April 22, 1833.

a week sooner than expected, when Knowles's new play, *The Wife, a Tale of Mantua*, was produced. The success of this piece promised to save Covent Garden from ruin; but as the burden of the performance fell on a single actress, Ellen Tree, it had to be given up within a week. On April 30 Laporte abandoned the theatre, leaving his actors to finish out the week (four nights) without a manager.[1]

Left once more without protection or employment, the actors determined to pursue their original design of going over to the Olympic, and trying their fortune with Knowles's new play. They, therefore, petitioned the Lord Chamberlain for permission to act at the Olympic for the remainder of the season, — between sixty and seventy nights. They had hoped to begin at their new quarters on Monday, May 6, but the Lord Chamberlain was tardy in giving his consent. Laporte now began to temporize. Although he had released all his actors, he proposed, at this juncture, to his forsaken performers "half the emoluments to which they would be entitled if the dramatic speculation had been profitable." But the actors declined to share further in the losses of one who cared so little for their welfare, preferring rather to throw

[1] See *Morning Chronicle*, April 25, 29, May 1, 3, 4, 6, 8, 1833, for an account of these strange proceedings.

themselves on the mercy of the Lord Chamberlain. The finesse of Laporte in offering the actors half-pay decided the Duke of Devonshire to grant the privilege of playing at the Olympic only on the condition that the Covent Garden manager had no objection to such a course. As might be expected, this requirement could not be satisfied, and although some of the performers had vowed they would not return to Covent Garden, stern necessity drove them back. The farce was enacted for a few nights more, of carrying on a losing venture to prevent a circumstance more dreaded by the patentee.

On the night of the 3d of May (1833), after the representation of *The Wife*, which was " excellently performed to a very crowded house," and most enthusiastically received, the audience was dumbfounded and chagrined at the opening sentence of the following address, delivered by Abbott:

" Ladies and Gentlemen, — To-morrow the play of *A Wife, A Tale of Mantua*, will be acted for the last time here [cries of O! No, no!]. The Performers of this Theatre having fortunately obtained a License from the Lord Chamberlain [great applause], propose opening with this popular play [cries of order, and applause], and upon their own responsibility [tremendous applause], at the Olympic Theatre [applause]. They respectfully yet confidently hope, that by your generous support, you will rescue the legitimate Drama [loud applause] of this country from total destruction. [Loud and lasting applause followed the annunciation.] " [1] The following night, Knowles himself came forward amidst thunders of applause, and announced the intention of the company to open the Olympic on the ensuing Wednesday (May 8).

But Laporte persisted in offering half-pay to the actors, thus standing as an effectual obstacle to the granting of the license. Finally, however, a license was promised for the remainder of the season, provided the whole company (about 300) were unanimous in the desire to enter into the undertaking. This condition was immediately complied with, and by the morning of the day announced for the opening, every box and available seat in the Olympic had been taken for the first performance.[2] As a counter-movement, Laporte announced his intention of opening the Covent Garden Theatre with a foreign troupe in opposition to the company at the Olympic.

[1] *Morning Chronicle*, May 4, 1833.

[2] In passing, it ought to be mentioned that it was due to the liberality of that remarkable woman, Madame Vestris, in offering the Olympic to the Covent Garden Company, that the performers were relieved for the remainder of the season. Yates also tendered the use of the scenery, wardrobe, etc., of the Adelphi.

This served to bring down the severest criticism from the public, who objected to the use of a house, dedicated to the service of the national drama, for the exhibition of foreign operas. But public opinion could do no more than express itself on the subject, it could not prevent the use of the patents for such purposes. "It is true," lamented the "Morning Chronicle" (May 10, 1833), "that as matters now stand it is not in the power of the highest authority in the drama to prevent the practice; but it is in the power of the public not to patronize it; and sure we are that this state of things cannot long continue."

Respecting the union of the patents, all doubts were removed on that score when, on the 27th of May (1833), Alfred Bunn published an address, officially announcing himself as sole lessee of the patent houses.[1] The fact alone was sufficient to arouse the antagonism of all enemies to monopoly, and this feeling was intensified, on the part of the actors at least, by the policy of retrenchment adopted by Bunn. However justified by business principles, no schedule of maximum salaries would be submitted to quietly by performers who had been used to demanding, and getting, their own terms. The Covent Garden Company, led by Knowles, re-

[1] Bunn, *The Stage*, i, 107.

fused to sanction with their assistance the monopoly as thus sealed. Some of them joined with Abbott and Egerton in a project to secure the Coburg during the summer, and to appeal for a license for a third winter theatre.[1] The most alluring bait was held out by Bunn to Knowles, but the latter indignantly refused to consider any overtures, preferring " to stand by his comates in exile." [2]

Bulwer's Dramatic Performances Bill was at this time making its way through the House of Commons, and many looked to it to relieve the distressed condition of authors and actors, brought about by the monopoly. In the mean time preparations went on to open the Coburg with the national drama, and Knowles himself headed a petition for the erection of a third theatre.[3] Never in the history of the patents had so many things been doing to work the utter ruin of the monopoly. The most painstaking and determined attitude was taken by the promoters of the petition. Knowles sought the coöperation of Macready,[4] but the actor had thus early learned prudence, and merely took

---

[1] *Morning Chronicle*, June 3, 1833.

[2] Bunn, *The Stage*, i, 115, footnote.

[3] The announcement of this appeared first in the *Observer*, June 9, 1833.

[4] Macready's *Diaries* under date June 12, 1833.

the matter under consideration. That the petition might certainly reach the King himself and receive a speedy answer, it was proposed to present it to him in person, on one of his levee days. Other details included the securing of a theatre, ready to be occupied as soon as the petition should be granted. So determined were some of the opponents to the monopoly that they did not scruple to advise that, if the petition were rejected, a third theatre should be started anyhow, legally or illegally. However, a more sober counsel prevailed, and the petitioners bided their time.

With all their hopes and careful preparations Knowles and his followers did not receive an answer from the King as soon as they had anticipated. Bunn memorialized the Crown against the petition for a third theatre, and felt his own importance sufficiently to think that he influenced the final decision.[1] It is probable, however, that the King reserved his answer to Knowles's petition, pending the fate of Bulwer's bill. The latter was defeated in the House of Lords on the 2d of August. On the 16th of the same month the petition for a third theatre was denied by the Crown.[2] One of the curious circumstances

[1] For this example of self–sufficiency, see *The Stage*, i, 122. For Bunn's petition, see *ibid.* 115–122.

[2] *Morning Chronicle*, June 10, August 19, 1833.

associated with the affair is that the signers
of the petition received no official notification of
the King's refusal to grant the request. All
that could be gleaned in the matter came through
persons connected with the patent houses.[1] The
petitioners themselves entertained strong doubts
of the trustworthiness of the rumored rejection
of their petition, for as late as the last of August we find Knowles writing from the provinces
(where he was playing in the "circuit") to London, "in some anxiety" to ascertain the facts in
the case. Finally, three weeks after the first
report of the King's denial to grant his sanction
to the petition, the committee appointed to represent the petitioners received official notice from
Mr. T. B. Mash, of the Lord Chamberlain's
office, "that under existing circumstances, it
is impossible that His Majesty can comply with
the prayer of the petition."[2]

As usual in such events, explanations were
numerous, and gratis, why the petition failed to
receive the King's approval. Some thought that
it had been injudiciously drawn up, containing, it
was alleged, too much argument. It was asserted
by others that Knowles failed to secure the

---

[1] This arose, no doubt, from a letter written to Bunn by the
Vice-Chamberlain, August 15, 1833. See Bunn, *The Stage*, i,
122.

[2] *Morning Chronicle*, September 2, 9, 1833, quoting *Observer*.

crown sanction to his third theatre project, because, forsooth, he had refused £500 from Bunn for a play, by which refusal he had virtually shown his insincerity as to his protestations regarding the "national drama."[1] As to Knowles's motive in refusing to be lured by so tempting an inducement as that just alluded to, it ought to be said in his justification, and to his credit, that he spurned the offer for two reasons. In the first place, he would hear of no compromise that did not include the Covent Garden actors,—and under Bunn's management there was little hope of this. And in the next place, Knowles was irreconcilably opposed to the union of the patent houses. On this point there is no misunderstanding the tone of the following laconic note from Knowles to Bunn, dated September 23, 1833:

" As I consider the present monopoly to be an insult to the public, an injury to the actor and the author, and an unwarranted departure from the purpose for which the Patents of Theatres Royal, Drury Lane, and Covent Garden were granted — namely, the maintaining of two distinct and rival companies of comedians, I think

[1] Tait's *Edinburgh Magazine* for December, 1833, in an article entitled, "The Stage and the Drama." Quoted in the *Morning Chronicle* for November 29, 1833. It is true that Bunn offered Knowles £500 for a full play, when the regular price was only £300. See *The Stage*, vol. i, pp. 115–119, footnote.

it due to my own respectability to state, in reply to your letter, that no consideration whatever can induce me to connect myself with either of these establishments." [1]

It is far more probable that the petition of Knowles for a third theatre was rejected on quite other grounds than those alleged. The fact that the answer to the prayer was postponed until after the fate of Bulwer's Dramatic Bill was known is significant. Had that bill passed, Knowles's petition had been needless. Its failure seemed to indicate the temper of Parliament relative to the theatrical situation. Likewise, the opinion of the Lord Chancellor in 1831, in the hearing of Arnold's case for an extension of privileges at the English Opera House, augured the defeat of the application for a third theatre. Again, the union of the patent houses under Bunn's management was looked on by many as a legitimate experiment made with the object of saving the patent houses from ruin, rather than an attempt to establish a tyrannical monopoly. The project of a third theatre party, if successful, might frustrate this hope. Moreover, the complaints of Knowles and his followers represented the temporary grievances of a select few, rather than the general cause of a free stage. At any rate, such seems to have

[1] Bunn, *The Stage*, i, 117, footnote.

been the interpretation placed on the petition by the Lord Chamberlain, as shown by his letter to the patentee, acknowledging the latter's memorial against a third theatre.

" I am desired by the Lord Chamberlain," writes the Deputy-Chamberlain to Bunn, " to express a hope you will employ as many of the Covent Garden performers as are deserving, and not confine your selection to the Drury Lane Company." [1] And, finally, the Duke of Devonshire was lukewarm, if not openly hostile, towards all attempts to invade the patent rights of the " great theatres." Enough of this attitude has appeared in the prosecutions of the minors to make it unnecessary to dilate further on the point here.

The " Observer," [2] with its usual cynical acuteness, consoled the defeated petitioners in the following strain, apropos of Bulwer's rejected bill: " We believe that the advocates for a third theatre now see the uselessness of proceeding farther in their enterprise at present, and are content to wait the issue of the experiment about to be tried at the two Winter Theatres. The opinion is, that it must fail, and that the public cannot again be brought to take an interest in theatricals, without some fresh and power-

[1] Bunn, *The Stage*, i, 122.
[2] *Morning Chronicle*, August 26, 1833.

ful excitement. How is that to be procured?
New plays we hear of none that have any chance
of producing the slightest sensation; and we
know more than one author, formerly in the
habit of writing original pieces, who positively
refuse to make any attempt in the present state
of the stage, declaring that they will not throw
away their time and talents. As to actors, from
what we have lately seen and heard, we believe
that there is scarcely a single new one worth
transferring from the provinces."

"The experiment about to be tried at the
Winter Theatres" was not calculated to relieve
the situation. The policy, outlined by Bunn in
his address, to reduce expenses at all hazards,
proved contradictory to the express object of
restoring the national drama. "We can conceive
of nothing more unjust or base," writes one of
the critics on Bunn's combining the two companies.[1] The maximum salary schedule made it
impracticable for the lessee to secure the best
talent for the stage. Ellen Tree absolutely refused to sign articles at either patent house, but
planned a lecture tour in the provinces instead.
Later she entered into an engagement with an
English company to act Shakesperean plays in
Germany. Charles Kean and Wallack were also
interested in this project of going to Germany,

[1] *New Monthly Magazine* for 1833, pt. ii, p. 247.

and about the middle of November (1833) the
company sailed for Hamburg. Powell came to
America and acted here very successfully during
the season of 1833–34. Sheridan Knowles, after
starring it in the provinces, contemplated a trip
to America for the same season, but he afterwards changed his mind and devoted himself as
actor and author to the service of the Victoria
(Coburg). The next year (1834), however, he
carried out his original plan, and came to the
United States.[1] "We are grieved to hear,"
breaks out the "Observer" (September 15,
1833), "and can scarcely believe, that the existing circumstances of the drama in this country
are likely for a time to banish from our shores
not only Ellen Tree, but Sheridan Knowles.
This indeed looks like the encouragement of our
national drama, when almost our only original
author is obliged to seek shelter and sustenance
in foreign countries! The Germans have a just
admiration of Shakespeare, and will no doubt
rejoice in the opportunity of seeing his plays
performed by English actors."

The effort to get relieved from the theatrical
monopoly lingered on for a few months. Serle
took up the cause after the rejection of Knowles's

[1] *Life of James Sheridan Knowles*, p. 118. For the movements of the "exiled actors" see also *Morning Chronicle* for
September 23 and November 18, 1833.

petition, and sought to enlist the leading actors
and dramatists. Macready entered into the plan
so far as to suggest, as some security to actors,
authors, and the public, a system of graduated
prices, based on the quality of the dramatic
exhibition, as indicated by the Lord Chamberlain on the license granted. Wallack furiously
attacked the plan, " contending for universal and
unrestricted license to act the drama in every
street." [1] A compromise was at last reached in a
plan which proposed to confine the classic drama
to the four large theatres of Westminster, restricting the performance of the regular drama
elsewhere to a great distance. Macready was to
confer with Arnold and Morris on the subject,
and, if they should enter into the proposed plan,
all parties were to join in a petition to Parliament.[2] But nothing came of this attempt,
and the matter was dropped until further development caused the authors to unite in
a final effort to defend themselves against the
monopoly.

[1] Macready's *Diaries*, December 25, 1833.

[2] *Ibid.* December 31, 1833. From the allusion to Arnold
and Morris, it appears that Drury Lane, Covent Garden, the
English Opera House, and the Little Theatre in the Haymarket, were the four theatres included in the plan.

CHAPTER XIV

THE last act of the tragi-comic drama was drawing to a close. The majors had ceased to persecute the minors, and were content to hear of "*Macbeth* at the Olympic, the *School of Scandal* at the Adelphi, or *Hamlet* at the Surrey," so long as they could defend themselves within their own stronghold; for the time had at last arrived when the minor managers invaded the ranks of the patentees, carrying off the great actors to "star" at the little houses.[1] The lesser managers were the better able to do this, as they depended largely on the talents of the leading performer and did not attempt to keep the average high for the whole company. Moreover their highest admission was only 5s., while the boxes at the patent houses were 7s. Kean was Kean at either price.

The tendency was greatly increased by the attitude of the Marquis of Conyngham, who came into the lord chamberlainship in 1836. From the outset, he was extremely hostile to the monopoly and correspondingly friendly to the

[1] Bunn, *The Stage*, i, 48, 49.

minors. The Haymarket Theatre, that had had
its license but recently extended to eight months,
was now given a further increase to ten months.
The season of 1839 at that theatre amounted
to 250 nights. It has already been mentioned
that the Strand was now licensed, and that the
Lyceum, Adelphi, and Olympic all received an
addition of two months to their licenses, while
Braham was permitted to open a new theatre,
the St. James. Add to these the sanction of the
Lord Chamberlain to the Opera Buffa (a minor
Italian opera house), the granting of the privilege of promenade concerts at the English Opera
House, extra favors shown the King's Theatre,
and, finally, the restriction of the patent houses
to English pieces only, and one may get some
notion of Lord Conyngham's policy respecting
the theatrical question. It took the greater part
of a century for the patentees to learn that the
Licensing Act (so much praised by Cibber and
the friends of theatrical monopoly at the time of
its enactment) might operate against, as well as
for, the patent houses. As pointed out by Chesterfield and others, that act made the Lord
Chamberlain the veritable sovereign over the
drama and the stage. Such a power might be
harmless, or it might be dangerous. For a long
period of years its exercise was considered most
beneficial by those it happened to protect,— the

patentees, and most oppressive by those it sought to exterminate, — the minors. But there was nothing in the provisions of 10 George II to prevent a reversal of the application of the power vested in the Lord Chamberlain. The turn in the lane had been reached at last.

The operations of the Lord Chamberlain's office to the undoing of the monopoly may best be seen in the Lenten controversy. This extended over a series of years, and forms one of the last spokes in the patentees' wheel of misfortune. I select this example for the reason, also, that it clearly illustrates the anomalous condition of the laws regulating the theatres, — one of the main arguments for the abolition of the monopoly. Early in 1831, C. Kemble (as patentee of Covent Garden) applied to the Lord Chamberlain for permission to perform the regular drama on Wednesdays and Fridays during Lent, but was denied the privilege.[1] The following year no such application was made, as it was thought that the patent theatres could not be kept open profitably. In 1833, however, both the patentees applied for Lenten privileges. The contemplated engagements which Captain Polhill had in view at that time rendered it important to his interests that permission to play during Lent without interruption should be

[1] Bunn says (ii, 194) in January, 1832, but this is a mistake.

conceded. Without awaiting the Lord Chamberlain's reply to this request, the Drury Lane manager, on the 25th of February, announced *Moses in Egypt* for the Wednesday following. The Duke of Devonshire thereupon sent his deputy (T. B. Mash) to learn of Polhill if he did not deem a former communication from the Lord Chamberlain sufficient (referring, no doubt, to the negative answer to Kemble's application in 1831). Polhill and his advisers showed considerable spirit on the occasion, talked of appealing to the people, and so on; whereupon a positive command on the subject was issued by the Lord Chamberlain's orders. On the following morning the Drury Lane lessee, accompanied by his manager (Bunn), called on the Duke of Devonshire and besought him to permit for one night the performance as advertised, after which, if anything in it were found objectionable, it would be withdrawn. But to this proposal the Duke gave a peremptory refusal, on the ground that, as the piece announced consisted of dancing, it could not be otherwise than objectionable. The matter here ended for a time. The " Observer " assumed that the Lord Chamberlain's decision " met with the entire and unqualified approbation of the highest authority." [1]

The peculiar thing about the circumstance

[1] *Morning Chronicle*, January 28, March 4, 1833.

relative to the Lenten prohibition is that it applied to the patent theatres only, inasmuch as the Lord Chamberlain's authority, as defined by the Licensing Act, did not extend beyond the liberties of Westminster. " The position in which the patent theatres are placed by the recent prohibition," observes the "London Times," " is not a little curious. The term ' monopoly' in their case has come to imply their not being able to do what the other theatres do. Thus at the Victoria and other minor theatres the course of the drama proceeds as usual, while at the Adelphi a series of entertainments, of which comic humor is the leading feature, are given without interruption ; while at Covent Garden a sacred drama, on the story of Jephtha, conveying solemn impressions, from some of Händel's finest music, is prohibited as a profanation of this period of fasting and mortification. There is doubt, it seems, where the odium should fix — on the Lord Chamberlain or on the Bishop of London. Let some intelligent Member of Parliament, for common respect to property deserves it, bring the question before the House of Commons, so that the blame may rest in the right place. The incident is enough to make us the laughing-stock of the whole continent." [1]

No further attempt was made by the patentees

[1] Quoted by *Examiner*, February 23, 1834.

to introduce performances on Wednesdays and Fridays during Lent until 1837, when Bunn proposed to bid defiance to the authority of the Marquis of Conyngham. The opera of *Fair Rosamond* was presented at Drury Lane on Tuesday, February 28, 1837. The success of the piece induced the manager to advertise it for Thursday and Friday of the same week. On Thursday, March 2, the Lord Chamberlain sent a letter to the Secretary of the Drury Lane Committee, forbidding the theatre to be opened on the following evening. This prohibition was explained on the ground that it was customary to permit only sacred entertainments on the Wednesdays and Fridays of Lent. The announcement for the Friday performance was recalled accordingly. But Bunn resented this tyrannical use of power, by preparing a petition[1] to Parliament, in which the facts were stated in respect to the closing of the theatre on the night in question. The memorial then submits to the House of Commons the partiality displayed in favor of the Adelphi, Strand, and St. James theatres (all of them as much within the jurisdiction of the Lord Chamberlain as Drury Lane), by allowing them to keep open on the evening prohibited to the patent house, and that too " to give a variety of entertainments of a mixed and ribald charac-

[1] Bunn, *The Stage*, ii, 198–204.

ter." In detail the Adelphi was open on the
Wednesdays and Fridays of Lent with an actress in "the delineation of the passions," with
comic singing by different persons. Among the
songs on these occasions was "Jim Crow," and
other negro melodies. The Bedouin Arabs were
also performers at the Adelphi; and a mono-
logue and scenic displays were among the attractions. The St. James had been open on the
same (Friday) evening with "comic songs,"
"imitations of the London actors," and a pantomime. The Strand had presented "A Wallet
of Whims and Waggeries," and a variety of
music, dancing, juggling, gymnastic exercises,
and scenic views.

Mr. T. S. Duncombe undertook the support
of Bunn's petition. The Lord Chancellor was
first approached in the hope that his influence
might be secured in behalf of the patentee.
From the communications which passed between
the Chancellor and Duncombe it appears that
the custom of observing Lent had ceased to exist
as regarded the minor theatres, but that it had
continued at Drury Lane "on account of its
having heretofore suited the lessee's convenience
to remain closed on those evenings." Duncombe
came near voicing the general sentiment on the
subject when he declared that, "when we know
what is going on in every portion of this metrop-

olis up to the days now in dispute, *all parties* consider the restriction attempted to be placed on Drury Lane Theatre as a gross piece of humbug, and, as I contend, a stretch of power on the part of the Lord Chamberlain's department unsanctioned by law."[1]

Pending the action of Parliament on his petition the manager of Drury Lane decided to open the theatre on Friday, March 17, in defiance of the Lord Chamberlain's prohibition. The communication containing this bold determination was shown to Sir John Russell, then Secretary of the Home Department, and to other members of Government. It was their opinion that if the parties interested in Drury Lane Theatre persisted in their intention of opening for performances on Wednesdays or Fridays in Lent, "they would expose themselves to all the penal consequences of persons playing *without a license ;*" and it was clearly intimated that a further prosecution of the subject by the manager of Drury Lane might endanger his patent.

The victory on this occasion, as formerly, was unquestionably on the side of the Lord Chamberlain ; but while the minors enjoyed to their full the situation, the general public was thoroughly indignant at the Lenten farce, which

---

[1] This most interesting episode has not been injured in the relating by Bunn. See *The Stage*, ii, 194, 215.

belonged to a bygone age. For once, though the fact produced no material benefits to the patentees, the popular sympathy was on the side of the monopoly. This was due, however, rather to the nature of the controversy than to any respect for patent rights. "There are no Oratorios this year, — pretenses 'most musical, most melancholy,' for keeping open the two Great Theatres on the nights called 'holy,'" remarks the "Spectator" (February 25) on the Lenten quarrel of 1837, " so that on Wednesday and Friday the two *greats* are deserted. Covent Garden looks like the mausoleum of the departed Drama — 'the tomb of all the Capulets;' and Drury like a great warehouse of stage properties. The sacredness of these 'holy days,' by the way, is of a very peculiar character; it is only profaned by dramatic performances at the theatres licensed by the Lord Chamberlain. The medley entertainments at the Adelphi, the St. James's, and the New Strand Theatre — which last Webster has engaged for the Lent nights only — bear the same relation to the regular performances on other nights as those evasive esculents, salt fish, parsnips, and pancakes, do to the flesh and fowl of other days. . . . Really, it is time that these conventional hypocrisies should be done away with. . . . A Protestant crusade against salt fish would be a fine thing: the Pope's bull would stand no chance against the roast beef of England."

In 1839 Bunn made a final attempt to give entertainments on the forbidden evenings. This time the proposed "show" was Van Amburgh's Lions. In an attempt to rid himself of the annoyance and tyranny of the Lord Chamberlain, the Drury Lane manager and his performers petitioned Parliament, on the 18th of February (1839), to be relieved from the authority of that official during Lent. As on the previous occasion, Duncombe took charge of Bunn's cause in the House, and though objections were raised to the irregularity of presenting a petition without first giving formal notice, he succeeded in getting a motion read to address the Queen, supplicating Her Majesty to order the Lord Chamberlain not to restrict theatres in Westminster from exhibiting amusements permitted to other theatres in the country. The motion, however, was lost by a very large majority.[1]

Failing in his effort to get the House to suggest the line of duty to the Crown, on the 28th of February, Duncombe contented himself with a motion to commit the sentiment of the members to the resolution, "That it is the opinion of this House that during Lent no greater restric-

[1] The vote stood 70 to 160. Hansard's *Parliamentary Debates*, 3d Series, vol. 45, cols. 577-583.

tions should be passed upon theatrical entertainments within the city of Westminster than are placed upon the like amusements at the same period in every other part of the metropolis." In presenting this resolution, Duncombe created much amusement for the House, at the expense of ministers and other high officials of state and church, by showing up the absurdity of the Lenten theory in the light of actual practice.[1] Relative to the theatrical controversy there was but one rational conclusion : to leave the Westminster theatres at the caprice of the Lord Chamberlain, in reference to Lent, was a piece of manifest injustice.

Lord John Russell was the main opponent to the motion. He stated that, after the question came before the House on the 18th of February, he had conferred with the Bishop of London, who gave as his opinion that the Westminster theatres ought to close on the Wednesdays and Fridays during Lent, out of respect to the established religion of the country. Lord John then reviewed the legislative acts which had led to the anomalous condition of the theatres respecting Lent. The Licensing Act gave the Lord Cham-

[1] The debates on Duncombe's motion of 28th of February are reported by Hansard, *Parliamentary Debates*, 3d Series, vol. 45, columns 1020–1045. Bunn (*The Stage*, vol. iii, ch. 1, especially pp. 128–152) gives a very complete account of the proceedings in and out of Parliament.

400 THE STRUGGLE FOR A FREE STAGE

berlain jurisdiction over theatrical entertainments in Westminster, and ever since the enactment of that law (and for the matter of that, long before), the custom of observing Lent in that portion of the metropolis had been practiced. By another act of Parliament the power to license theatres outside of Westminster, within a radius of twenty miles from London, was vested in the magistrates. While it had turned out that those places of entertainment outside of Westminster had been exhibiting performances on " holy days," nevertheless, they were constantly liable to severe penalties for being illegally established. If managers within the jurisdiction of the Lord Chamberlain complained of the hardship of being compelled to close on Wednesdays and Fridays during Lent, their attention was called to the provision in their licenses restricting them on the days in question. Furthermore the antiquity of the custom would seem a sufficient reason for the observance. Lord John acknowledged the lack of uniformity in the practice of the custom, but maintained that the rest of the metropolis should conform to Westminster rather than the latter should follow the rest of the city in abolishing the convention.

The majority of the House disagreed with the Secretary of the Home Department. It was declared an absurdity and an injustice to insist

on a religious observance anywhere, if not every-
where, in the Kingdom; and it was denounced
as sheer hypocrisy to maintain one religious
law for the rich and another for the poor. Some
went so far as to assert that the whole Lenten
farce was of Popish origin, and no part of the
Protestant forms. That part of Sir John's speech
referring to the Bishop's advice was pooh-poohed;
the members knew all that before, and they
knew also that the voice of the people would
support the motion before the House, in spite of
the Bishop's testimony, and in spite of the Government's attitude (as represented by Lord John
Russell). The time had passed for making English people look upon Wednesdays and Fridays
as different from the other days in Lent. The
debate on the resolution grew exceedingly warm.
The position of the Government seemed at utter
variance with the popular mind. The Chancellor of the Exchequer (Mr. T. S. Rice) joined
Lord John Russell in his opposition to the measure; while D'Israeli, of course, supported the
motion. But party lines were by no means followed in the debate, and when the House divided
it was found that the resolution had a majority
of 20, the vote standing 92 to 72.

Supported by this action of the House of Commons Bunn announced the opera of *Farinelli*
at Drury Lane for Friday, the 8th of March

(1839). But to the patentee's unbounded surprise and chagrin an interdiction came from the Lord Chamberlain's office (March 6) forbidding the performance. And this time the command was "by direction of Her Majesty's Ministers." [1] The quarrel was taken up immediately by the public prints, and the whole transaction on the part of the Lord Chamberlain was characterized as trumpery.[2] On the same day of this prohibition Duncombe called for the correspondence between the Lord Chamberlain and the Drury Lane manager on the subject,[3] and five days later (March 11) brought in another motion to the effect that the House had learned "with regret and surprise" that Her Majesty's Ministers had seen fit "to interfere with the wholly unfettered discretion which the legislature had been pleased to vest in the Lord Chamberlain, . . . by directing that officer . . . so as to defeat the manifest object of a resolution of this Commons House of Parliament." In discussing this motion Duncombe charged the Ministers with directing the actions of the Lord Chamberlain in closing the theatres, and that by so doing they had not only infringed the prerogative of

[1] Bunn, *The Stage*, iii, 140.

[2] See *Morning Chronicle* for February 27, 1839. Article quoted by Bunn, iii, 141–145.

[3] Hansard's *Parliamentary Debates*, 3d Series, vol. 45, col. 1318.

the Crown, but also "had been most disrespectful to the House of Commons."

Lord John Russell did not deny that he and other members of the Cabinet had advised the Lord Chamberlain in what he had done, because they had not deemed a mere resolution of Parliament superior to the laws of the land. Furthermore, taking into consideration the contradiction of sentiment shown in the two votes taken in the House (the first on the 18th, the second on the 28th of February), he saw no reason to suppose that the resolution embodied the deliberate opinion of the members. The contradiction of the existing theatrical laws in the metropolis was admitted, but the discrepancy was placed to the blame of the minors, and not the majors, in violating the statutes. At this point, it is interesting to note that Sir John Russell stated that it was the purpose of the Government to correct the deficient laws regulating theatres in London, either by introducing a bill, or by providing, in some of the police measures then before the House, for magistrates to have the power to grant licenses for theatrical entertainments, as well as for music and dancing. On this phase of the subject he gave it as his sincere opinion that "the power of procuring good and respectable theatrical entertainments should extend throughout the metropolis." [1]

[1] *Parliamentary Debates*, 3d Series, vol. 46, 229–243.

By this strategic move toward conciliation, satisfying, in a degree, Duncombe's insistence on some definite promise that the regulations respecting Lent should be removed the following year, the motion was prevented from passing. But the airing of the Lenten controversy made clear the necessity of some immediate regulation whereby favor should be shown impartially to majors and minors.

The Lenten restrictions were not the only indignities which the "inviolable patents" had to suffer at the hands of the Lord Chamberlain. The character of the performances themselves was limited to the English tongue. In May, 1837, Bunn secured Madame Pasta for a few nights in Italian opera, but the announcement was met with a mandate from the Chamberlain's office forbidding everything at Drury Lane except English entertainments. This order referred to the "Opera Arrangement" of 1792, by which no Italian operas were to be given at either of the patent houses, but only at the King's Theatre.[1] It was retorted that by that arrangement the Opera House was to be opened on Tuesdays and Saturdays only, and that recently the Chamberlain had violated the treaty of 1792 by

[1] On the accession of Victoria to the throne (1837), the Opera House in the Haymarket became "The Queen's Theatre," or "Her Majesty's."

permitting the Italian Opera House to be open "week after week" for six nights in the week, and, in addition, to give six successive morning concerts, besides German and French operas, French plays, and even English performances. But it was useless to point out to the Marquis of Conyngham that "arrangements" and "laws" and "settlements" had been broken time and again by all parties, and hence were dead letters; that official was determined to be his own interpreter of these things.

No longer able to endure the galling yoke of Lord Conyngham's tyranny, the Drury Lane manager, in his extremity, dared even to approach Windsor Castle. But instead of getting an audience from His Majesty, he received a note instead, which coolly stated that if Mr. Bunn's visit was with reference to the theatre, he must carry his affair to the Lord Chamberlain. Bunn, it should be remembered, was, in a sense, a member of the King's household, since he belonged to the corps of gentlemen-at-arms. Nevertheless the sovereign took such umbrage at the circumstance that he remarked that "if Mr. Bunn attempted to interfere with His Majesty's prerogative in regard to the patent theatres, he should be under the necessity of requiring him to leave the corps of gentlemen-at-arms."[1]

[1] Bunn, *The Stage*, ii, 222–229.

This prohibition respecting Madame Pasta came at the very time when the licenses of the leading minors under the Lord Chamberlain's jurisdiction were extended, and, for this reason, operated as a double hardship on the patentees. The House of Commons was appealed to, through T. S. Duncombe and Sir Benjamin Hall, to amend the Licensing Act; but the bill was so modified in the House of Lords as to increase rather than diminish the Lord Chamberlain's power. Before final action could be taken on the measure His Majesty died, and Parliament was dissolved.

The antagonism of the Lord Chamberlain to the patent theatre found a new opportunity for exhibiting itself at the close of the season of 1836–37. The twenty-one year license issued to the Drury Lane Committee in September, 1816, had just expired. When Bunn proposed to open Drury Lane in the autumn of 1837 he received a message from the Chamberlain's office demanding on what authority he based his actions. In answer the Drury Lane manager brought forward the Killigrew patent, which had been purchased, finally, from the Covent Garden proprietors December 13, 1813, as already related. This was the first time since the old parchment had gone to sleep in 1682 that it was claimed to be of active worth (with the possible exception of the brief period when John Rich controlled Covent Garden and Lincoln's-Inn-Fields). And it was the first time since the days of Charles II that it was positively known (by the general public) to be in existence.[1] Its reappearance came too late to be of any material benefit to its owners, while the circumstance was in no sense calculated to relieve the strained relations between the patentee and the Lord Chamberlain.

One more illustration will serve to make clear the widening breach between the patent theatre and the office which had so long defended the monopoly of amusements. In 1838, M. Spontini contemplated a series of German operas to be given in London the following year, and, as he afterwards claimed, got a promise from the Lord Chamberlain to issue him a license for that purpose. In the first year (1833) of Bunn's lesseeship at the patent house Spontini had been introduced so successfully in opera at Drury Lane that Bunn now (1839) conceived the plan of assuming the responsibility of the German opera venture, and arranged with Spontini accordingly. As the latter required an advance payment of his salary (£1000) the Drury Lane manager,

---

[1] *The Stage*, ii, 280–81. Bunn attributes the animosity of Lord Conyngham to this circumstance, since, by the appearance of the "dormant patent," the annual fee of £100 to the Lord Chamberlain ceased. *The Stage*, iii, 92.

although feeling protected by his patent, thought to make assurance doubly sure by sounding the Lord Chamberlain on the subject of the German opera. That official requested Bunn to put his case in writing. As Bunn was at that time lessee of the English Opera House also, he deemed it wise to apply for the opera license at that theatre, and not run the risk of compromising his patent rights at Drury Lane by tacitly admitting the superior power of a license to his patent. But, as it turned out, he had as well saved his shrewdness for some other occasion; for he was notified in unequivocal terms that the Lord Chamberlain " had decided not to grant a license for German Opera," and that " only English entertainments of the stage were sanctioned at the Theatres Royal, Drury Lane and Covent Garden." [1]

In defense of his rights the Drury Lane manager asserted that the Lord Chamberlain had exceeded his power in attempting to close a playhouse on the ground that it had no license to represent a particular piece, since, it was claimed, the Act of 10 George II gave to that official of the King's household authority only to prohibit plays, making no mention of licensing them. For example, the opera of *Fair Rosamond* was not licensed on its first representation

[1] Bunn, *The Stage*, iii, 79–93.

(February 28, 1837), — the Chamberlain had stated merely that he did not prohibit it.[1] But Bunn must have known that this was a mere quibble over terms, and that the practice of a hundred years was strongly against him. The fact is, that so long as the Lord Chamberlain exercised his authority to the disadvantage of the minors, and to the consequent favor of the patent houses, the monopoly made no complaint of tyranny; but as soon as the tables were turned the injustice of the situation was quickly appreciated by the patentees.

It is a relief to hasten to the end. The truth must be told; the monopoly in theatrical amusements had run its natural course; "the wheel had turned full circle." The old Killigrew patent that had been dubbed "dormant" had, in reality, "died and made no sign;" and the contentions for the decade (1832–1842) were merely over the details of the funeral. The patentees were the first to realize the hopelessness of their situation. For long they had maintained successfully that the grants of Charles II to Killigrew and Davenant conferred upon the holders of those documents a monopoly of the drama, limiting all other houses of theatrical amusements to a narrow range of performances. The reverse of this had now come to pass; and the resistance of Man-

[1] *The Stage*, ii, 196.

ager Bunn to the altered state of affairs in the theatrical kingdom only served to confirm the change. The struggle had been a long one, and in the main disheartening; but the dawn of the new century brought a gleam of hope to the struggle for a liberated stage. Reformation along many lines filled the air, and a free theatre for the regular drama came in on the crest of the wave of the general movement.

As usual in such cases, the fact was assured before legislation gave the final stamp of recognition. The end was prefaced also by a petition from nearly all the leading dramatic authors praying for a law to protect their profession. In the discussion in the House of Commons on this petition Lord Mahon took occasion to review the existing conditions of the drama and the stage. The mischief to the dramatic art, it was declared, had resulted from the legislation on the subject. The penalty provided by the Act of 10 George II had been, said Lord Mahon, a dead letter from the day of its enactment; for at first the actors were too poor to pay the fine, and later they defied it. It was this contradiction of law and practice that had produced the state of affairs they were importuned to correct. If it were asked, what need was there for modifying the laws, since the minors had invaded with impunity the sacred precincts of the patent monopoly? it was answered, that so long as the laws might be enforced the safety of the drama was endangered, and the position of the actor made precarious; for "nearly every actor who trod the boards of our theatres was performing under the risk of a penalty of £50 a-night." In like manner, theatres, unless sanctioned by a license from the Lord Chamberlain, were held to be illegal in courts of law; in consequence of which anomalous condition contracts of authors, actors, and others with managers of unlicensed theatres were made always with the possibility of being declared null and void. Herein lay a new argument in favor of a legally free stage.

Supplementing and abetting this evil was that of the monopoly, repugnant to the sentiments of the public, and to the interests of the monopolists also. If the argument were raised that the patent theatres were necessary for the encouragement and defense of dramatic genius, Lord Mahon desired to call attention to the facts, namely, that "nearly all the best dramas produced since the establishment of the patents had been brought forward irregularly or unwillingly. Johnson forced Goldsmith's *She Stoops to Conquer* into the theatre. Tobin died regretting that he could not succeed in having the *Honeymoon* performed. Lillo produced *George Barnwell* in an irregular theatre after it had been rejected by the holders of the patents. *Douglas* was cast back on Home's hands. Fielding was introduced as a dramatist to the public at an unlicensed house, and Mrs. Inchbald's comedy had lain two years neglected when by a trifling accident she was able to obtain the manager's approval." While the public was thus not served by the monopoly, the managers of the patent houses fared no better. Statistics were produced showing that "the monopolists were reaping only bankruptcy and ruin." [1]

As a result of this petition from the dramatists the House ordered returns of copies of any communications that had been addressed to the Secretary of State for the Home Department, in the course of the year, complaining of the laws regulating the drama. On the 26th of the following July (1843) a bill was brought in known as the Theatre Regulation Bill. The speed with which this was carried through both Houses of Parliament shows the ripeness of the time for settling the theatrical controversies of a century. If petitions were presented against the measure, or if objections were raised to it in debate, they were all for the purpose of making sure that the vexed question should be settled forever ; for all par-

[1] *Parliamentary Debates*, 3d Series, vol. lxiv, cols. 791–800. The petition of the dramatic authors was presented to the House of Commons by Lord Mahon in June, 1842.

ties were finally agreed that the incongruous and unjust theatrical regulations were no longer to be borne. Five days after its first reading the bill was read a second time without debate in the House of Commons (July 31); and on the 4th of August it was considered by the Committee of the whole House.

The low state of the national drama was admitted by all those who spoke on the measure. Sir J. Graham made the assertion that the chief plays of the country were to be seen at the Haymarket Theatre only. The patent theatres were closed for such a period of the year that but for the Haymarket it might be said that Shakespeare's plays could not be represented in London for several months in the year. As far back as 1833 we read the following in the "New Monthly Magazine" [1] relative to the Haymarket: "We recommend a visit to this theatre to all who have a liking for the old comedy. It is the only place where we can get a glimpse even of its skirts." In 1835 the "Examiner" (July 26) speaks thus of *The Rivals* at the same theatre: "We have seen it better played in all its parts, but we never saw it go off better. . . . We must say generally of the entertainments of this theatre that they are deserving of every support. It is the only theatre now where we catch a glimpse

[1] *New Monthly Magazine*, pt. ii, p. 518.

of the good old comedy." And again on August 16, 1835, to the same effect.

Duncombe testified that he thought the Regulation Bill would operate to the benefit of the patent houses. Indeed, he said, he happened to know that Drury Lane Theatre had been leased in consequence of the introduction of the bill.[1] Mr. Duncombe had made a canvass of authors, actors, and managers, and all had concurred in the opinion that the conflicting and injurious laws ought to be altered. In discussing the clause in the bill relative to the question of what licenses the Lord Chamberlain should be empowered to grant, the speaker thought it ought to include the counties of Middlesex and Surrey. Otherwise the vitiating principle then in practice might recur, and the measure would fall short of its intended purpose. The objection raised to this suggestion was that, by inserting such a clause, the magistrates of the two counties named would be placed on a different legal basis

---

[1] The allusion is to Bunn. At the close of the season 1835–1836 the union of the two houses was broken, Bunn giving up Covent Garden. After the disgraceful squabbles between Bunn and Macready (April-May, 1836), the latter went over to Covent Garden and became its lessee the following year, in opposition to Drury Lane. Bunn remained at Drury Lane until 1839, when he left it, a bankrupt. On the passage of the Theatre Regulation Bill, he again, for a short time, assumed control of Drury Lane.

from the justices of the rest of the Kingdom. The amendment was therefore passed by.

The bill was reported on the 5th of August, passed its third reading without debate on the 7th, and on the same day was carried to the House of Lords and read the first time. Three days later it went through the second reading, followed on the 11th by consideration in the Lords' Committee. Lord Beaumont moved to strike out the clause providing for Shakespeare's plays to be represented, and the Earl of Glengall brought up the antiquated argument of "inviolable patents." Arnold, of the Lyceum, petitioned to know whether it was the intention of the bill to allow the minors to play the regular drama when they pleased, and if so, whether the English Opera House would be included among the minors; if not, he opposed the bill. This petition brought on a request from the representative of the patent interests (Earl Glengall) for the privilege of the patent houses to act Italian opera. To this the Marquis of Clanricarde retorted facetiously that he looked upon the bill merely as a police measure, to exclude from amusements all that might be offensive to public decency and morals, adding that it was no part of the Lord Chamberlain's duties to say whether the language of a performance should be English, Irish, Iroquois, or Italian.

There was no real objection to the spirit of
the bill, only everybody wanted to make sure
that his individual interests were included under
the protective wings of the measure. They had
so long been vexed by narrow and contradictory
laws that they could not afford to take chances
now. Some thought that the only change made
in the Lord Chamberlain's power by the bill was
an extension of it to a radius of twenty miles.
The general construction, however, placed upon
the measure by the Lords, as by the Commons,
was that the Chamberlain's duty was the defense
of morals, and that, otherwise, managers should
be left free.

On the 15th of August the bill came up for
its final reading. One objection only was raised
to it as originally prepared, namely, to that
clause empowering the Lord Chamberlain to
prohibit, at his pleasure, the representation of
any play whatever in any theatre in his jurisdiction. This was thought to invest that official
with a power too inclusive, and hence too dangerous. Two main benefits were intended by all
parties concerned : the protection of public peace
and morality, and the widest possible freedom
to the drama in every quarter. The power proposed to be given to the Lord Chamberlain
would assuredly do away with the confusion attending the operation of the laws as they then

existed, — but it might also operate to limit the legitimate freedom of the stage. Lord Campbell moved, therefore, to amend the clause in question by introducing it in the following words:

"Be it enacted, that for the preservation of good manners, decorum, and of the public peace, it shall be lawful for the Lord Chamberlain, for the time being," etc. (the remainder of the clause to be left intact).

It was at once objected that the amendment turned the restriction to the opposite extreme. As a middle course, the Lord Chancellor proposed this alteration in the wording of the beginning of the clause: "Whenever in the opinion of the Lord Chamberlain it was necessary for the promotion of good manners and decorum, or of the public peace, to forbid the performance of any stage play, farce, etc." As thus amended, and with this slight and single alteration, the Theatre Regulation Bill was read a third time in the House of Lords (August 15), returned to the Lower House for final approval, and passed to Her Majesty for the royal assent, which was given on Tuesday, August 22, 1843.[1]

At last the theatrical monopoly had been legally destroyed, though, except for its general

---

[1] For the history of this bill see Hansard's *Parliamentary Debates*, 3d Series, lxx, 1350; lxxi, 7, 232, 233, 296, 313, 471, 544, 545, 588, 589, 689, 690, 987.

attitude of the dog in the manger, it had been a monopoly only in name for many years. Excepting Macready's noble attempt to revive the Shakesperean drama at Covent Garden in 1837–1838, the patent houses had sunk to the level of their minor rivals. Had the wise counsel of the editor of the "Prompter" been followed in 1735, to restrict the minors to the legitimate drama, the false position which the patent houses had been forced to assume for the last fifty years of their existence would have been reversed, and, though the monopoly was sure to fall sooner or later, the patentees might have enjoyed the last years of their " exclusive privileges " in some degree of comfort. But it was too late to change the history of theatrical monopoly in London. " The ' Patent' monopoly has finished its work," writes the " Spectator " (June 10, 1843) in the style of an obituary notice prepared in advance. " The 'legitimate drama,' for the support of which the two great theatres were endowed with exclusive privileges, has ceased to exist — at least in so far as they are concerned. The degenerate successor of the elder dramatists, that at the Restoration was confined to the fostering care of these two dry nurses, has been overlaid by their huge, overgrown bulk ; they treated it like a spoiled child, surfeited it with sweet-meats, bedizened it with fine clothes, and amused it with all sorts of toys, including a Noah's Ark full of animals; but while its hireling guardians became bloated with pampering, and ostentatious with importance, their puny charge dwindled away to a shadow, until it could not be recognized as the offspring of that healthy and vigorous stock which produced a Shakespeare. In a word, the 'legitimate drama' has fallen a victim to protection. Mr. Macready, its fast and best friend, tried every effort to revive it; but in vain."

It might be supposed that, with the barriers finally down, the old fear apprehended so often by the patentees in the event of a free stage would be realized, namely, the rise of theatres in every street. Sufficient evidence has appeared in the course of this narrative to show that London was not famishing for places of theatrical amusements in 1843. The last one built before the enactment of the law just considered was The Princess, in 1840; and, strange as it may seem, London was not to have an addition to her long list of playhouses for over twenty years. In that period both of the old patent houses were to sink to the low level toward which they had been surely drifting since the early part of the century; and one of them, Covent Garden, was to be again visited by fire (1856).

It might be surmised, also, that with the

legitimate drama open to all comers, the competition for public favor in that species of theatrical amusement would begin at once on the passage of the Theatre Regulation Bill, and be so fierce as to force all the weaklings to the wall. But in this also we are disappointed in our guess. The law caused no alteration whatever in theatrical conditions: it only provided for possibilities. Some few, indeed, did undertake the championship of the Elizabethan drama, but in a short time felt under the necessity of falling back into the old tendencies. Wallack, at the opening of the season of 1843–44, tried to give the plays of Shakespeare a "local habitation" at Covent Garden; but after an experience of two weeks' performances to empty benches he was compelled to abandon the project.[1] One thing, however, the law of 1843 did accomplish: it put to rest the interminable quarrels of the majors and minors, and wiped out the blot of theatrical monopoly.

[1] Wallack blamed (correctly, probably) his actors for the failure to revive Shakespeare's plays. *Spectator*, October 21, 1843.

CHAPTER XV

FROM a survey of the struggle from 1660 to 1843, to free the English stage from the patent monopoly granted by Charles II, it will appear a much easier task to point out the causes of the downfall of the patent houses than to explain why the theatrical monopoly was permitted to exist so long. It was a graft so utterly foreign to the England of the nineteenth century, if not, indeed, of the eighteenth century, as to challenge our wonder why it was not lopped off a hundred years and more before it was finally abolished. It may be that the inert temper of the English people, the mere habit of permitting an old institution to continue, in some degree accounts for the old age of the monopoly in theatrical amusements. But a careful analysis of the facts related in the foregoing chapters will, I think, go a long way towards clearing up the phenomenon. An examination of the leading theatrical events connected with our subject will disclose six main periods, each of which stands for a more or less distinct significance in the development of the idea of theatrical monopoly; though of course these divisions overlap and intermingle. In making this epochal analysis, I would emphasize the most general tendencies only.

In the first place, it will appear that, from the granting of the patents to Killigrew and Davenant to about 1720, the ruling sovereigns of the realm never thought for a moment that the grants of Charles II in anywise limited the crown prerogative over public amusements. Charles himself was the first to exercise his authority without regard to his former patent grants, when he united the patents in 1682. William III was advised by his counselors that one King cannot bind a succeeding Prince in the matter of granting theatrical privileges; and as a result of this opinion, Betterton and his followers received a license from the Crown to establish a company of comedians independent of the patent house. Northey and Pemberton, in 1704–05, sustained this decision; and we have seen how Queen Anne exercised her prerogative to a degree equal to that of the second Charles himself, — licensing Swiney and Collier, silencing Rich, and even sanctioning his ejection from the Drury Lane Theatre. George I was no less certain of his power in the matter. He granted a patent to Steele, reissued a license to Cibber, Doggett, and Wilkes, permitted John Rich to open

Lincoln's-Inn-Fields Theatre, prevented Colley Cibber from performing, revoked Steele's patent, and disbanded the company of comedians at Drury Lane. Every one of the four sovereigns, during this period of fifty years, exercised the crown prerogative over public amusements at will, and to its full extent, as occasion demanded. Furthermore, with the single exception of Sir Richard Steele, no question was raised as to the authority of the Crown in theatrical matters.

In 1720 it is safe to say that the English King had no doubt that he possessed the same legal control over the patents granted by Charles II as that which the Merrie Monarch had exercised. So thoroughly was this fact established that for years no occasion arose demanding an application of the crown prerogative over the patent theatres. It seems to have been an object of the three sovereigns succeeding Charles II to crush the spirit of exclusive privileges in public amusements, and to keep the whole matter well under the control of the Lord Chamberlain. This thoroughly accomplished, that which so often happens under similar circumstances happened then: the power fell into disuse as soon as there was no occasion for its exercise. In the place of it sprang up independent (that is, unlicensed) theatres, which were tolerated rather than sanctioned by Government. These were the Haymarket and Goodman's Fields; and there can be no better proof that the patentees regarded their patents inferior and subject to the crown prerogative than the quiet submission to this new competition. It was only when the liberty permitted to the unlicensed theatres was degraded into scurrilous attacks on Government, and insults to public decency and morals, that a readjustment and a redefinition of the theatrical situation was demanded. The Licensing Act of 1737 was the result. As has already been explained, this aimed at a legal, *i. e.*, a parliamentary, recognition of the authority of the Crown over public amusements, as it had been practiced by Charles II, Anne, and the first George. But in the expression of what was in reality an established fact in the common law, namely, the absolute authority of the Crown over theatrical amusements, the Government committed itself to a practical recognition of the exclusiveness of the grants of Charles II. In this consisted the real illiberality of the act, though at the time its opponents feared the effects of the absolute power secured to the Lord Chamberlain. As a matter of fact, it was this unlimited power, sanctioned by law, in the hands of the Lord Chamberlain, that was to bring about the final abolition of the monopoly. The period, then, from 1720 to 1737, ending in the passage of the Licensing Act, has two meanings, diametrically opposed to each other. Legally — and in the long run, in reality — it emphasized the necessity and the fact of the absolute authority of the Crown over theatricals, — such as had been exercised from 1660 to 1720. In its immediate effects it was a violent reversal of the policy maintained by the monarchs from Charles II to George I, for it gave a legal recognition — the first thus far — to the patent theatres, and destroyed all other competition.

1720 should have been the natural end of the monopoly granted by Charles II, but the opportunity went by, and the Licensing Act did what even Charles II could not do,— it sealed the exclusive privileges in theatricals, and laid the foundation of an illiberal policy on the part of Government, and a century's struggle for a free stage. The practices and arrogant spirit of the patentees after 1737 clearly show the Licensing Act to be the real birth of theatrical monopoly in England.

From 1737 to 1787, the third period in our investigation, the monopoly is distinguished by an absolutism scarcely approached by any other period of equal length during its existence. If the half-century from 1660 to 1720 marks the constant buffeting of the patentees at the will of the Crown, the fact is offset by the domination

of the monopoly over theatrical affairs in London
for the fifty years succeeding the enactment of the
Licensing Act. That the Act of 1737 was largely
responsible for this turn of affairs can be no
better illustrated than by a comparison of the
revolts of 1733 and 1743 — one before the passage of the act in question, the other after. The
former, though led by the disreputable Theophilus Cibber, was a complete victory for the actors
over the patentees, as shown by the decision in
the Harper case, which caused the immediate
ruin of the patentee, Highmore, who was in all
legal justice in the right. The revolt of 1743
was led by no less respectable and influential
persons than Macklin and Garrick; but the
Licensing Act was so sufficient a protection to
the patentee, Fleetwood, that Garrick, in the interests of prudence, was impelled to beat a hasty
retreat, and even the vindictive and indomitable
Macklin was forced into ultimate submission.
The pusillanimous Theophilus Cibber was silenced with a threat, whereas, ten years before,
he had flaunted his impudence with impunity.
So soon had been reversed the theatrical affairs
of London, by the interpretation of a law to
meet the interests of private individuals. But it
should not be lost sight of that there was another
possible construction to be placed on that act.

The period from 1737 to 1787 was one of com-

parative security to the monopoly, and the one
during which it was really established. Few
attempts were made during this half-century to
perform the legitimate drama outside the two
patent theatres, and when such performances
were given they were usually if not always " by
permission " of the patentees. While the accident of Foote's patent at the Little Theatre in
the Haymarket was, for the moment, a return to
the crown authority, showing conclusively that the
power to grant theatrical patents was located
precisely where it was in the time of Charles II,
nevertheless it should be observed that in Foote's
case the patent was granted only for the lifetime
of the patentee, and that it was reduced to an
annual license when transferred to Colman in
1777 ; also that the monopolists were first consulted before the patent was granted to Foote,
the result of which was that the season at the
Haymarket was limited to the four summer
months. To consider what might have happened
in case the patentees had refused to give their
consent to the granting of Foote's patent can
result in nothing more than speculation. Certain
it is, however, that they saw the error they had
fallen into in opening their safeguards to any
sort of competition, a mistake which they tried
to rectify by inaugurating the war of encroachment on the season of the summer theatre.

This third stage of the history of the patents ends and the fourth begins with the wild attempt of John Palmer to establish the Royalty Theatre (1787). This was the first great practical test of the efficacy of the Licensing Act in defending the interests of the theatrical monopoly; and we have seen how satisfactory its operation was to the patentees. This circumstance also brings out the importance of a new element in theatrical history, which was to develop into greater and greater prominence in the struggle against the monopoly—namely, the conflict of anomalous theatrical legislation — the acts of 10 George II (Licensing Act) and that of 25 George II (empowering magistrates to license musical performances, etc.). What the outcome of this episode might have been had some one with a character and reputation less shadowy than that of Palmer been at the head of the Royalty scheme, or had some one less watchful and with less political influence than Sheridan been back of the patent houses, is also a matter of conjecture; but it is probable that the result would have remained unchanged, inasmuch as the monopoly had a half-century of established precedent in its favor.

At any rate the Royalty attempt stands for the awakening of a tendency which dominated the period from 1787 to 1810 — the movement for the establishment of a third theatre for the representation of the national drama under the protection of Government. This movement had its culmination in the famous proceedings before the Privy Council in 1810, on the petition for a third theatre. This climax was approached by certain preliminary efforts, such as the attempts of Colonel Greville from 1802 onwards, proposals for joint-stock companies, and subscription theatres of various kinds, as well as plans for a national theatre, English opera, and so forth. The attempt to establish a third theatre in London in 1810 was the first approach to the breaking down of the monopoly by way of crown sanction, just as the efforts in Parliament in 1811 and 1812 were the first endeavors to reach the same result by means of legislative action. The outcome of this attempt to establish a third theatre seemed to fix more firmly than ever the habit of suffering the theatrical monopoly. But it would be rash to say that the findings of the Privy Council on that occasion, and the rejection of the bill by Parliament in 1811 and 1812, had the effect of more firmly establishing the monopoly itself. The very opposite is nearer the truth; for in the discussions and arguments which were brought out at that time, the weaknesses and questionable practices of the patentees were laid bare, and " exclusive privilege " in theatricals received a shock from which it never fully recovered. The proceedings in the Council and in Parliament did show, however, that the monopoly was not to be destroyed by means of any third theatre scheme—a plan which at best could relieve the situation only temporarily. Furthermore, had all the most favorable conditions imaginable been ripe for such a movement, it is scarcely likely that it would succeed in the King's Council; for if the Crown possessed the power to grant the petition prayed for by the third theatre promoters, then it is altogether likely that the Crown would reserve that power to be exercised by its "own will and mere motion," as it had done on former occasions.

However, a set of influences had long been at work undermining the monopoly, and these came out into strong relief during the period from 1810 to about 1832. The conflicting legislative acts regulating the theatres have already been mentioned. These were aggravated by the rise and development of the minor theatres, those that were prohibited from representing the legitimate national drama. These minor establishments began to creep into existence about the outskirts of London, especially on the Surrey side, back in the eighteenth century, at the very time when the patent houses were so secure

within the stronghold of the Licensing Act.
These minors sprang up under the provisions of
the Act of 25 George II, for the licensing of music
houses and for regulating places of public amusement. So long as Government, represented by
Chamberlains such as the Earl of Salisbury,—
who, it should be remembered, served in that capacity from 1783 to 1804, — was friendly to the
patent monopoly, there was little to fear by the
latter. At such times — which include nearly
three quarters of a century after the passage
of the Licensing Act — the laws were almost
invariably interpreted as existing for the protection of the patent theatres. But so soon as a
Lord Chamberlain should be found sufficiently
independent to shake himself free from the iner-
tia, the doom of the monopoly was struck. Such
a Chamberlain was Lord Dartmouth (1804–
1812), who, though he did not openly attack
the patent privileges, permitted the undercur-
rents already at work to take their course.

As a result, therefore, of this leniency of Lord
Dartmouth the minor theatres multiplied with
such rapidity and vigor as to become firmly
rooted before the end of his reign. Their rise to
an important place as a factor in the struggle
for a free stage is the main characteristic of the
period under review (1810–1832). It has been
pointed out at length how the manipulation of

the species of entertainment known as "burletta"
(falling originally under the Act of 25 George
II, permitting musical performances) gradually
opened the door of competition to the minors.
This process was hastened by the lowering of
theatrical representations at the patent houses,
so that by 1820 there was little difference between the performances at the best of the minors
and the average melodramatic spectacle at the
" great houses ;" while by 1832 the minors were
as certainly established as if there had been
a special law legalizing their existence. Had a
Lord Chamberlain with the views of the Earl of
Dartmouth appeared in the eighteenth century,
there is reason to presume that the struggle
might have been materially shortened. The period from 1810 to 1832 is in many respects the
most important in the long history of the patent
monopoly ; for it was a practical proof of the
weakness of a concern that had to be supported
by extraneous means and not by merit alone.

Finally, the period from 1832 to 1843 is characterized not so much by the destruction of the
theatrical monopoly as by the strife over the
method by which it should be silenced. The union
of the two patents in 1833 was the signal for attacks
from every quarter upon the two old theatrical concerns. The third theatre project was revived by
Knowles — but it is safe to say that that particu-

lar scheme of relief from the monopoly had been finally disposed of in 1810. Bulwer had, the year before (1832), caused the practices of the patentees to be scrutinized in the Select Committee on Dramatic Literature, and it has been shown how this investigation was followed up in 1833 by the introduction of the Dramatic Performances Bill. Why that measure failed has already been discussed. During all these furious attacks on the monopoly the patentees were carrying on a suicidal warfare against the minors, to whose rescue the Marquis of Conyngham stepped in, and, by his incessant zeal against the patent houses, promised to end the work begun by Lord Dartmouth. For a time it seemed that no outside force would be needed to exterminate the monopoly, for the contests between the patent houses themselves threatened to destroy them both; while the Lenten prohibitions were thrown in to make assurance doubly sure. After the noise of the final conflict had ceased, which had raged for the decade (1832–1842) between the monopoly on the one side, and authors, actors, the minors, and the general public on the other, Parliament came in (1843) and, with an echo of the reform movement, gave legislative sanction to the verdict that the monopoly had died a natural death.

BIBLIOGRAPHY

BIBLIOGRAPHY

[*Note.* — In the following, no attempt is made to give more than a list of those titles which were found most useful in the preparation of this work, and especially those which, hitherto, have not been published in connection with theatrical history. A complete bibliography of the general subject is, probably, too great a task for one to accomplish. The most satisfactory compilation thus far is Mr. R. W. Lowe's " A Bibliographical Account of English Theatrical Literature." New York and London, 1888.]

AN ACCOUNT OF THE PROCEEDINGS BEFORE HIS MAJES-TY'S MOST HON. PRIVY COUNCIL, upon a Petition for a Third Theatre in the Metropolis; with the Arguments of Counsel, and Copies of all the Petitions and Documents. Pp. 117 + Appendices A–S. London, 1810.

BAKER, DAVID ERSKINE.
Biographia Dramatica, or, A Companion to the Playhouse : containing Historical and Critical Memoirs, and Original Anecdotes, of British and Irish Dramatic Writers, from the commencement of our Theatrical Exhibitions ; amongst whom are some of the most celebrated Actors. Also an Alphabetical Account of their works, the Dates when printed, and occasional Observations on their Merits. Together with an introductory View of the Rise and Progress of the British Stage. A New Edition. Carefully corrected; greatly enlarged; and continued from 1764 to 1782. 2 volumes. Dublin, 1782.

BAKER, H. BARTON.
The London Stage: its History and Traditions from 1576 to 1903. 2 volumes. London, 1904.

BEDFORD, ARTHUR, M.A.
A Sermon preached in the Parish Church in St. Bu-

tolph's, Aldgate, in the City of London, on Sunday, the Thirtieth Day of November, in the Year of Our Lord 1729. Occasioned by the Erecting of a Play-House in the Neighborhood. Pp. 40. London, 1730.

BESANT, SIR WALTER.
London in the Eighteenth Century. London, 1902.

BETTERTON, THOMAS.
See Lowe, R. W.

BIOGRAPHIA DRAMATICA.
See Baker, David Erskine.

BLAND, MISS.
See Jordan, Mrs.

BOADEN, JAMES.
Memoirs of Mrs. Siddons. Interspersed with Anecdotes of Authors and Actors. 2 volumes. London, 1827.

Memoirs of John Philip Kemble. London, 1825.

The Life of Mrs. Jordan. London, 1831.

Private Correspondence of David Garrick. London, 1831–32.

BOULTON, WILLIAM B.
The Amusements of Old London. Being a Survey of the Sports and Pastimes, Tea Gardens and Parks, Playhouses and other diversions of the People of London from the 17th to the beginning of the 19th century. Twelve colored illustrations. 2 volumes. London, 1901.

BULWER, EDWARD, LORD LYTTON.
See Report on Dramatic Literature.

BUNN, ALFRED.
The Stage. Both before and behind the Curtain. From Observations taken on the Spot. 3 volumes. London, 1840.

THE BUSKIN AND SOCK; being controversial Letters between Mr. Thomas Sheridan, Tragedian, and Mr. Theophilus Cibber, Comedian; Just published in Dublin. Pp. 56. London (reprint), 1743.

THE CASE BETWEEN THE MANAGERS OF THE TWO THE-ATRES, AND THEIR PRINCIPAL ACTORS, fairly stated and submitted to the Town. London, 1743.

CHETWOOD, W. R.
A General History of the Stage, from its Origin in Greece down to the Present Time. With the Memoirs of most of the principal Performers that have appeared on the English and Irish Stage for these last Fifty Years. With Notes, Antient, Modern, Foreign, Domestic, Serious, Comic, Moral, Merry, Historical, and Geographical, containing many Theatrical Anecdotes; also several Pieces of Poetry never before published. Collected and Digested by W. R. Chetwood, Twenty Years Prompter to His Majesty's Company of Comedians at the Theatre-Royal in Drury-Lane, London. London, 1749.

CIBBER, COLLEY.
An Apology for the Life of Colley Cibber, Comedian, and late Patentee of the Theatre-Royal. With an Historical View of the Stage during his Own Time, Written by Himself. *The Third Edition.* To which is now added, A Short Account of the Rise and Progress of the English Stage: Also, A Dialogue on Old Plays, and Old Players. London, 1750.

CIBBER, SUSANNAH MARIA.
An Account of the Life of the Celebrated Mrs. Susannah Maria Cibber, with interesting and amusing Anecdotes. Also the two remarkable and romantic Trials between Theophilus Cibber and William Sloper. London, 1887.

CIBBER, THEOPHILUS.
An Apology for the Life of Mr. T— C—, Comedian.

Being a Proper Sequel to the Apology for the Life of Mr. Colley Cibber, Comedian. With an Historical View of the Stage to the Present Year. Supposed to be written by Himself. In the Stile and Manner of the Poet Laureat. London, 1740.

See The Buskin and Sock.

A Lick at a Liar ; or, Calumny Detected. Being an Occasional Letter to a Friend from Theophilus Cibber, Comedian. Pp. 23. With an Advertisement. London, 1752.

A Serio-Comic Apology for Part of the Life of Mr. Theophilus Cibber, Comedian. Written by Himself. In which is contained, A Prologue, an Epilogue, and a Poem, wrote on the Play of *Romeo and Juliet* being first revived in 1744; Also some Addresses to the Publick, on different Occasions; Likewise original Letters that passed between the late Sir Thomas De Veil, and Mr. Theo. Cibber, (Relating to the Stage Act) On a stop being put to the playing at the *Haymarket*. Interspersed with Memoirs and Anecdotes concerning the Stage Management and Theatrical Revolutions, in the Years 1744, 1745, and 1746, &c. And cursory Observations on some Principal Performers; Particularly Mr. Quin, Mr. Ryan, Mr. Delane, Mrs. Woffington, Mrs. Ward, and Miss Bellamy; Mr. Garrick, Mr. Barry, Mrs. Cibber, Mrs. Clive, Mrs. Pritchard, and others. Pp. 71–108. n. p., n. d., [London, 1746].

COLMAN, GEORGE, The Younger.

Random Records. 2 volumes. London, 1830.

THE CONDUCT OF THE STAGE CONSIDERED. Being a short Historical Account of its Origin, Progress, various Aspects and Treatment in the Pagan, Jewish, and Christian World. Together with the Arguments urg'd against it, by Learned Heathens, and by Christians, both Antient and Modern. With short Remarks upon the Origin and pernicious Consequences of Masquerades. Pp. 43. London, 1721.

CONSIDERATIONS ON THE PAST AND PRESENT STATE OF
THE STAGE ; with Reference to the late Contests at
Covent Garden ; to which is added a Plan for a new
Theatre for the purpose of HEARING Plays. To the
Right Honourable George, Earl of Dartmouth, Lord
Chamberlain of His Majesty's Household. Pp. 54 +
Appendices A and B. London, 1809.

COOKE, WILLIAM.
Memoirs of Charles Macklin, Comedian, with the
Dramatic Characters, Manners, Anecdotes, &c., of the
Age in which he lived: forming an History of the Stage
during almost the Whole of the last Century. And
a Chronological List of all the Parts played by Him.
2d edition. London, 1806.

See Foote, Samuel.

THE COVENT GARDEN JOURNAL. Compiled by John
Joseph Stockdale. 2 volumes. London, 1810.

CUMBERLAND, RICHARD.
Memoirs of Richard Cumberland. Written by himself.
New York, 1806.

The Minor Theatre. 16 volumes. London, n. d. Contains copies of the plays which were acted at the
minor theatres in London.

DAVIES, THOMAS.
Memoirs of the Life of David Garrick, Esq. Interspersed with Characters and Anecdotes oɩ his Theatrical Contemporaries. The Whole forming a History
of the Stage, which includes a Period of Thirty-Six
Years. From the last London edition. Boston, 1818.
The Dedication bears date of April 22, 1780.

DIALOGUES ON THE DRAMA, between "Smith and Johnson." In "Morning Chronicle," beginning September
22, 1830.

DIBDIN, MR. [CHARLES.]
A Complete History of the Stage. 5 volumes. London,
[1800.]

DIBDIN, CHARLES, JR.

History and Illustrations of the London Theatres :
comprising an account of the Origin and Progress of
the Drama in England ; with historical and descriptive
accounts of the Theatres Royal, Covent Garden, Drury
Lane, Haymarket, English Opera House, and Royal
Amphitheatre. London, 1826.

DIBDIN, THOMAS.

The Reminiscences of Thomas Dibdin, of the Theatres
Royal, Covent Garden, Drury Lane, Haymarket, &c.,
and Author of the Cabinet, &c. London, 1827.

DICKENS, CHARLES.
See Mathews, Charles James.

DORAN, DR. [JOHN.]

Annals of the English Stage, from Thomas Betterton
to Edmund Kean. Actors — Authors — Audiences.
2 volumes. New York, 1865.

DOWNES, JOHN.

Roscius Anglicanus, or, an Historical Review of the
Stage from 1660 to 1706. A Fac-simile Reprint of the
Rare Original of 1708. With an Historical Preface by
Joseph Knight. London, 1886.

" DRAMATICUS."

An impartial View of the Stage, from the days of
Garrick and Rich to the Present Period ; of the
Causes of its degenerated and declining State, and
shewing the necessity of a Reform in the System, as
the only means of giving stability to the present Property of the two Winter Theatres. London, 1816.

EBERS, JOHN.
Seven Years of the King's Theatre. London, 1828.

EGAN, PIERCE.

Life in London. Illustrated by colored Drawings by
George Cruikshank. London, 1821.

Life of an Actor. The Poetical Descriptions by T.

Greenwood. Embellished with Twenty-Seven Characteristic Scenes, etched by Theodore Lane. London,
1892. The Dedication (to E. Kean) bears date of
December 18, 1824.

ELLISTON, ROBERT WILLIAM.
See Raymond, George.

FARREN, WILLIAM.
A Full and Accurate Account of the Destruction of the
Brunswick Theatre, with the Statements of . . . Wil-
liam and Percy Farren. London, 1828.

FITZGERALD, PERCY.
A New History of the English Stage, from the Restora-
tion to the Liberty of the Theatres, in Connection with
the Patent Houses. From Original Papers in the Lord
Chamberlain's Office, the State Paper Office, and other
Sources. 2 volumes. London, 1882.

FOOTE, SAMUEL.
Memoirs of the Life and Writings of Samuel Foote
Esq. ; the English Aristophanes : to which are added
the bon-mots, repartees, and good things said by that
great wit and excentrical genius. London, n. d. [1777.]

Memoirs of Samuel Foote. With a Collection of his
genuine Bon-mots, Anecdotes, Opinions, &c., mostly
original. And three dramatic pieces, not published in
his works. By William Cooke, Esq. London, 1805.

GARRICK, DAVID.
Mr. Garrick's Answer to Mr. Macklin's Case. [Lon-
don, 1743.]

Memoirs of the Life of David Garrick. See Boaden,
James ; Davies, Thomas ; Knight, Joseph.

GENEST, JOHN.
Some Account of the English Stage from the Restoration in 1660 to 1830. 10 volumes, Bath, 1832.

GILDON, CHARLES.
A Comparison between the Two Stages, with an Ex-

amen of the *Generous Conqueror ;* and some Critical
Remarks on *The Funeral,* or *Grief Alamode, The False
Friend, Tamerlane,* and others. In Dialogue. London,
1702.

HAWKINS, F. W.
See Kean, Edmund.

HAZLITT, WILLIAM.
A View of the English Stage ; or, a Series of Dramatic Criticisms. London, 1818.

HILL, AARON.
See Newspapers and Periodicals, " The Prompter."

HOWARD, FREDERICK, EARL OF CARLISLE.
Thoughts upon the Present Condition of the Stage, and
upon the Construction of a New Theatre. A new edition, with additions. Pp. 47 + Appendix. London,
1809.

HUNT, JOHN.
Critical Essays on the Performers of the London Theatres ; including General Observations on the Practice
and Genius of the Stage. By the Author of the Theatrical Criticisms in the weekly paper called the News.
London, 1809.

AN IMPARTIAL EXAMEN OF THE PRESENT CONTESTS BE-
TWEEN THE TOWN AND THE MANAGER OF THE THE-
ATRE. With some Proposals for accommodating the
present Misunderstanding between the Town and Man-
ager. Offered to the Consideration of Both Parties.
By Mr. Neither-side. Pp. 24. London, 1744.

THE INTELLIGENCER.
(A collection of 19 pamphlets. No. 3 is " A Vindication of Mr. Gay, and the Beggar's Opera.") London,
1729. (Printed in Dublin.)

JACKMAN, ISAAC.
Royal and Royalty Theatres. London, 1787.

JACKSON, RANDLE.

See An Account of the Proceedings before His Majesty's most Hon. Privy Council, etc.

JORDAN, MRS.

Public and Private Life of that Celebrated Actress, Miss Bland, Otherwise Mrs. Ford, or, Mrs. Jordan ; Late mistress of H. R. H., the D. of Clarence ; now King William IV, founder of the Fitzclarence Family ; Delineating the Vicissitudes attending on her Early Life ; The Splendour of her noon-tide Blaze, as Mistress of the Royal Duke ; and her untimely Dissolution at St. Cloud, near Paris, resulting from a broken Heart. Accompanied by numerous Remarks and Anecdotes of illustrious and fashionable Characters. By a confidential Friend of the Departed. London, n. d.

KEAN, EDMUND.

The Life of Edmund Kean. From Published and Original Sources. By F. W. Hawkins. 2 volumes. London, 1869.

The Life of Edmund Kean, English Tragedian ; with Critical Remarks on his Theatrical Performances. By Sheridan Knowles, Esq. London, 1833.

KEMBLE, JOHN PHILIP.

See Boaden, James.

KIRKMAN, JAMES THOMAS.

Memoirs of the Life of Charles Macklin, Esq. ; principally compiled from his own Papers and Memorandums ; which contains his Criticisms on and Characters and Anecdotes of Betterton, Booth, Wilks, Cibber, Garrick, Barry, Mossop, Sheridan, Foote, Quin, and most of his Contemporaries. 2 volumes. London, 1799.

KNIGHT, JOSEPH.

David Garrick. With etched Portrait from the Gainsborough Painting. London, 1894.

See Downes, John.

KNOWLES, JAMES SHERIDAN.

See Knowles, Richard Brinsley ; and Kean, Edmund.

446 BIBLIOGRAPHY

KNOWLES, RICHARD BRINSLEY.
The Life of James Sheridan Knowles, by his son Rich-
ard Brinsley Knowles. Privately printed for James
McHenry. London, 1872.

LAWRENCE, JAMES, KNIGHT OF MALTA.
Dramatic Emancipation, or Strictures on the State of
the Theatres, and the consequent Degeneration of the
Drama ; On the Partiality and Injustice of the London
Managers ; On Many Theatrical Regulations ; And on
the Regulations on the Continent for the Security of
Literary and Dramatic Property. Particularly Deserving the Attention of the Subscribers for a Third Theatre. Original, 1813. (Printed in the "Pamphleteer"
for December, 1813, ii, 370–395.)

LOWE, R. W.
Thomas Betterton. London, 1891.

MACARTHY, EUGENE.
A Letter to the King, on the Question now at issue between the Major and Minor Theatres. London, 1832.

MACKLIN, CHARLES.
See Cooke, William ; and Kirkman, James Thomas.
Reply to Mr. Garrick's Answer. To which is prefix'd,
All the Papers, which have publickly appeared, in re-
gard to this Important Dispute. Pp. 36. London, 1743.

MACREADY, WILLIAM CHARLES.
Macready's Reminiscences, and Selections from his
Diaries and Letters. Edited by Sir Frederick Pol-
lock. New York, 1875.

MALONE, EDMOND.
An Historical Account of the English Stage. (In Vol.
I of "The Plays and Poems of William Shakespeare.")
London, 1790.

MATHEWS, CHARLES JAMES.
The Life of Charles James Mathews. Chiefly Auto-
biographical, with Selections from his Correspondence

and Speeches. Edited by Charles Dickens. With Portrait. 2 volumes. London, 1879.

THE NATIONAL DRAMA, or the Histrionic War of Majors and Minors. With folding caricature Frontispiece. London, 1833.

NEWSPAPERS AND PERIODICALS.
See *post*, p. 452.

O'KEEFE, JOHN.
Recollections of the Life of John O'Keefe. Written by himself. 2 volumes. London, 1826.

OULTON, W. C.
A History of the Theatres of London, containing an Annual Register of New Pieces, Revivals, Pantomimes, &c. With Occasional Notes and Anecdotes. Being a Continuation of Victor's & Oulton's Histories. From the Year 1795 to 1817 inclusive. 3 volumes. London, 1818.

History of the Theatres of London : containing an Annual Register of all the new and revived Tragedies, Comedies, Operas, Farces, Pantomimes, &c., that has been performed at the Theatres-Royal, in London from the Year 1771 to 1795. With occasional Notes and Anecdotes. 2 volumes. London, 1796.

PEPYS, SAMUEL.
Diary. January 1, 1660–May 31, 1669. First edited by Lord Braybrooke, 1825.

PLACE, FRANCIS.
A Brief Examination of the Dramatic Patents. (Extracted from the "Monthly Magazine" for March, 1834.) London, 1834.

POLLOCK, SIR FREDERICK.
See Macready, William Charles.

THE PRESENT STATE OF THE STAGE IN GREAT BRITAIN AND IRELAND, and the theatrical Character of the principal Performers in both Kingdoms, impartially considered. Pp. 55. London, 1753.

A PROPOSAL FOR THE BETTER REGULATION OF THE STAGE, with some Remarks on the State of the Theatre among the Antient Greeks and Romans. (Dedicated to "The Managers of Both Houses.") London, 1732.

QUIN, JAMES.
The Life of Mr. James Quin Considered. With the history of the Stage from his commencing actor to his retreat to Bath. Illustrated with many curious and interesting anecdotes of several persons of distinction, literature, and gallantry. To which is added a supplement of original facts and anecdotes, arranged from authentic sources. Together with his trial for the murder of Mr. Bowen. (A reprint from the edition of 1766.) London, 1887.

RALPH, J.
The Case of our Present Theatrical Disputes, Fairly Stated. In which is contained, a succinct Account of the Rise, Progress, and Declension of the Antient Stage ; A Comprehensive View of the Management of the *Italian*, *Spanish*, *French*, and *Dutch* Theatres, with some free Remarks upon our own. Pp. 64. London, 1743.

RAYMOND, GEORGE.
The Life and Enterprises of Robert William Elliston, Comedian. Illustrated by George Cruikshank and "Phiz." (Portrait of Elliston, and 5 full-page illustrations.) London, 1857.

REPORT ON DRAMATIC LITERATURE, with the minutes of the evidence. Folded sheet. Pp. 250. London, 1832.

A REVIEW OF THE PRESENT CONTEST BETWEEN THE MANAGERS OF THE WINTER THEATRES, THE LITTLE THEATRE IN THE HAYMARKET, AND THE ROYALTY THEATRE IN WELL-CLOSE SQUARE. To which are added several authentic papers. London, 1787.

REYNOLDS, FREDERICK.
The Life and Times of Frederick Reynolds. Written
by himself. 2 volumes. London, 1826.

SHERIDAN, RICHARD BRINSLEY.
See Account of Proceedings before . . . Privy Council,
1810.

SHERIDAN, THOMAS.
See Buskin and Sock.

SIDDONS, MRS.
Memoirs of Mrs. Siddons. By James Boaden. 2 volumes. London, 1827.

STEELE, SIR RICHARD.
The State of the Case between the Lord Chamberlain
of His Majesty's Household and the Governor of the
Royal Company of Comedians. With Opinions of
Pemberton, Northey, and Parker, concerning the The-
atre. Pp. 31. London, 1720.

The State of the Case between the Lord Chamberlain
of His Majesty's Household, and Sir Richard Steele,
as represented by that Knight, Restated, In Vindication
of King George, and the most noble the Duke of Newcastle. With a true Copy of King Charles's Patent, to
Sir William D'Avenant, for erecting a Play-house, &c.
London, 1720.

STERLING, EDWARD.
Old Drury Lane. Fifty Years Recollections of Author,
Actor, and Manager. 2 volumes. London, 1881.

STOCKDALE, JOHN JOSEPH.
See Covent Garden Journal.

TAYLOR, W.
A Concise Statement of Transactions and Circumstances Respecting the King's Theatre in the Haymarket. By Mr. Taylor, the Proprietor. Together with
the Official Correspondence upon the same Subject between the Rt. Hon. The Lord Chamberlain and Earl
Cholmondeley, &c. Pp. 46. London, 1791.

THEATRICAL BIOGRAPHY : or, Memoirs of the Principal Actors of the Three Theatres Royal, Drury Lane, Covent Garden, Haymarket. 2 volumes. London, 1772.

THEATRICAL CORRESPONDENCE IN DEATH. An Epistle from Mrs. Oldfield, in the Shades, to Mrs. Br—ceg— dle, upon Earth ; containing, A Dialogue between the most Eminent Players in the Shades, Upon the Late Stage Desertion. Pp. 24. London, 1743.

THEATRICAL MONOPOLY : being an Address to the Public on the alarming Coalition of the Managers of the Winter Theatres. London, 1779.

THIRD THEATRE.
See An Account of the Proceedings before . . . the Privy Council, 1810.

THORNBURY, WALTER.
London Theatres and London Actors. In " Belgravia," January, 1869–February, 1870.

TOMLINS, F. G.
A Brief View of the English Drama, from the earliest Period to the Present Time ; with Suggestions for alleviating the present Condition of the Art and its Professors. London, 1840.

Major and Minor Theatres. A concise View of the Question, as regards the Public, the Patentees, and the Profession, with Remarks on the Decline of the Drama, and the means of its Restoration. To which is added the Petition now lying for signature. By one of the Public. London, 1832.

Past and Present State OF DRAMATIC ART AND LITERATURE. 2d edition, London, 1839.

A VERY PLAIN STATE OF THE CASE ; or, The Royalty Theatre Versus The Theatre Royal. (In refutation of " A Review of the Present Contest, etc.," q. v. Attributed to George Colman, the Younger.) London, 1787.

VESTRIS, MADAME.

Memoirs of the Life, Public and Private Adventures, of
Madame Vestris : of the Theatre Royal, Drury Lane,
Covent Garden, Olympic and Haymarket, with interesting and amusing Anecdotes of celebrated Characters
in the fashionable World, detailing an interesting variety of singularly curious and amusing Scenes, as performed before and behind the Curtain. To which is
added the amorous Confessions of Madame Vestris,
carefully selected by Charles Mallory W—m—e, Esq.,
from a series of Letters written by Madame to Hand-
some Jack, in which will be found most curious Anecdotes of many eminent roues and debauchees of the
day ; with various others of public notoriety. London,
1839.

VICTOR, BENJAMIN.

The History of the Theatres of London and Dublin.
From the Year 1730 to the Present Time. To which is
added an Annual Register of all the Plays, &c., performed at the Theatres-Royal in London, from the Year
1712. With Occasional Notes and Anecdotes. By
Mr. Victor, Late one of the Managers of the Theatre-
Royal in Dublin. 2 volumes. London, 1761.

The History of the Theatres of London and Dublin,
&c. Being a Continuation of the Annual Register of
the new Tragedies, Comedies, Farces, Pantomimes, &c.,
that have been performed from the Year 1760 to the
Present Time. London, 1771.

WATERS, E.

The Opera Glass : exhibiting all the curious proceedings of the King's Theatre ; together with the original
letters and papers, which have passed between the
present proprietors, since the death of Francis Goold,
Esq., joint proprietor with Mr. Taylor in the above
property. London, 1808.

A Statement of Matters, Relative to the King's Theatre.
Pp. 27. London, 1818.

WILLIAMS, J. M.
See Newspapers and Periodicals, " Dramatic Censor."

WILLIAMS, MICHAEL.
Some London Theatres, Past and Present. (A compilation from magazine articles.) London, 1883.

WRIGHT, JAMES.
Historia Histrionica. A Dialogue of Old Plays and Old Players. (In Dodsley's Collection of Old Plays.) London, 1699.

WROTH, WARWICK, assisted by Arthur Edgar Wroth.
The London Pleasure Gardens of the 18th Century. London and New York, 1896.

WYNDHAM, HENRY SAXE.
Annals of Covent Garden Theatre. London, 1906.

NEWSPAPERS AND PERIODICALS

THE ANNUAL REGISTER, or a View of the History, Politicks, and Literature for the Year (1758–   ). The Annual Register was commenced by R. Dodsley, and continued by his house down to 1790, when the stock and copyright were sold. Since then, it has appeared in numerous editions and with the imprint of various publishers. Some of these editions are made up from all the preceding editions. The seventh edition, together with the New Series, which began in 1863, is complete and continuous. Since 1838 the word "Literature" has not appeared in the title, and in 1863 the sub-title was changed to "A Review of Public Events at Home and Abroad." Since 1790 the Annual Register has been published simultaneously from the houses of the various owners of the stock.

BELGRAVIA, a London Magazine. London, November, 1866–   In progress.

THE BRITANNIC MAGAZINE; or, Entertaining Repository of Heroic Adventures. 12 volumes. London, 1793–1807.

THE BRITISH MAGAZINE AND REVIEW: or, Universal Miscellany of Arts, Sciences, Literature, History, Biography, Entertainment, Poetry, Politics, Manners, Amusements, and Intelligence Foreign and Domestic. London, July, 1782–December, 1783.

THE CABINET ; or, Monthly Report of Polite Literature. 6 volumes, with 42 plates. London, 1807–1808.

THE COUNTRY JOURNAL ; or, The Craftsman. By Caleb D'Anvers, of Gray's-Inn, Esq. 14 volumes. London. Weekly. Original dates, December 5, 1726– April 17, 1736. See Gray's-Inn Journal.

THE COUNTRY LITERARY CHRONICLE AND WEEKLY REVIEW. See Literary Chronicle.

THE CRAFTSMAN. See The Country Journal.

THE DAILY COURANT. 7 fol. volumes. No. 1, March 11, 1702. Flourished for over thirty years. *The first London daily.*

THE DAILY UNIVERSAL REGISTER. See The Times.

THE DRAMATIC CENSOR ; or, critical and biographical illustration of the British Stage. For the Year 1811. Involving a correct register of every night's performances at our Metropolitan theatres, and published with a view to sustain the morality and dignity of the drama. Edited by J. M. Williams, LL.D. 1 volume. Columns 1–493. London, 1812.

THE DRAMATIC CENSOR : or, Critical Companion. 2 volumes. London, 1770.

THE DRAMATIC CENSOR ; or, Weekly Theatrical Report. Comprising a Complete Chronicle of the British Stage, and a Regular Series of Theatrical Criticisms, in every Part of the Drama. By Thomas Dutton, A. M. 2 volumes, 26 numbers. London, January 4–June 28, 1800. Two more volumes were added in 1801, when the title was changed to " The Dramatic Censor ; or, Monthly Epitome of Taste, Fashion, and Manners."

THE EDINBURGH LITERARY JOURNAL ; or, Weekly Register of Criticism and Belles Lettres. 6 volumes. Edinburgh, November 15, 1828–January 14, 1832.

THE EDINBURGH SPECTATOR, A Journal of Literature and the Fine Arts. Semi-weekly. 10 numbers. Edinburgh, February 15–April 7, 1832.

THE EXAMINER : A Sunday paper, on politics, domestic economy, and theatricals. London, 1808–1836. 4to down to 1830, fol. since 1830.

THE EUROPEAN MAGAZINE AND LONDON REVIEW. By the Philological Society of London. 87 volumes. London, 1782–1825. After vol. 50, " Philological Society " does not appear on title-page. In September, 1825, a New Series was commenced and continued to July, 1826, when The European Magazine was united with The Monthly Magazine, q. v.

FOG'S WEEKLY JOURNAL. London, September 28, 1728–January 1, 1732. Fog's Journal was a continuation of Mist's Weekly Journal (q. v.), a Tory paper, started in 1716, in opposition to Read's Weekly Journal, which was conducted in the interests of the Whigs. Defoe was connected with Mist's Journal for a number of years.

FRASER'S LITERARY CHRONICLE, and Register of British and Foreign Literature, Science and the Fine Arts. Complete in One Volume. Containing Reviews of New Books, together with various original Articles, Poetry, the Drama, Fine Arts, &c., &c., &c. Weekly. London, December 5, 1835–May 28, 1836.

FRASER'S MAGAZINE FOR TOWN AND COUNTRY. Monthly. 80 volumes. London, 1830–1869. New Series, volumes 1–26, 1870–1882.

THE GENERAL MAGAZINE AND IMPARTIAL REVIEW. Including a History of the present times, and an account of new Publications, interspersed with original and selected Tales, Essays, Biography, Poetry, &c., &c., &c., with a Monthly Chronicle of Events. London, June, 1787–December, 1792.

THE GENTLEMAN'S MAGAZINE; or, Monthly Intelligencer. Vol. I, No. 1, January, 1731. In progress.

GOLD'S LONDON MAGAZINE. See The Theatrical Inquisitor.

GRAY'S-INN JOURNAL. By A. Murphy. Weekly. London, September 29, 1753–September 21, 1754. From a manuscript note prefixed to the copy in the British Museum we learn that "This volume contains the last 52 numbers of the *Gray's-Inn Journal*, all that were printed in this size. The preceding numbers were published in *The Craftsman*."

GRUB-STREET JOURNAL. Weekly. 400 numbers in 2 volumes. London, January 8, 1730–August 25, 1737. The Grub-Street Journal was started by a Non-Juring clergyman by the name of Russel. In 1737 it became The Literary Courier, under which title it had a long career.

THE LADY'S MAGAZINE; or, Entertaining Companion for the Fair Sex. Appropriated solely to their Use and Amusement. Monthly. 50 volumes. London, August, 1770–December, 1819. New Series, 10 volumes, January, 1820–December, 1829. See Lady's Monthly Museum.

THE LADY'S MONTHLY MUSEUM; or, Polite Repository of Amusement and Instruction; being an assemblage of whatever can attend to please the fancy, interest the mind, or exalt the character, of the British Fair. London, July, 1798–June, 1806. New Series, 1807–1811.
Continued as

THE LADIES' MONTHLY MUSEUM, ETC. Improved Series. 1817–1828.
Continued as

THE LADIES' MUSEUM, 1829, 1830. New and Improved

Series, 1831, 1832. Incorporated with The Lady's Magazine, (q. v.), 1832, and

Continued as

THE LADY'S MAGAZINE AND MUSEUM OF BELLES LETTRES. Improved Series, enlarged, 1832–1837. United with The Court Magazine and Monthly Critic and

Continued as

THE COURT MAGAZINE AND MONTHLY CRITIC, AND LADIES' MAGAZINE AND MUSEUM OF THE BELLES LETTRES. London, 1838–1847. Volume 27 of The Court Magazine contains a statement that The Ladies' Magazine was first published in 1756.

THE LITERARY CHRONICLE AND WEEKLY REVIEW: Forming an Analysis and General Repository of Literature, Philosophy, Science, Arts, History, the Drama, Morals, Manners, and Amusements. London, 1819–1828. New Series, May–July, 1828, which became incorporated with The Athenæum.

THE LITERARY COURIER OF GRUB-STREET. See Grub-Street Journal.

LLOYD'S EVENING POST. Monday, Wednesday, Friday. London, Vol. I, No. 1, July 22, 1757 ; Vol. XLVI, No. 3591, June 28, 1780.

THE LONDON CHRONICLE. To be continued every Tuesday, Thursday and Saturday. Vol. I, No. 1, January 1, 1757 ; Vol. CXXXI, July 15, 1822. Afterwards united with The London Packet.

THE LONDON MAGAZINE AND MONTHLY INTELLIGENCER. London, 1732–1783. From 1735 to 1746 the title was "The London Magazine and Monthly Chronologer."

THE LONDON MAGAZINE. Monthly, 1820–1824. New Series, 1825–1828. Third Series, 1828–1829. January–August, 1825, title appeared as "London Magazine and Review."

THE LONDON PACKET. See London Chronicle.

MIST'S WEEKLY JOURNAL ; or, Saturday Post. London, 1716–1728. In the latter year, after an almost incessant persecution by the Whig Government, Mist was under the necessity of abandoning the name of his journal, and of reducing its tone. The name was changed to " Fog's Weekly Journal," q. v.

THE MONTHLY MAGAZINE, AND BRITISH REGISTER. London, 1796–1826.

Continued as

THE MONTHLY MAGAZINE : or, British Register of Literature, Sciences, and the Belles Lettres. New Series, 1826–1834.

Continued as

THE MONTHLY MAGAZINE OF POLITICS, LITERATURE, AND THE BELLES LETTRES. 1835–1838.

Continued as

THE MONTHLY MAGAZINE. 1839–1843.

THE MONTHLY VISITOR, and Entertaining Pocket Companion. By a Society of Gentlemen. London, January, 1797–April, 1803. After January, 1801, the title became " The Monthly Visitor, and New Family Magazine."

THE MORNING CHRONICLE. Daily. London, 1768–1854.

THE MORNING HERALD. Daily. London, 1780–1869.

THE MORNING POST. Daily. London, 1772–1803.

THE NEW MONTHLY MAGAZINE AND UNIVERSAL REGISTER. London, 1814–1820.

Continued as

THE NEW MONTHLY MAGAZINE AND LITERARY JOURNAL. 1821–1836.

Continued as

THE NEW MONTHLY MAGAZINE AND HUMOURIST. 1837–1871.

Continued as

THE NEW MONTHLY MAGAZINE. New Series, 1872–
1879. New Third Series, 1879–1881. New Series,
1882–1884.

THE PAMPHLETEER. Respectfully dedicated to Both
Houses of Parliament. To be continued occasionally,
at an average of four or five annually. London, 1813–
1826.

THE PROMPTER. Tuesday and Friday. 173 numbers.
No. I, Tuesday, March 12, 1734 ; No. CLXXIII, Friday, July 2, 1736. In 1784 E. Malone wrote on the
fly-leaf of his copy of The Prompter (now the property
of the Yale University Library) : " I have never seen
another copy of this work. This paper was written by
Aaron Hill, Esquire. He was occasionally assisted by
Wm. Popple, who was buried at Hampstead, Feb. 13,
1764. This Mr. Popple was Governor of Bermudas
[or rather perhaps his brother]." The British Museum
has a complete copy of The Prompter, with the exception of Nos. 138 and 158 which are wanting.

THE SPECTATOR. [By Addison, Steele, and others.]
Innumerable editions. Original edition, daily, London,
1711–1714.

THE SPECTATOR. A weekly Journal of News, Politics,
Literature, and Science. London, 1828–

TAIT'S EDINBURGH MAGAZINE. 1st Series, 4 vols.,
1832–1834 ; 2d Series, 28 vols., 1834–1861. In June,
1834, Johnston's Edinburgh Magazine was incorporated
with Tait's.

THE TATLER. The Lucubrations of Isaac Bickerstaff
Esq. [*i. e.* Steele, Addison, and others]. 271 numbers.
Weekly. London, April 12, 1709–January 2, 1710.

THE TATLER. A daily Journal of Literature and the
Stage. 3 volumes. London, September 4, 1830–December 31, 1831.

THE THEATRE. To be continued every Tuesday and Saturday. By Sir John Edgar [*i. e.* Sir Richard Steele]. 27 numbers. London, Saturday, January 2, 1720–Saturday, April 2, 1720. No. 28 was added by Steele in his own name. The Theatre was published by Steele in defense of his rights, at the time when the Crown revoked his patent.

THE THEATRE. By Sir Richard Steele ; to which are added the Anti-Theatre ; The Character of Sir John Edgar ; Steele's Case with the Lord Chamberlain ; The Crisis of Property ; with the Sequel, Two Pasquins, &c., &c. Illustrated with Literary and Historical Anecdotes. By John Nichols. London, 1791.

THE THEATRICAL EXAMINER ; or, critical remarks on the daily performances, with bills of the plays. London, 1823–1828.

THE THEATRICAL GAZETTE ; or, Nightly Reflector of the Theatres Royal, Covent Garden and Drury Lane. London, 1818.

THE THEATRICAL INQUISITOR ; or, Literary Mirror. By Cerberus. 16 volumes. London, 1812–1820. New Series, 1 volume, 1821. Discontinued in 1821 and combined with Gold's London Magazine.

THE THEATRICAL OBSERVER. Daily. London, 1821–1876.

THE TIMES. Begun January 1, 1785, as "The Daily Universal Register." On January 1, 1788, the title was changed to "The Times Universal Register." London, 1785–

TOWN-TALK. In a series of Letters to a Lady in the Country. To be published every Saturday. [By R. Steele.] 9 numbers. London, December 17, 1715–February 13, 1715–16. No. 6 contains copy of Steele's theatrical patent.

THE TOWN AND COUNTRY MAGAZINE; or, Universal Repository of Knowledge, Instruction, and Entertainment. Monthly.   London, 1769–1791.

THE UNIVERSAL MAGAZINE OF KNOWLEDGE AND PLEASURE.   Monthly.   London, 1747–1803.

Continued as

THE UNIVERSAL MAGAZINE.   New Series, 1804–1814.

Continued as

THE NEW UNIVERSAL MAGAZINE.   1814, 1815.

THE UNIVERSAL MUSEUM; or, Gentlemen's & Ladies' Polite Magazine of History, Politicks and Literature. Monthly.   London, 1762–1764.

Continued as

THE UNIVERSAL MUSEUM AND COMPLETE MAGAZINE OF KNOWLEDGE AND PLEASURE.   1765–1770.

THE WASP.   A Literary Satire.   Containing an exposé of some of the most notorious literary and theatrical quacks of the day, etc.   Weekly.   12 numbers.   London, Saturday, September 30–Saturday, December 16, 1826.

THE WEEKLY JOURNAL; or, Saturday's Post.   See Fog's and Mist's.

INDEX

INDEX